The Ridiculous Misadventures of a Single Girl

GABRIELLE STONE

Come play online!
@theridiculousmisadventures
@gabriellestone

The Ridiculous Misadventures

of a Single Girl

Table Of Contents

To the ones who only deserved the unhealed
version of me—I will always be grateful
for the purpose you served.
To the ones who waited for this version of me to heal...
Thank you.

Hold Up!

This crazy ride is the official sequel of
Eat, Pray, #FML.
If you haven't yet read where the journey began...
Start there.

The Ridiculous Misadventures of a Single Girl

It all started with a kiss. One seemingly harmless, simple fucking kiss—and oh, how long ago that kiss now seems. If you're reading this, it's because you came on a seriously life-altering journey with me. In fact, you probably feel like we're best friends by now—and I love that. In a way, we are. I mean, you know my deepest darkest secrets. My ridiculously embarrassing moments. My highs, my lows, my scars, and my wounds. You really *know me*. You watched me find out about an affair, witnessed my marriage crumble, and screamed, *"Oh my God, don't do it!"* as I fell—hard—into the arms of a damaged man. You were with me for my biggest heartbreak, my most terrifying decision, and the greatest adventure of my life. You traveled with me, ate (*a lot*) with me, cried, laughed, and healed with me. And, if you're like 95% of the other readers, when it was done, you dropped to your knees, looked up to the heavens, and screamed: *WHAT THE FUCK HAPPENED AFTER EUROPE?*

Well, my new best friend, you're in luck. Mostly because my life continued to be a wild escapade filled with life lessons, uninhibited experiences, chaotic relationships, and a whole lot of healing. But also because I'm just crazy enough to write about it one, more, time. So once again, buckle up for the ups, the downs, the growth, the travel, and of course, the men—new and old—because this is *The Ridiculous Misadventures of a Single Girl.*

The Ridiculous Misadventures of...
HOMECOMING

My backpack hit the floor, and I stepped inside. I was home. Fuck. Not only was I home in Los Angeles, I was actually *home* in the house I grew up in because I am now a pending divorcée at the ripe age of twenty-eight. Winning. I was so jetlagged and tired I could barely think straight. My mom threw her arms around me as I sort of collapsed into hers. A month was a long-ass time for us to not have seen each other, maybe the longest ever. I was happy to see her. I was *not* happy to be home.

We sat down in the kitchen, and she hit me with a million questions about the grand adventure I had just returned from. I answered each with as much excitement as my exhausted body could muster up. But I knew what question was eventually coming, and *that* I wanted to avoid like a kid sitting down for the birds-and-the-bees talk. And then, of course, it came.

"So what's the status of you and Javier? Did you get closure going to see him?" she asked. *No, Mother, I had wild sex for five nights, rebroke my heart, and ended up deciding we were now best buds like Timon and fucking Pumbaa.*

"We're going to be good friends." I focused extremely hard on not rolling my eyes at that ridiculous fucking statement.

"Well, did he ever give you a reason for what the hell happened?" She popped her hip out and failed at hiding her anger toward him.

"Yeah. He just went to bed in love with me and woke up not."

She scoffed. Can you blame her?

"When he fell in love with me, he had a ton of grief come up that had been stuffed way down. It isn't a satisfying answer to any of us, but it is what it is. We care about each other a lot. So we're going to just be friends." A month in Europe and one thing hadn't changed, apparently. I was still defending him.

"Okay...did he at least apologize for the insane situation he dragged you through?" she continued. I knew her feelings were valid. But for the love of God, I had *just* gotten home and that alone made me want to burst into tears.

"Of course. I don't expect you to understand. I just don't really want to talk about it." I aimed to redirect the conversation.

"Well, I've been waiting to hear what the hell has been going on!" My attempt failed.

"That's it! That's what's going on!" Ugh, tears, stay down.

"God, it's just unbelievable. It's such a cop-out. He played you." She scoffed again.

"*Mom*! Can we not do this? I literally just got home!"

"And you didn't think you would need to tell me what the hell the situation is? You're not the only one who's been on a roller coaster, Gabrielle!" Although she had a point, the epically bad timing was not appreciated.

"Look, I understand that you don't get it, but that's the only answer I have! I was so worried about coming home and being unhappy. This is the *last* thing that I wanted to walk into!" Ah, hello tears, join the welcome-home party.

"You know, maybe it's best that we just don't discuss him anymore, and you keep me separate from your friendship or whatever it is with him." She started to leave the kitchen.

"Mom, that is so unfair! Why are you being like this right now?" I knew the answer. She was angry. Really fucking angry. And rightfully so.

I walked into my room, sat on my bed, and cried. I was in the same *exact* situation I had been in right before I left: crying on my bed, feeling fucking helpless.

After a hard cry, I washed my face and got ready for bed. I sent my mom a text.

2

Me: The last thing I want is to not be okay with you right now, during all that I am trying to heal from. I know that all of this has hurt and affected you just as much as me in different ways. But please, take a step back and see that tonight, after just coming home, was not the time or place to get into it. I just wanted to catch up and talk about happy things I wanted to share with you. I didn't want to be upset and feel how I felt before I left. The situation is done and there is no reason to continue to bash him and upset me. I'm trying to heal, and the one thing that will not help me is fighting with you. I love you.

Mom: It's fine. Goodnight. Going to sleep. Love you.

My mother has never been the best texter. As I snuggled into my bed (which was so goddamn comfortable after a month of random beds and hostel bunks), I tried to talk myself out of this dark hole I found myself in. Thought Onion? The jet lag is too real. *Shut up, Gabrielle, do it now.* Fine. Superficial thought?

- I'm "friends" with the man I love, I'm miserable, and I'm home.

Okay, slightly dramatic. But considering the last three months, I'll let myself have it. Authentic thought?

- As much healing as I did on my trip, I still feel substantially broken.

That thought was devastating to me. It was one of the subconscious fears I'd discovered back in Sicily. Nothing like a fear coming to fruition to smack you upside the head. Do I even want to venture into the subconscious layer?

- I am *not* fucking okay.

Damn. I knew this was a possibility. I had just been *really* hoping it wouldn't be the case. I'd *needed* this trip to fix me. I'd needed this to be my *Eat, Pray, Love.* To come home feeling like I could take on the world. Yet the last three months—everything I had gone through and definitely this trip—had proven over and over that no matter what, in the long run, I would *always* be okay. So why did the fear of not being okay in this moment terrify me so damn much? I went to sleep hoping my dreams would take me somewhere else. Anywhere else.

Around 5 a.m., I opened my eyes to complete and utter darkness. I sat up and struggled to make out my surroundings. My brain came to and started wondering where I was. Barcelona? No. Mykonos? No. San Vito? Definitely not. Oh, that's right, I'm back in Los Angeles. Back home. Fuck. My. Life.

The Ridiculous Misadventures
of...
REALITY

I was sick. Like, really fucking sick. Not the "Oh, you should get some rest and drink tea" type sick, but the "You should be fucking quarantined" type sick. Alas, after a month of impressively minimal sleep, enough shitty food to feed a small country, and enough alcohol to keep the Titanic afloat, my body shut, the fuck, down. And of course, I had booked a film that was shooting in a week and a half. Not *nearly* enough time to work off the crepes, cannoli, gyros, paella, gelato...God, I'm hungry.

The other activity on the calendar? A farewell BBQ at Javier's parents' house. We had discussed it in San Vito, and it was in fact actually happening. It would be the last time I saw my newly dubbed "friend" for four months while he went to Mexico to film. I took a massive amount of DayQuil, slapped makeup on my running nose, and headed out the door.

"Where are you off to?" My mom came over to give me a hug. We were now in the "let's not talk about Javier and pretend everything is totally fine because I love you" phase, and I was *not* about to divert from that.

"Heading over to hang with Tess and Elizabeth," I lied. I *hate* lying to my mom. Besides the fact that we're very close and I don't ever feel the need to hide anything from her, it just made me feel like I was doing something *wrong*. And I wasn't. Let's also take a moment to recognize that I am a twenty-eight-year-old woman who is now lying about where she is going because she lives at home after finding out her husband was a sociopath. I'm such a catch.

"Ok, baby. Love you." She gave me a hug. Way to make it worse, Mom.

It had been four days since I had returned home from Europe. Being sick was making the already awful reality even worse. As I drove over to Javier's parents' house, I gave myself a pep talk. *This is fine. You are fine, Gabrielle. He's not even that great of a guy.* Except he's gorgeous, sexy, funny, successful...*Hello, brain, you are failing me right now.* Lord, here we go.

I have to admit, I was really excited to throw my arms around his mom. She was one of the people who had helped me get through the past month. I parked, took a deep breath of here-the-fuck-goes-nothing, grabbed my purse, and headed inside.

I walked in, trying to ignore the fact that the last time I had stood in this house, I was meeting his mother for the first time and thinking about how many fun times we would have here in the years to come. What a laugh that was now. I walked into the kitchen and found his mother, Ana, beaming at me.

"Gabriella!" She threw her arms around me. We stood there hugging for a few moments. It was such a crazy journey she and I had been on, even though the majority of it had happened over text messaging. We had just bonded instantly.

"Oh, it's so good to see you. I'm so happy you're here!" She wanted to know all about my trip and see all the photos. Javier came into the kitchen and laughed at his mom and I squealing like college roommates. As she headed outside to continue setting up, I handed Javier a bag that I had brought containing a book he'd lent me, one of his shirts, and the photobooth picture of the five of us from the first night we had gone dancing. He grabbed the photo from the bag and looked at me with sad eyes. I shrugged back at him with a forced smile. *Yes, you can keep that photo of the kiss that started it all. And know what an idiot you are for letting me go.*

His mom and I sat in the kitchen catching up, and Javier would periodically come in to chat with us. He was constantly joking and throwing sarcastic jabs at me, like a kindergartener poking his class-mate with a stick.

"Do you have any idea how many fat jokes I've endured from your son?" I laughed.

"What?!" She scolded him with her eyes.

"Oh, come on, you know I'm kidding!" he said to me.

"Javi, what is wrong with you?" she defended me.

"I know, I know, I'm an idiot." As he walked to the backyard, she threw her arms up and facepalmed her forehead. I laughed. She loved me and was so frustrated that her son had let someone like me go and had handled everything the way he had.

Later on, one of his friends I had never met showed up. We quickly discovered in our conversation that we were both going through quite ugly divorces.

"Have you ever been salsa dancing with this fool?" his friend asked, referencing Javier. "Every time I go with him, chicks are just under a freaking spell. He's like…" He started making dramatic salsa dancing gestures with sound effects. "And then he just walks away, and they're left out of breath, saying, 'No, come back!'" He laughed. Clearly, he was *not* one of the friends who was aware of the past three months or who I was. I looked at Javier and rolled my eyes while smiling.

"She's like the last person to say that to, trust me." Javier laughed.

"Pretty accurate with how you are off the dance floor too," I jabbed.

His friend began telling me about a book he'd found that gives compatibility for two people based on their birthdays.

"It's called *The Secret Language of Birthdays*. Trust me, I never even go on a date now without checking that shit out first." He chuckled. "Once I put mine and my ex-wife's info in, I was like, goddamn, we were doomed from the start!"

"Oh, I would *love* to see what warnings there are about my ex-husband." I laughed.

"There's an app. I'll pull it up!" He opened up his phone.

"It probably says fucking run," Javier commented as we all laughed.

I told him the required information, and he typed it all in.

"Okay, ready?" he said.

"Oh, yes."

"They both have dark tendencies that their relationship may trigger, for better or for worse," he started.

"Yeah. For worse." We all laughed.

"Extramarital involvements between these individuals, whether with each other or outside their relationship, are especially tempting to both partners. Marriages will generally prove too much for this combination, since the practical burdens of everyday life do not really suit their preference for the easy pursuit of pleasure." My mouth hung open.

"Easy pursuit of pleasure is right! You should see her ex's girl's Instagram!" Javier said. Like most, Javier had been highly entertained by watching my ex-husband Daniel's Instagram as he went from totally normal human to social media white-boy wannabe. It was true. He was an entirely different person. If you put one of his recent photos next to one from our wedding, you wouldn't even think it was the same human.

"Where were you before my marriage?" We were laughing so hard I had tears coming down. "You could have saved me so much bullshit and so much money."

"Put mine and Gab's in," Javier said. My face instantly reacted as if someone had told me there was no more wine. I have no poker face.

"Oh, yeah, cause that's exactly what we need to know," I replied.

"No, come on, put ours in," he instructed his friend.

Are you guys fucking ready for this shit?

"These relationships are among the few combinations where the partners can be both friends and lovers before, during, and after their love affair. There is a deep understanding and loyalty in this relationship and a mutual respect, especially on the mental plane. Yet, as well as these two get along, it may not be in the cards for them to marry or even live together, since ease does not necessarily entail either emotional depth or the ability to commit." He paused.

"OH MY FUCKING GOD," I said involuntarily. "Emotional depth and inability to commit. Javier, did they interview you for this?" I laughed.

"It's like they know my life the last month," he joked back. "Okay, what else?"

"Even if these two meet when either or both of them is involved with another steady partner or spouse, the seductive pull of a love affair between them will usually be so great that neither can resist," his friend continued reading.

"That sounds fucking awful," I stated.

"Jesus," Javier concurred. "So we're just screwed." He chuckled.

We all sat down to eat. So many times Javier's mom would look at me with a look that said *What is wrong with my son?* And I would return the look with *Ugh, Ana, I know.* Javier's sarcastic jabs continued, which was his weird way of flirting. Alas, even with all the weirdness that was going on and my still most definitely broken heart, we all laughed until we cried, had amazing conversations, and had a wonderful time together. Around 10 p.m., my jet lag came up to me and karate kicked me right in the face. I was *so* tired. And when I get tired, I can't really handle my emotions. I've been like that since I was a little girl.

I said goodbye to Ana and Javier's dad. Everyone else had already left by then.

"I'll walk you out, Gabs," Javier said.

Once we were at my car, we realized that this really was the last time we would see each other until he returned from Mexico.

"Crazy I'm not going to see you for four months," I said.

"I know. But I'm sure I'll come back when I have time off, and I'll FaceTime you when I get there." He hugged me. We stood there with our arms around each other for a long time. When we finally pulled away, my eyes were filled with water. "What's wrong?" he asked, concerned.

"Nothing, I'm fine. I'm just really tired," I said through tears. "God, it's going to be so weird when one of us starts dating someone." I laughed.

"Yeah, I know," he said solemnly.

"Like, 'Hey, just so you know, I'm super good friends with my ex.'" We both laughed.

"I don't even like calling you that." He put his arms around me again, and we stood there for another long moment, just breathing in each other's arms. "Are you okay?" he asked.

"Not really," I said as more tears came. Ugh, damn you, jet lag.

"What is it? What can I do?"

"Nothing. I'm just really tired. All this shit with my mom is really affecting me. And this fucking divorce. Every time I get an email from his lawyer, I want to puke. I'm just not happy I'm home," I admitted.

"Everything with your mom is going to be fine. You're going to be fine. The divorce will end, and you'll be able to put that jackass behind you."

"Yeah." None of that made any of it better. "This is all just hard for me. To just switch all my feelings for you off."

"It's hard for me too. I have to catch myself from flirting with you."

"You're so annoying! How can you say you just have friendship feelings for me and you have to catch yourself from flirting with me?" I laughed at the stupidity of it all.

"I don't know. I'm just saying it's hard for me too. I'm really going to miss you, Gabs." He hugged me yet again. Standing there in that moment, I don't think either of us fully realized what was in store for us.

"Okay, I'm gonna go." We had now been doing this song and dance of stalling, talking, hugging for over an hour.

"Okay. Are you okay to drive?" he asked.

"Yeah."

"Call me when you get home, okay, Plum?" Another hug.

"Yes, Veto." Don't let go.

"I love you, Gabs."

"I love you too." Another few moments. Then I released my arms from him.

I got in the car and drove down the street. *Don't cry. If you start to cry, it won't stop. And you're too tired to cry. It's fine. Everything is fine. You're friends.* To attempt to hold back the gallons of tears behind my eyeballs, I figured I'd bust out a Thought Onion on my forty-five-minute drive home. Superficial thought?

- WHY ARE YOU SUCH AN IDIOT, JAVIER?!

Yeah. Well. Fair assessment of where I was at in the moment.

- Is he just *that* scared of having something as amazing as what we had?

I mean, look at the facts. This man was telling me he felt nothing but friendship feelings toward me. Yet he'd wanted to have intensely intimate, passionate sex with me while we were in Sicily. Then he asks his friend to put us in the relationship book to see our compatibility. And finally, he tells me he has to stop himself from flirting with me. Yeah, dude, totally sounds like a normal friendship thing to me.

- He's just not ready.

Yep. There it was. There was no fucking reason to analyze it. Regardless of all the mixed signals and confusing elements, it was *that* simple. He was not ready to be in a full-on, deep, committed relationship. Had I been looking for that right after handing my husband divorce papers? *Hell* no. But I knew I wanted it the moment I woke up camping on the beach with him. I was ready if it was with him. And now, knowing it was no longer in the cards, I was not ready for anything like that either. I was ready to be *fucking single*.

As I pulled up to my mom's house at midnight, I continued to tell myself that I was fine. I had made it all the way home without crying. I called him, as promised.

"I'm home. Go to sleep." I sighed, sitting in the driveway.

"Good. Get some sleep, Gabs. So happy you came."

"Me too. Goodnight, Veto."

"Love you, Plum."

"Love you too."

Oh. Hey there, surge. I hung up and sat in my car, staring at my phone in my hands. No. Time to stop bullshitting yourself, Gabrielle. You are, in fact, *nowhere* near fucking okay. I knew in that moment that something had to change. He was not my best friend. He was not someone who could casually tell me he loved me. He was the person who had completely broken me and flipped my world upside down. And for the love of God, *it was time to get my fucking balance back.*

The Ridiculous Misadventures of...

DIVORCE

woke up not knowing what time it was but recognizing the feeling in my body all too well—depression. That feeling when you open your eyes, mad at yourself for waking up, because you're reminded of how fucking awful you feel. All I wanted to do was hide under my covers and force myself back into a temporary happy coma. Unfortunately, I had a shoot coming up, and my I'm-heartbroken-and-therefore-eating-like-an-asshole weight was not going to magically fall off by itself. And I was still *so* sick. Like I could really lose even *one* cannoli in a week.

I just felt...numb. Javier was on his way to Mexico, which was probably for the best. Time to get out of this awful funk, get back to feeling good physically, and redirect my focus to my career. Off to the gym I went.

After barely making it through a mile run while the antibiotics in my system punched at my stomach lining like Rocky Balboa, I headed over to the weights.

While on my last set, I rested on the bench, bopping to some energetic reggaeton song on my playlist. I happened to glance to my right where the group fitness room was and locked eyes with someone. I had never met her before but knew *exactly* who she was—and she *damn* sure knew me.

Laurel. Yes, just then, at 24 Hour Fitness, I locked eyes with the blonde nineteen-year-old who had been sleeping with my husband for six months. Seriously, I don't know if my life is a sitcom or a horror story.

Our gazes were locked for a solid three seconds as she stared at me like a deer in headlights until I chuckled and looked away. Still, I felt the surge. My body was having a physical reaction. There I was, wearing a green hat and a Spiritual Gangster T-shirt, feeling beyond uncomfortable in my post-Europe body and not able to swallow or breathe properly, staring at the teenager I had unknowingly been sharing bodily fluids with for months. I'm sure you all just read that and went "Ew..." Yeah, imagine how I felt.

Still, I had to laugh. Honestly, without even knowing it, she had done me a huge favor. Even with how broken and depressed I was currently feeling, I knew one thing for sure: I was *so* thankful to not be trapped in a toxic marriage to Daniel. The affair really had been an out for me. I wasn't sure where my life was heading, but I was *damn* glad it wasn't going to be with him.

I finished my last set and turned to head to my next machine. There he was, not fifteen feet away from me. Yes, ladies and gentlemen, like the movie that is my life, Daniel and Laurel.

I didn't hesitate. I didn't think twice. It wasn't even a question that I was going over there. So, without knowing what the hell was going to come out of my mouth, I marched straight up to the man who was still legally my husband and his girlfriend.

"What's up, dude," I said, planting myself between them, ironically arranging us in a triangle like the one we were once in.

"Hey, what's up..." He leaned over and gave me a *side hug* while he tried not to show his complete panic and shock.

"Not much. I was just wondering when you were gonna get around to signing our divorce papers so we could actually, you know, get divorced," I said matter-of-factly. Laurel stood there, eyes wide. Hold on, dear, Mom and Dad are fighting.

"Uh...I mean I signed the stuff my lawyer gave me," he stumbled.

"Right...well, because you hired a criminal justice attorney and *not* a family law attorney, none of it was done correctly so nothing has moved forward." I turned and looked straight at Laurel.

"I'm sure you'd like us to get divorced, right?" I smiled. Before she could even try and come up with a response, I turned back to Daniel. "So, could we maybe get that going?"

"I, um...yeah, yeah I'll get it done." Sheer and utter panic. Hilarious.

"Thanks, I would *really* appreciate it," I said with a fake smile and just enough sarcasm to fool a therapist. Then I turned back to Laurel. "I'm Gabrielle, by the way. But you know that." I grinned. As she opened her mouth to force an overly cheery, "Hi," I was already five steps away from them.

I have no idea what lies Daniel filled her head with. But I do know that she knew. The day after I left my house, she posted a photo announcing their relationship, so I know that she knew *exactly* who the fuck I was. And quite frankly, she was right to look terrified. I could probably beat Daniel's ass if it really came down to it, much less a 5'5" Barbie the size of my thigh. But I would never jeopardize my career and dreams to make her feel smaller than I already knew she felt. No, instead, I simply took my power back. Because after all, a black eye or a broken nose only lasts so long. A best-selling book? That shit will last a lifetime.

The Ridiculous Misadventures
of...
BEST FRIENDS

After Javier had been in Mexico for two weeks, FaceTiming me to show me his apartment and new hairstyle for his role, I had solidified the fact that I did not want, nor need, another best friend. Let me clarify—I didn't need a best friend who made my heart ache every time I saw his pretty fucking face, heard his stupid sexy voice, or got a text saying, *I love you*, to which my brain would scoff and say in a tone mimicking a five-year-old's, *But only as a fucking friend.*

At this point in the story, half of you reading this are probably ready to throw this book across the room and scream, "JESUS, GIRL, GET THE FUCK OVER IT." The other half, those that have been in that type of infatuated, deep, not-so-healthy type of love are saying, "Yeah, girl, I totally fucking get it." To be clear, I am totally with *all* of you. And because I felt all these things too, I knew what needed to happen next.

I had not started to feel better and I sure as shit wasn't healing, so it was time to make some serious changes, and step number one was cutting off what was making my heart continually hurt—*him*.

I knew the conversation that needed to happen. There was no way I was going to be able to get everything out over the phone or FaceTime because we always ended up laughing. I'm a big believer in writing down your feelings—here's why.

1) You can make sure you communicate everything you want to in a clear, effective way. You don't have someone

else interjecting, and you can correct things you might wish you could take back later.

2) It forces the person on the other end to really take in and digest what you're saying—they are forced to hear you instead of thinking about a rebuttal, reason, or excuse. I've found it also allows time for them to reflect on your words instead of immediately going on to the next topic.

So I decided to write my feelings in a message before having a conversation about it all.

Me: I don't even really know how to start. I've been doing a lot of thinking, reflecting, and attempted processing around everything that's gone down in the past month. You know I'm not okay. I wish I could say I was certain of a way to fix that or knew what would magically make it fine, but I don't. What I do know is that what I'm currently doing isn't working. If I'm being brutally honest with you, I feel that you are scared to death to love and be loved—because you think that person might die like your brother—and I get that. I have dealt with that fear since my dad died. I understand it, I sympathize with it, and I know how real it feels, especially subconsciously. But I hope you can recognize the incredible things and people you're going to lose if you don't find a way to let that go, because it is a debilitating belief to carry. In my eyes, you closed a door that wasn't ready to be shut—out of fear. But for whatever reason, you chose to shut it, and here we are. You know how I feel about you. You know I love you—but I just can't do this. I can't pretend that I just became a best friend…that my heart isn't hurting. And I can't pretend that I'm okay. There has always been a small part of me that thought you'd wake up and want to be together— and I can't allow whatever part that is to exist anymore. It's not fair to my heart or soul to not move forward, whether I think it's your mistake or not. And that's just not possible when I'm talking to you every day. Letting you go is terrifying to me. Not having you in my life is heartbreaking to me. I can only trust that over time we will be able to be that "person" that we've so clearly become to each other. But right now, I don't see any other option. I'm not saying that if you ever truly needed me that I wouldn't be there—I think you know that isn't the case. But I need some time and distance from you and the constant communication because I can't keep letting myself feel this way.

There. I had sent it. At least operation *mending my fucking heart* had been set in motion. I knew another conversation needed to take place, but at least I had made it known what needed to happen—what the next steps would be.

The next day that phone call took place. As I answered the FaceTime and looked at the person who I had gone through so much with in such a short amount of time, my heart was ready to beat out of my chest.

"Hey, Gabs," he said, smiling yet somber on the inside.

"Hey." I forced a smile back.

"Look. I totally understand everything you're saying. I wish it wasn't so hard, and I wish things were different. Of course I don't want to not talk to you. I love you, and you're so important to me. You changed my life. But I will do whatever you need to feel better and to make us stronger in the future. So if I need to give you space, I will give you space," he said.

"Thank you. It's just scary for me, I guess. I've gotten so used to having you here going through all of this with me."

"Yeah, I know. It's scary for me too."

We talked through more of how we were both feeling and then transitioned into totally off-topic things—because we knew this would be the last time we would be talking for a while.

After two hours had passed, I finally said, "Okay, I'm going to go. I hope the shoot goes well."

"Thanks, Gabs. I love you. Reach out anytime."

"I love you too." We looked at each other.

"Is it okay if I call you on your birthday?" he asked. I thought about it. My birthday was a little over a month away.

"Sure," I answered.

"Sure?"

"Yes, that's fine." I chuckled.

"Okay. I love you," he repeated.

"Okay. I love you too." I hung up.

I had finally done it. I had done what everyone had been scream-ing at me to do all of book one and cut off communication with Javi-er. *You can do this, Gabrielle. You're fine, and it's for the best.* So then why do I feel like I just lost a freaking limb? Ugh. Superficial thought?

- He's going to go find some hot incredible woman in Mexico, and I will be here, heartbroken.

Superficial indeed—but isn't that always the superficial fear when you let go of someone that was once yours? Authentic...

- What if he totally forgets about me and what we had, and we can never even have a friendship in the future?

That was definitely accurate—although I think deep down I knew that wasn't true. So then, what's the subconscious thought?

- I won't ever find what we had again.

Yep, as much as I hate to admit it, the golden subconscious nug-get was not about something I needed to heal or fix—it was a giant fucking fear. More importantly, now that I had figured out what the subconscious fear was, I needed to figure out a way to heal it. How the hell do you heal such a deep-rooted subconscious belief? First off, I needed to figure out what it was triggering in me.

- You let Dad go—*and he never came back.*

In this case, I was terrified to let this man go. Clearly. And it wasn't just him. This was a pattern for me—and when there are pat-terns in your life, it means you need to start paying attention to what they could be trying to tell you. How had these patterns manifested in my life you ask?

- I tend to hold on to things even when I know they're not good for me.
- I have an irrational fear that when I can't get ahold of someone, they're dead. (That may sound ridiculous to some people, but have your high school sweetheart say, "I'll call you when I get home," and never call—well, you get it.)
- And the obvious one—Javier. I kept in touch with him my entire Europe trip, went to see him and was intimate with him, and now, I was still terrified to let him go.

Looking at this, I realized something: all of our subconscious beliefs are related to an earlier event that *taught us to think this way*. Usually this happens from very big events, life-changing experiences, and incidents that really left a mark on us. Sometimes, they happen later in life, but more often than not, they originated when you were still a child. I call these Origin Experiences. A lot of my Origin Experiences (that have to do with men, at least) trace back to losing my father at such a young age.

Now, how on earth do you begin to heal a belief that's been with you for over twenty-five years? You get quiet, shut your eyes, and have a conversation with yourself—at the age of your Origin Experience. The more you can talk to and comfort the little child that is living inside of you, the more you can begin to let go of the things that were instilled in their being. So I sat there and spoke to little six-year-old Gabrielle. *You can let anything go, and it will always come back if it's good for you. You can let something go without it dying. You can safely let go.*

That subconscious layer of the onion was very real for me—one that, quite frankly, I had never felt before. In fact, every breakup I had ever gone through, I always knew deep down that something or someone better would eventually be on their way. So why did this short-lived romance make me feel like I would never recover?

The next few months would be a wild mess of trying to ignore my depression, forcing myself to date, and soothing my broken heart with too much alcohol. So buckle up, be prepared, and maybe take notes to keep all the men straight. Down the deep, dark rabbit hole we go.

The Ridiculous Misadventures

of...

THE BEGINNING OF FATE

That fateful September 4th, 2017, I had received hundreds of messages after I had posted the photo of me at the airport, announcing my divorce. Incredible sentiments from women I didn't know who said it had given them hope, support from random acquaintances and distant friends, and inspired people who asked me to please continue to share my journey. But there was one message that was a complete blast from the past. And although I was touched to receive it, I didn't think too terribly much of it when I was boarding the plane, brokenhearted and secretly panicked.

The message was from a man named Tyler. We had worked together back in 2010 on a film where I played his younger sister. He was fifteen years older than me, and we had totally bonded on a soul level while we were on set. We had quickly established the nicknames Jacky D (due to the immense amount of Jack Daniel's he consumed during our boring off days) and Peanut (which he insisted he call me in the film, and well, because, next to him, I look like I'm the size of a fucking peanut.) He was dating his then fiancée Christine, and I was with my college boyfriend Wyatt at the time and totally in love. We hadn't seen each other since filming, but we kept in touch on Facebook. He had sent his congratulations to me on my wedding, and I to him on the birth of his daughter. So, when this message came in before I boarded my plane, it simply made me smile warmly.

Tyler: Peanut...I just read your post. My heart is with you on your journey. You're truly an amazing person and the universe knows this. You deserve the world and everything in it. Safe journey and forever smile inside your heart. Jacky D

Me: Aw. Love you, dude.

Tyler: Love you too, girlie. Let me know when you get back... let's have a visit. Miss your face!

Me: Yes. Please.

Why is this all important, you may be asking? Well, because on October 20th, 2017, as fate would have it, I happened to visit one of my favorite clubs—and who just happened to be working behind the bar? Tyler. How do I even begin to accurately describe Tyler? He's 6'3", half Persian and half Irish, but looks more like a Roman God that stepped off the pages of a rugged Ford truck advertisement. He had a tan complexion, crystal baby-blue eyes that could easily impregnate you upon first glance, and an obnoxiously suave wink-and-smile combo—and somehow, like my favorite red wine, got freaking better with age.

"Peanut!" I heard over the loud music.

"Jacky?!" I ran over to meet him at the side of the bar. He scooped me up, squeezed me tightly, and twirled me around.

"You're back!" he said.

"You're here!" I exclaimed.

"My buddy owns this place. I work a few nights a month."

"Shut up! This is our spot. We're here all the time!" I shrieked.

My friends were all standing back at the bar, watching this exchange take place. Jess, who was already buzzed from taking shots at home, came over and introduced herself. Just then, one of the other bartenders walked over to ask Tyler a question.

"Gabs!" Jess smacked my arm. "He's so fucking hot!" she said way too loudly and way too close to where Tyler was standing. I rolled my eyes and begged her to go back and wait for me where our group was. "Ugh, fine," she protested as she began to dance her way back to everyone.

I turned back to Tyler, smiling, hoping he hadn't heard my drunk, yet accurate, friend blabbing.

"How's Christine?" I asked.

"Oh..." He looked at me slightly confused. "We split like two years ago."

"Oh my God, I had no idea."

"Yeah, we didn't really publicize it on social media." He chuckled. "It's for the best. We weren't happy and it was time. But we have Blue now, so no regrets."

"Of course. I've seen photos on Facebook. She's adorable. Shame you guys made such an ugly kid." I smiled. He smiled back.

"So how was your trip? Do I need to find both those idiots in a dark alley? What the hell happened?"

"Dude, honestly, it's such a joke of a story. As is, you know, my life." I laughed, only half thinking it was funny.

"Well, we have to get dinner so I can hear all about it. For now, let me get your group a round on me, and don't you dare pay for a drink the rest of the night." He smiled.

"Jacky, you totally don't have to do that," I assured.

"I know I don't have to. Come on, sky's the limit for Peanut." He hugged me and headed back behind the bar.

After I got our entire group a round of drinks, we headed over to dance for a bit. I was immediately interrogated about who the tall, dark, and annoyingly handsome guy was.

"Gabs, he's freaking gorgeous! Is he single?" a slightly more drunk Jess asked.

"Okay, besides the fact that I *just* got back from a trip trying to mend my broken heart, *after* a freaking awful divorce that is still not yet finalized, he's like my older brother. It's not like that." Speaking the words out loud, I could hear the bullshit dripping from them— Tyler was *really* hot. And charming, and apparently no longer married, so we had that in common.

Throughout the night, I found myself finishing my drinks more quickly than normal for the sole purpose of getting to go back to the bar so we could talk more while he made me another sugary, delicious, yet for sure a hangover-in-your-future cocktail. He would do his wink-and-smile combo, which made me question how many times he had devastated women with that single perfected talent. After the four-month shit show I had just experienced, my internal alarm was flashing like a goddamn firetruck. *There is no way someone that good-looking and that suave can be a good guy.*

Unfortunately, my desire to flirt with my once on-screen older brother led me to consume many cocktails, which caused me to eventually drunk text Chris.

Chris and I had been in constant touch since he had kissed me farewell at the Barcelona airport, and, as promised, he was coming to visit me in LA in a few weeks. For a moment that night in the club, I drunkenly thought to myself, *Why are you out drinking and substance soothing? You're not okay, Gabrielle. You're nowhere near okay.* When I was eighteen and my high school sweetheart died suddenly, I learned the hard way how wrong things can go when you choose to substance soothe. In fact, since then, I had been diligent about not drinking when I was dealing with any type of trauma. After the divorce, I would go out dancing with my friends but wouldn't have a sip of alcohol. So why did I choose to neglect that majorly important rule now, when I was even deeper in the trenches of depression? Don't worry, it will come back to bite me in the ass...

I vaguely remember saying goodbye to Tyler that night, and hopefully I thanked him profusely for the nine—yes, I said nine—free drinks that I would 100% be regretting in the morning. I was definitely starting to spiral into a not-so-healthy way of coping with my delicately fragmented heart. But that night, a tiny little seed was planted and, unbeknownst to me, it was the very small beginning of what some might call—fate.

The Ridiculous Misadventures of...

JAKE

It was late October when I found myself looking for answers in all the wrong places. What are those places, you might ask? Alcohol. Men. Work. Basically, anything that was outside of where all the answers were—*within myself*. Might I remind you that in *Eat, Pray, #FML* I included the self-love cocktail in the *epilogue* for a reason. "While I had begun to scratch the surface of the concept of loving myself, I can't tell you that I fully and truly realized how to do it on my grand European adventure. This monumental discovery came well after my return home, after more heartache, gallons of tears, and a shit-ton of soul-searching." Well, y'all, we have not reached that fucking point of this book yet.

For some random—or divinely ironic—reason, all the men that were coming into my life had some type of characteristic about them that brought up things from my past. Some bigger than others, but still, it was enough to notice what some might call coincidence and others may call mirrors—and Jake was no exception.

Not only did Jake share the same name as my high school sweetheart who had passed away, he'd first come into my life when I was younger, and we did a performance together where he played the role of my *father*. Let's not even begin to delve into that fucked-up psychological rabbit hole, which I'm sure Freud would have a field day with. However, it started off totally with friendship intentions. He, like so many others, had reached out to me on September 4th when I posted about my divorce.

Jake: Hey, Gab. Wanted to touch base with you. I, too, went through my wife having an affair and divorce. If you ever want to connect and talk or not talk about it…either way.

I had responded from London:

Me: Wow, I had no idea. I'm so sorry to hear. But huge blessings in the long run. Thanks for reaching out.

Jake: Of course. Whenever you're back in town, let's connect. If you're open to it. Many blessings and well wishes in your healing process.

Me: Would love to. Back October 4th.

I had forgotten about this exchange and tentative plans until a photo of Jake popped up on my Facebook feed. I needed a friend—and a drink. And it would be nice to have a discussion about all the fucked-up things cheating and divorce bring that they fail to mention when you're spewing loads of bullshit at the altar. Jake and I were in the same acting class when I was much younger. He had always been kind of like an older brother to me (*yeah, okay, sensing a theme here…*). I was a kid at sixteen when we met, and he was twenty-seven, so that was of course the dynamic you would expect.

I was in the type of depression where you need to fill your calendar up with as many stimulating things as possible because if you stop moving for too long, you might just slump into your bed and never get out again. These calendar items consisted of nights out drinking and dancing, dragging my ass to the gym to try and undo what Europe had done, and day dates with my girlfriends. Why not add in a once-brotherly figure who had been through the same whirlwind shit show I'd been through? So, a few days after my unexpected run-in with Tyler, I reached out to Jake.

We decided to meet that Saturday to catch up over a drink. While I was getting ready, my phone dinged with a text message. I picked it up and felt the surge when I saw the name on my phone screen: Javier. He casually told me that he was working with the set decorator from *Moulin Rouge* and how amazing her stories were.

Uh, okay, dude. Did we not just have a GIANT discussion about how we are going to *not* be communicating? It's been like...*three days*. Yes, *Moulin Rouge* was my all-time favorite movie—but did you really need to send a generic and not incredibly important text after all we had just addressed? Come on.

I threw my phone aside without a response, got in my car, and drove to meet my old friend.

I met Jake outside the bar, which I quickly learned he was a regular at. He smiled and hugged me before escorting me to a seat at the center of the bar. Jake was tall and the definition of masculine, with the deepest voice you've ever heard and an artistic bad boy vibe. I had known a few of his girlfriends in the past, and he was always described as intense. I can now confirm that description.

The first hour was spent detailing our wild cheating and divorce stories while sipping on some delicious craft cocktails. We had some crazy similarities in our stories, and it was really nice to vent to someone who had been through it and totally understood all of my feelings around it. When I'm not trying to flirt with someone, I talk the same way I talk to my good friends. I call them dude, don't really filter anything I'm saying, and might even be described as "not lady-like," although what the fuck does that even mean? So that's exactly how I approached the entire night.

The second hour and second round of drinks shifted into some unexpected compliments, a different look in Jake's eye, and me trying to convince myself that there was no actual way that this forty-year-old was flirting with me. How could he even look at me as a full-grown woman when he had known me at sixteen?

"I think you're a badass for still taking that trip," he said.

"Well, thank you. It changed my life, and I'm about to publish a freaking book about it. So, I'm glad I went."

"Don't think I didn't see all those pics you were posting. I may or may not have checked out that Mykonos photo more than once." He smiled at me.

I actually found myself kind of blushing. Here I had shown up looking somewhat ragged from the long night I'd had before and dropping f-bombs and *dudes* like I was talking to one of my girl-friends. I was caught very off guard but was not entirely mad about it. Jake was charismatic and spiritual, two qualities that made him attractive to any normal woman and easy to spend four hours at a bar with.

I still wonder if he had known that he was interested in me when he suggested we get together or if it happened circumstantially once we were there. Either way, once he pointed out the small spark, it was then blatantly obvious as it grew into a flame.

When the bar was nearing closing time, and I was in serious need of sleep, Jake fought me for the tab, and I quickly lost. He said goodbye to those he knew in the bar and then walked me to my car.

"It was really great to see you," he said.

"You too. I had a great time." I smiled.

"Good." He smiled back as he towered over me. Then he lifted his hand to tilt my chin up—*and fucking kissed me.* Well...that was wildly unexpected.

I drove home thinking about the shocking yet really exceptional kiss that I couldn't have predicted in a million years. I also thought about the words I had written while sitting in a café in Rome.

After I finally handed Daniel the papers I was...fine. Even my mom and friends were surprised how okay I was. I'm emotionally aware enough to know that if I had been in a depressed and aw-ful state when Javier came into the picture, it wouldn't have been healthy at all.

I still stand by those words and emotions. When Javier entered my life, I was, believe it or not, *okay.* I wasn't heartbroken, and I wasn't crying myself to sleep at night. In fact, I felt a great deal of relief and gratitude toward my ex-husband. Daniel had made it so easy for me to walk away—and gave me a second chance at life. Of course, I was navigating the betrayal and disrespect, but I was doing pretty damn well. But now? That was *so* not the case. Javier had broken my heart in a way that Daniel never could have, and I knew that I was not in *any* state to be seriously dating or looking for a relationship. In fact, it had become abundantly clear that I had, for the first time in twenty-eight years, put up a wall around my heart. If one thing had stuck with me from this heartbreak, it was that I didn't *ever* want to make *anyone* feel the way that man had made me feel.

I arrived home to a text.

Jake: Thank you for a pleasantly surprising evening and your sweet kiss. All of it. Please let me know that you arrived home safely.

Me: You're welcome for all of the above. I had a great time pleasantly surprising you. Home safe and sound.

Jake: If you're open to it, I'd love to hang again in the future.

Well, well...what a dilemma you have, Gabrielle.

*****

I must admit, I was doing an exceedingly excellent job at keeping myself so goddamn busy that I wouldn't sink into the quicksand pit of depression that was sitting right in front of me. Chris had booked his ticket to come to LA in a few weeks, I was heading to New York for a film festival in a few days, and now I had Jake showering me with unexpected attention. So, in my attempt to avoid this impending pit of soul-sucking sadness, I accepted Jake's invitation to see him again.

Jake: Good morning, beautiful.

Why does every woman receive a text like this from a man who is totally all about you, ready to completely swoon over you, and then immediately think: *Hm, I wonder what that dick who left me before Europe is doing?* It's really ridiculous. We do it to ourselves sometimes.

I met Jake that night at a cute little restaurant, where we had a great conversation with witty banter, which I always love. At one point, when I was in the middle of some sarcastic jab, I caught a look in his eye—a very specific look that I've seen from a few different men in my life. From my college boyfriend, Wyatt, right before we fell head over heels for each other. From Daniel, when he first laid eyes on me at the club we met at—before he more or less stalked me until I agreed to go out with him. And from Javier, that night we went dancing when we both realized how fucked we were. Seeing that look on Jake's face? Made me totally fucking panic. *Hard.*

After dinner, we went next door to a bar, and Jake grabbed us two beers. He definitely had that bad boy swag that every girl pines over, but on the inside he was a total softy and very spiritual. As I leaned against the high-top table we were standing at, I continued to see that look dance across his face, so quickly that I didn't know when to interject to try and put the brakes on it. Somewhere in the conversation, he made a comment about the sexual tension between us—and this is what ended up coming out.

"I have to be honest with you, Jake. I am broken right now. Like, really broken. Trying to date me right now would be like walking into a brick wall face-first." I took a giant gulp of my beer.

"I appreciate you telling me that. I'm definitely not looking to get my heart broken."

"That's probably one of my biggest fears right now—making anyone feel the way that Javier made me feel. I would never want to cause you any hurt," I shared honestly.

"Thank you for that."

"So, I feel like crossing that line into being physical would just be..." I trailed off.

"Walking straight into a brick wall headfirst?" He chuckled.

"Yeah." It was strange. My body, ego, and need for a mental distraction really wanted to go home and fuck the spiritual bad boy's brains out—but I knew that it would be so much more for him, and I was not capable of giving him that.

"Okay. Thank you for being so honest with me. You're pretty incredible, Gabrielle Stone, you know that?" He smiled and took another sip of his beer.

"I don't know about that." I smiled back.

A few beers later, we headed back to Jake's place, where my car was parked.

"You want to have some water and chill for a bit before heading home?" he asked.

"Sure," I agreed.

If any of you are screaming, "DON'T DO IT, GABRIELLE, IT'S A TRAP!" you are absolutely, 100% correct. Well, it wasn't an intentional creepy guy move, but it was basically him thinking that he could climb the giant brick wall instead of running straight the fuck into it.

We did end up hooking up that night, but we didn't have sex. It was the first time I had been physical with anyone since Javier and I'd had wild passionate sex in a little Airbnb in Rome. Still, the wall that had been built around my fragile heart held sturdy—it was going to take someone incredibly strong to knock that shit down. But it became clear that Jake had heard what I had said and had chosen to deliberately disregard it and move right ahead anyway.

What was with these men hearing me clearly tell them what I needed and then blatantly disregarding it like it didn't freaking apply to them? I had told Javier I needed space, only to be sent a text days later about nothing of any fucking importance. I had clearly told Jake that crossing the physical line was a bad idea, that I was broken, and he went right ahead and did it anyway. But more importantly, why was I allowing this behavior? Onion. Superficial?

• I'm a people pleaser.

Yes, it's always been in my nature to avoid the awkward *don't kiss me I just told you to chill the fuck out* talk. Authentic?

• If I put my foot down, they'll abandon me.

Accurate. I always want to have the option to be the one to leave—not vice versa. But there has to be something so much deeper. What's the subconscious?

- I don't truly demand my worth.

Ah. There is it. I did in my twenties, before the man I was married to taught me that I was worthless and not good enough. Even though I had felt like I had rediscovered my worth on my Europe trip, I apparently wasn't able to unequivocally demand, expect, and not settle for less than it.

After he kissed me goodbye that night, I got into my car and felt a giant pit of anxiety in my stomach. I drove home kicking myself for being able to vocalize what a hurricane I was and then allowing him to just say *fuck it* and dance in the rain.

So, I did what any rational brokenhearted woman who isn't ready to accept a man wanting to shower her with love and affection would do—I boarded a plane to New York City.

The Ridiculous Misadventures
of...
MARCUS

The film that I had directed and starred in the prior year was just finishing up its festival run. It had screened in sixteen festivals, racked up twenty-two nominations, and received twelve awards. And its final screening just so happened to be in New York. What else happened to be in New York, you ask? *Marcus.*

I was planning on staying with Brooke, a girlfriend of mine who lived in the city. Coincidentally, a group of my best girlfriends from high school were all going to be there at the same exact time. Over the years, it's gotten harder to spend time with my high school girls because we now live all over the globe, so I was excited for a trip filled with film, quality girl time, and you know, maybe a side of the hot guy I rolled around with in Mykonos.

After the film had screened at the festival, we headed out to celebrate. New York has an entirely different vibe than LA—you either totally love it or you completely hate it. I was still undecided at the moment.

We all clinked glasses, toasted to another successful screening of my directorial debut, and sipped on cocktails that made LA prices look like piggy bank change. As I gulped on my fancy overpriced drink, I thought about what the hell I was doing with my life. I still felt like my heart was fucking bleeding from three different puncture wounds from Javier. I was planning on seeing Marcus when I knew that wasn't going anywhere. I was navigating through feelings about my Barcelona romance with Chris. And to top it all off, I had romantic texts from Jake coming in which should have made any woman swoon but made me want to sprint in the opposite direction. Ding. Another came in.

> Jake: I am about to drift to dreamland. I wish you sweet dreams. Kisses to you, beautiful Gabrielle. You're a remarkable being. I hope to spend more time getting to know more of you.

Those are the types of text messages we dream about getting as little girls. The kind of compassion and deep feelings we crave as empathic human beings. But for where I was at in my life, and all that I was still trying to heal from, this was the absolute last thing I needed.

The next day I met with my girls, whom I hadn't seen since before my entire life went up in flames when my ex-husband's penis somehow slipped and found itself in the barely legal vagina known as Laurel. They knew all about the divorce and the romance (and epic downfall) of Javier, and had followed along with my Europe trip. But of course, the moment we all sat down at the cozy New York City restaurant, their opening line was: *TELL US EVERYTHING.*

I was so tired of this story. I was so tired of having to admit that I wasn't magically over this stupid man. I wanted to be over it all. Unfortunately, the biggest component of a winning healing recipe is what none of us have the patience for—time.

"So how long has it been since you guys stopped talking?" one of my girlfriends asked.

"Umm...I don't know, like almost two weeks?" I realized.

"Are you guys still following each other on social media?"

"Yeah. He still watches all my stories," I admitted. "But every time I see a photo of him, it mildly feels like I'm getting punched in the face." I laughed at myself.

"So unfollow him," another much blunter friend stated matter-of-factly.

"I just don't want it to seem like there's bad blood between us. I don't hate him, I just have to let my heart heal," I said.

My friend then grabbed my phone off the table, opened my Instagram, and muted his posts so that they wouldn't show up on my feed.

"There." She handed my phone back to me. "Now you don't have to see his dumb face anymore." She smiled.

I smiled back at her, knowing that she was damn well right. I needed to not see his dumb (yet obnoxiously good-looking) face anymore. The first rule of getting over someone is to stop torturing yourself by looking at shit that reminds you of them. So, for any of my brokenhearted ladies reading this right now, open your phone, mute, block, delete, and commit. It's the only way. *Do it now.*

Later that night, I met Brooke at a bar. As we entered, we passed a psychic who was set up in the entryway that led into a swanky speakeasy that was dripping with Gatsby vibes in all the best ways. After some very fancy cocktails, Brooke and I were just tipsy enough to drop twenty-five dollars on an arbitrary psychic reading in a random New York City bar.

I sat down to go first, and she looked at me intensely, reading my energy, which I'm sure was quite loose after the few cocktails that had accumulated over the evening.

"You've had quite a journey the last few months." She shuffled the cards in her hands.

I immediately sobered up a little bit. Why is it that every god-damn psychic I see can automatically read into my fucking soul? She spread the cards over the table in front of us, pulled one out, and flipped it over, facing up. Brooke and I sat staring at what was so clearly a picture of a devil. And this, friends, is where I learned I would soon die.

Kidding, obviously, but like...what the hell else do you think when a psychic flips a devil card over on the table?

"The relationship that just ended for you...you need to fully let go of it. Whoever he was, he was an addict in regards to you—like a form of sexual obsession—and because of this, he won't stay gone. He'll keep popping back into your life because what the two of you had together was like a drug," she said.

I looked over at Brooke, deadpan. Her mouth was hanging open. Well, looks like I'll be getting my twenty-five dollars' worth. She flipped a second card over.

"You're not going to fully have closure until the next time you see him. But I urge you to distance yourself from him," she said sternly.

Well, I guess I'll be waiting for closure for a long time, considering he just went to Mexico. Great.

"Be aware, just because he returns does not mean he's changed. It does not mean things will end up differently—but we definitely haven't seen the last of him." I sat there, stunned, feeling like I had just been delivered an evil omen. *Whatever, I'm sure not all psychics are entirely accurate.*

Another card.

"Who in your life just experienced a volatile divorce?" she asked.

At this point, *my* mouth was now hanging on the floor.

"Uh, that would be me," I answered.

"Oh. Interesting. But that's not the addictive relationship. The divorce was before," she said accurately.

"Yes," I confirmed.

Another card.

"You just came back from a trip, yes?" I nodded. "You're contemplating leaving the country again. If the opportunity arises, go. It might not be right away, but when it comes, go."

That made sense—I had been wanting to run away from home since my plane had landed from Europe.

"You also have a big project that is either just being completed or is about to be?"

"Yes," I answered.

"Don't confine it to one box. This is going to be big across multiple platforms. Is it a movie?" she asked.

"No, a book."

"Ah, well...I wouldn't be surprised if it ended up on screen eventually. But it's going to help a lot of people—you were meant to create it." She winked at me.

Do not forget this information, Gabrielle, I told my mildly drunk brain. I must say that was way more than I was ever expecting from a random psychic sitting in the entryway of a bar. Four months before having closure seemed painfully long. But what was worse about this piece of information? It meant I would be seeing him again—and at that moment in a bar in New York City, I had no fucking idea in what a big way it would be.

The next day I ventured around the city while Brooke was at work. That night would be the one and only night I'd be seeing Marcus. I stopped and had a delicious bagel with lox and people watched in the chaotic streets of the city. I was beginning to realize that I might be on the completely hate New York side of the coin. Maybe it was the dense city, the hustle and bustle, or the overwhelming amount of cement and concrete that felt suffocating to me. It just didn't really make me feel alive. Then again, neither did Los Angeles, it just happened to be home. I was constantly dreaming of Europe, or wherever I could potentially escape to on my next solo adventure. South America? Probably not the best idea considering my track record with Latin men. Asia maybe? Anywhere but home.

It was more than just a newfound love of travel. Call it intuition or perhaps subconsciously knowing where my answers were, but I was being pulled to just...leave. Was it healthy? Probably not—but if you feel the desperate need to run away, more often than not, you have a pretty life-changing destination to arrive at.

While I walked, staring up at the giant buildings around me, lost in my thoughts, my phone rang. It was Tyler.

"Hello?" I answered.

"Hey, you, how's it going?" His rugged voice came through the other end.

"It's going!" I laughed. "I'm in New York right now for a film festival."

"Oh, that's right! How's New York treating you?"

"Jury is still out on that one. How are you?"

"I'm good. Wondering if I can take you to dinner when you're back." I couldn't help but smile as I walked the busy streets.

"I'll have to check my schedule, but I think we can make that happen," I teased.

"Good. Pencil me in. I know you're in high demand and all."

"Yeah, I'm just warding all the men off constantly. With divorce papers. And plane tickets." We both laughed. "I'll give you a call when I get back?"

"Sounds good. Be safe out there, Peanut."

"Will do, Jacky D." I hung up and continued adventuring around with a little more pep in my step than before.

That night I threw on jeans, a T-shirt, boots, and some shade of I-no-longer-give-a-fuck lipstick, and Brooke and I headed out to meet Marcus and the rest of the Vodka Soda Boys. We walked into a bar that was rowdy as ever from Sunday night football. I looked to my left and locked eyes with Marcus the same way we had in the club in Mykonos. He flashed his charming frat boy smile, and Brooke and I headed over to where their group was.

Marcus put his arms around me and kissed my cheek as he handed me a beer.

"Welcome to New York, Gabrielle," he shouted over the loud music.

"Long way from Mykonos." I laughed.

"Crazy that you're here." He smiled.

We all danced, drank, and had a great final night out in NYC. Once the bar died down, we headed to some delicious pasta joint that I loathe doesn't exist in Los Angeles.

"Here's a set of house keys." Brooke handed me keys as she headed off with one of Marcus's friends, who was counting his lucky stars to be taking her home.

"You don't need those." Marcus smiled.

"Why is that?" I smirked, knowing the answer.

"You're coming with me. I only have you for one night." He put his arm around me, and we began to walk the still very alive streets of the city at 2 a.m.

We arrived at his very typical, less than stellar, two-dudes-living-in-New-York apartment. It was always very clear to me the type of relationship that Marcus and I had. While we had fun and enjoyed each other's company, it was never going to actually go anywhere. However, what it did do, and very well I might add, was make me feel like the freaking powerful woman that I was. I hadn't slept with anyone since I had been with Javier that final night in Rome, and that last night in New York City, I wanted someone to worship me the way that Javier did in bed.

After saying goodnight to his roommate and realizing that I needed to start dating men that lived in grown-up adult apartments, we headed to his room, more specifically, his mattress on the floor.

Making out with Marcus (who most definitely *did* smoke cigarettes back home) felt like kissing that bad boy in high school you snuck out late to see after your mom went to bed. He grabbed a condom, and we had the type of hook-up sex where you don't even think *Does this angle make me look good* or *I wonder if they're enjoying this* because it was purely physical. In the weirdest way, Marcus gave me exactly what I *thought* I needed that night—to feel totally worshiped and powerful—all three times.

The next day I said goodbye to Brooke and boarded my plane to LA. As I sat on yet another runway, waiting to take off, I realized something. Just because I was able to escape the sadness and anxiety I was experiencing for a few days, that didn't mean that any of my problems were cured. Quite the contrary. It had become soberingly clear that I was in fact running from something. I just hadn't quite consciously come to terms with what that something was. At the end of the day, you can run, drink, fuck, and even fly away from your problems—but eventually you have to face the damn music... and go home.

The Ridiculous Misadventures
of…
CHRIS

I love that people who read *Eat, Pray, #FML* became so invested in the characters. Over the last few years, I've become accustomed to getting the same handful of questions from my readers. Here are the top three that almost every person is dying to know:

1. Do you still talk to Javier?
2. What happened when you came home?
3. DID CHRIS EVER COME TO LA?!

Since question #1 will be given much more explanation and #2 is quite literally what this book is about, I will finally give you all the chapter you've been waiting for since finishing the section about Barcelona—*what the fuck happened between me and Chris?*

Since Europe, Chris and I had kept in constant touch through phone calls and texts. The twenty-three-year-old who had been so instrumental in my healing journey, and had left such an imprint on me (and, clearly, all of you, as well), was finally coming to LA in early November. I had seen in NYC that Marcus was definitely the typical frat guy he had appeared to be, and I was wondering how this rendezvous with the one person I had developed feelings for was going to play out. We had plans for a fun weekend around LA and rented an Airbnb in Hollywood (because I was not about to say, "Hey, Mom, a younger guy I slept with in Barcelona is going to come stay with us for a few nights"—God, I have to move out).

On November 9th, I picked him up at LAX. He came out, dropped his bag, and gave me a hug and a kiss.

"I can't believe I'm here," he said, looking into my eyes.

"Welcome to LaLa Land, Mr. Barcelona." I smiled up at him.

Standing there in Chris's arms, I thought to myself, *If anyone can help me break this Fort Knox wall down and let my heart breathe, it's him.*

That night we grabbed drinks at a cute little bar before heading to dinner in Hollywood. We reminisced about our time in Barcelona and talked about the traveling we did after and what was going on in our lives now.

"So what's going on with you and Javier?" he asked. Seriously— even the men I was dating knew what a catastrophic shit show this man had become in my life.

"I actually told him I needed some space. My heart just wasn't healing, and it was too hard to try and be his friend right away. We haven't spoken in almost a month."

"Damn. I mean, yeah, I think you totally made the right call. How's the book coming?"

"Almost done! I had to finish up all of the things leading up to the trip. Mostly the divorce."

"That's probably so weird to go back and write about," he said.

"Actually, not really. I'm so disconnected from it all and so thankful I got out."

"Well, cheers to you making a badass book out of it all. Honored to be a part of it." He winked and raised his glass for a toast.

I smiled and took a sip of my drink. After two rounds at the bar, I insisted I pay since I knew he would be paying for dinner, which wouldn't be cheap. Chris hadn't earned the name TripAdvisor for nothing—he wanted to go to all the delicious LA hot spots, and Beauty and Essex was the epitome of that.

We headed in through the speakeasy entrance, where we snapped a picture, and into the beautiful dining room. We talked a ton about our histories, work, and everything that you would normally discuss on an intellectually stimulating date.

"If I didn't live in San Francisco, I would definitely want to make you my girlfriend," he said with a smile. I looked across the table at the man who had made my heart skip a beat in Barcelona, had opened my eyes to what everyone else had been clearly seeing, and had surprised me in more ways than one. Chris was the perfect package. He had a great job, he was smart, caring, and well-traveled. In any other year of my life, I would have been ready to fall face-first into a relationship with him. But this wasn't any other year.

"I am totally not ready to be another girlfriend," my panic answered for me. "But that's really sweet. And I agree, long distance sucks." I attempted to recover.

As I looked at the man across the table that so many of my readers had fallen in love with, smiling at the broken woman he had crossed paths with in Barcelona, something became clear to me. Not even he was going to be able to break down this wall. And as much as I wanted to reciprocate the feelings that he was so clearly still having, I was just too freaking broken to feel anything—and it was going to take someone really extraordinary to change that.

Many more cocktails and a delicious meal later, we hopped into an Uber and headed back to our Airbnb. Somewhere in the Uber, the alcohol kicked in and, once we were home, we were both a lot drunker than we'd realized. We got changed, got into bed, and started to make out. Once we were both naked, it was clear that we were in no condition to be having sex. Thankfully, Chris being the good guy that he is, put his arm around me and held me until we both passed out.

I woke up to Chris the next morning while he was still sound asleep. As I lay there staring at the ceiling, I thought about the big Thought Onion I had uncovered back in Mykonos. My need for the physical desire of a man stemmed from not wanting to be abandoned. I gave up a sacred piece of myself in order to protect myself. But something like that runs so much deeper—what was the Origin Experience?

• My dad dying. I'm not safe without Dad—without a man.

That may sound crazy to some people—how on earth can your father dying lead to seeking physical validation from men? Anyone reading this who has lost a father knows all too well how complicated the repercussions of such a trauma are. Then I looked at some of the ways this pattern had showed up over the years in my life.

- Being friends with mostly boys in my elementary years.
- Always having a boyfriend and being in a relationship.
- Using sex as a tool to make myself not feel abandoned.

I'd realized it back in Mykonos. Yet, here I was, *clearly* still repeating that pattern. I didn't truly feel safe and protected by myself—I had always sought that from a man in my life. So as Chris slept soundly next to me, I spoke to my little six-year-old self. *Gabrielle, you don't need any man or physical affection to feel safe or worthy. You are safe and incredible and strong all by yourself. I'm here; you don't need to be scared.*

That night we met a few of my friends at our favorite dance spot. Everyone was so excited to meet the infamous Chris from Barcelona. We had a blast dancing all night and yet again drank a bit too much. At one point, Chris and I decided to head out to another famous LA spot—Roscoe's Chicken and Waffles. As we accommodated our drunk munchies, we continued to talk about life. Chris was really easy to talk to, and we had always been open with each other. It was a comfort having the person who had unknowingly helped me so much on my trip there with me. As he smiled at me across the table, I wondered what the hell was wrong with me. I had met him, across the world, after what was arguably one of the most difficult and gut-wrenching times of my entire life—and I hadn't felt like a brick wall. In fact, I had totally opened up to, connected with, and had feelings for this person. Yet here I was, months later, realizing that even the man who changed my course was no match for the broken pieces left unhealed inside of me. Those pieces were not going to be glued back together by any man—those pieces were going to have to be fixed by me.

While we stuffed our faces with a massive amount of delicious calories, my phone went off. It was a text from Jake.

Jake: Goodnight, Stone. Missing you.

It became intensely clear to me right then that what I was doing was not working. I had all these really amazing men orbiting around me and yet I didn't truly want anything with any of them. No one was able to break through or even slightly crack the wall that was now firmly and comfortably protecting my heart. And although I would be up front and tell people I wasn't ready for anything serious, brutally honest at moments, it was still beginning to create exactly what I didn't want—to make anyone feel the way Javier had made me feel. So, at Roscoe's Chicken and Waffles, I attempted a mildly drunk Thought Onion. Superficial thought?

- You're just having fun! Stop worrying about it. Men flirt and date around all the time. Why can't you?

While that thought might seem (and be) valid in many ways, it was still a very good insight to the fact that what I was doing was *not* working for me. Authentic?

- You're falling back into old habits of always needing a man in your life.

That was partially true—however, in the past, I would have been in a full-on relationship with one of these people showering me with love and attention, not feeling like I needed to hightail it in the other direction. So there must be something underneath it all—subconscious thought?

- You're not ready—and if you're not ready, who the hell are you?

My whole life I have felt most comfortable and powerful when I'm in control of what is going on in my life. When I am *ready*. If there is an issue, I can fix it. If I have a goal, I can achieve it. There is very little I haven't been ready to control in my life—and the things on that list have been fucking catastrophic. Death. Grief. Infidelity. Divorce. Heartache. So as I sat there, staring at the man who helped me heal across the world when I was so broken, I realized something. It's not going to matter if it's Marcus or Chris or Channing fucking Tatum straight out of *Magic Mike*—I am not ready to give myself to anyone because I haven't fixed *me* yet. As much as it pained me to say it, I was still very much *broken*—and the fact that I didn't know *how* to fix myself, that I couldn't *control* what I was feeling, that I for some reason *could not* love myself, was absolutely terrifying. Because if I can't fix myself, if I can't control it, who the hell am I?

When I woke up the next morning, I revisited my Thought Onion from the night before. As I lay there next to Chris, what I had been fighting the past two days had fully become clear to me—and I was actually pretty bummed about it. This was going to become a friendship and not much more. It wasn't just because he lived in a different city, or even that he was younger—it actually had nothing to do with him at all. I knew whatever I had felt in Barcelona had changed. I don't think he was ready to let me go at that moment—and for that I felt sorry.

We hiked up to the Griffith Observatory and spent the morning looking out over the epic views. I was leaving later that day to shoot a film in Arizona, and the only way to describe how I was feelings was—anxious. I had no idea what about, but it felt like a dark and ominous cloud could be seen in the distance and, somehow, I just knew that it was heading for me.

"You're going to get through this, Gabrielle." Chris snapped me out of my daze as we sat on top of the lookout.

"What?" I asked, confused.

"All of it. You're going to get through it. You might not be able to let anyone in right now, but whoever eventually gets in is going to be one lucky guy." He smiled at me.

Damn. I had done my best to have a good weekend and not show my brokenness, or the apparently obvious wall I was now hiding behind. I wiped away a hidden tear.

In that moment, the thing that grew most was our friendship. And for all the #TeamChris fans out there, I'm happy to tell you that we still have that friendship. He has since moved to LA, which has allowed us to have some awesome friend dates. We often laugh at all the questions that are asked about him. But after that weekend, I knew that anything more than a friendship wasn't in the cards for us. Alas, like Marcus, he had not filled the awful void that seemed to be growing inside me.

As I sat on the plane that evening, I knew that cloud of anxious dread I felt creeping toward me was about to arrive—and unfortunately, it was *so* much worse than I thought.

The Ridiculous Misadventures of...

HAPPY FUCKING BIRTHDAY

Something happened in Arizona. Something *really* happened in Arizona. But it wasn't obvious—it was a small little seed that was planted without me even consciously realizing it. Often in an artist's life, the work you do somehow mirrors something personal to you. Sometimes it's something that you're going through, things you need to heal, or a part of yourself that you have yet to discover. I did a film once where my character had a car accident and when she came to, she was upside down in the wrecked car and had to pull herself out. I showed up on set that night, not thinking too terribly much about the scene, and immediately burst into tears. The wrecked car looked *identical* to the car Jake had crashed and died in. That night, while being extremely difficult, also ended up being immensely therapeutic. It was as if I was faced with one of my biggest fears and then had to quite literally pull myself out of it.

On set in Arizona, it was no different. I was playing a character who had fallen madly in love with a man who everyone close to her warned her about—he ended up betraying her by leaving her, killing her father, and taking everything she valued. He'd never been the man she thought he was, and she ended up tragically jumping off a bridge to her death. Obviously, this is the overly dramatic movie version, but...*sound familiar?* One late-night shooting, we were filming a dream sequence that didn't have any dialogue, and the director was talking me through the different emotions he wanted to see me experience.

"He never loved you. He doesn't want you anymore. Everyone was right. How could you let this happen? Your heart is broken. He left. Your dad is gone. Everyone is gone."

Needless to say, I was fucking bawling (which was great for the footage), and I was obviously aware enough to realize how many fresh wounds those words poked at. And that's when the seed was planted.

That seed of old wounds then grew over the next week leading up to my twenty-ninth birthday, and the familiar depression that my soul had been dangerously teetering on the edge of came to a head. I went from wobbling on the rim to fully falling into the deep, dark hole that suffocates you while you're awake. The type of depression that can only stem from grief. And the scariest part? *I just wanted to freaking sit in it.*

"I don't want to do anything for my birthday," I said to my mom.

"What if we just have some of your close friends here to hang out?" she offered.

It was really weird. I have always wanted to be surrounded by people on my birthday. In fact, I often feel anxiety around making sure my birthday is fulfilling and fun. But this year, I just wanted to hide under the covers and cry.

The other thing that was buzzing around in the back of my mind like an annoying-ass fly that wouldn't just fucking die? The fact that Javier was supposed to be calling me on my birthday. We hadn't spoken in a month, and, to be honest, if I was clear on *anything* at that point, it was that talking to him would *not* help where I was currently at in life.

After my mom insisting that I at least have my close friends over—the ones who I could be sad and depressed around and not feel judged for it—and me agreeing, I made another decision. I was going to put my goddamn phone in a drawer and not take it out *all freaking day.*

On November 20th, 2017, I woke up just after 6 a.m. with anxiety. Waking up with anxiety is one of the worst ways to start your day, and it is physically impossible to go back to sleep when your exhausted body is in such an uncomfortable state of unrest. I desperately needed to do something with my racing mind and building anxiety—so I tossed my phone in my drawer and went to the gym.

Turns out, like most times, my mother was right. It actually ended up being a really great evening with a few of my close friends. We played a bunch of ridiculous games, drank some wine, and laughed ourselves stupid. I was really thankful for those people that night.

Once everyone had cleared out around midnight, I headed to my room to do what I had been dreading doing the entire day—look at my phone. *Maybe I'll just leave it there and never talk to anyone via technology again*, I thought to myself. Not really practical, Gabrielle. I started to sift through the dozens of texts, phone calls, and social media messages that had come in throughout the day.

There was a text from Tyler, which made me smile: *Happiest of birthdays to you, pretty one. Dinner soon.*

A voicemail from Chris that made me kind of sad: *Hey, Gabs, just calling to say happy birthday. Hope you're having an awesome day and weekend. Uh...yeah, last weekend was awesome. Missing you a little bit. Call me soon, bye.*

A voicemail from Jake that made me blush: *(guitar strums—followed by a fully sung rendition of Happy Birthday) That's my, uh, terrible version of Happy Birthday (laughs). That's it, that's what you get, so enjoy.*

And last, but certainly not least, the one birthday bomb I had been dreading the entire day—from Javier: A missed call. Then his voice as I hit play: *Hey, Gab, I tried calling you on my break. I'll try and get you later today. Happy birthday either way! Thirty is a big one.* Another missed call.

The surge. FIRST OF ALL, I had just turned *twenty-nine* and wouldn't be thirty for another year. This freaking man, who was supposedly *in love* with me and had thought (as brief as it had been) that I was *the one*—who couldn't live life without me as his best goddamn friend—DIDN'T KNOW MY FUCKING AGE? My blood started to boil. I had moved past the denial and pain stages of my heartbroken grief and shimmied right on into *anger*. I was *angry* at Javier. For disrupting my life, shattering my heart, confusing the hell out of me, not abiding by the space I had asked for, and now, as trivial as it may seem, not knowing how fucking old I was.

I decided then and there that I would use that anger to get me out of this deep fucking hellhole of depression. I would use it to *get the fuck over him.* I would use it to pick myself up, dust myself off, and succeed. *Happy birthday, Gabrielle. He just gave you the one gift you truly needed.*

The Ridiculous Misadventures
of...
IT'S NOT A DATE

While I had committed to getting myself out of this colossal and unceasing pit of depression I had found myself in, it is *so* much fucking easier said than done. But I was committed, so to jump-start the process, I made a list of things that I knew made my soul happy—that I was completely capable of giving myself. Nothing needed from a man, a friend, or anyone other than me. I taped the list onto my mirror and vowed I would complete at least one thing off that list every single day—meditating, dancing, creating, going to the gym, healthy eating. All things that I knew made me feel good mentally. And here, without me even realizing it, in the hopes of saving myself, the self-love cocktail was born.

I also called some of my closest friends and scheduled a proper celebration of turning—say it with me now—*TWENTY-NINE*. We scheduled dinner at one of my favorite restaurants and dancing at our favorite bar after. I felt accomplished for at least planning something that was meant to be fun—I hadn't really gone out anywhere in the last three weeks.

Something else I needed to do? Man up (well...woman up) and tell the men in my life that I wasn't going to be able to give them anything in return. Don't get me wrong, I had been very up front and honest about where I was at every step of the way, but there was definitely a gray area with Jake and Chris where I was figuring out what exactly my feelings for them were. So, like ripping off a three-day old Band-Aid, I did. First, to Jake.

Me: Thank you for the birthday message. It put the biggest smile on my face. I've been a wreck honestly, put my phone in a drawer for the whole day.

Jake: Happy to make you smile. Anything I can do? Or want to talk about?

Me: It's just really frustrating. After the divorce I was fine…really fine. But this whole thing with Javier really messed me up. It's like he said, "What's her biggest issue? Abandonment? Cool, boom." And I've just been coming to terms with how much anger I have toward him for doing this to me and making me so not okay.

Jake: Well, Daniel abandoned too. I'm sorry. Getting through the burn-off of anger to the truth of your inner world and the reason we attract these things is gold. It ain't easy but in my experience it's the only thing that works for me to heal and grow and ultimately attract the things I truly desire.

Ugh. Ain't that the fucking truth.

Me: Yeah. I think I just need to be alone right now.

Jake: I hope you can find peace.

That one simple sentence—*I think I just need to be alone right now.* It's always easy to preach it, until you have men wanting to restore your faith in humanity ready to sweep you off your feet. I really was like a brick fucking wall. And although I know Jake would have liked to take a sledgehammer and make things go a very different way, having him give me permission to walk the other direction was more valuable than he will ever know.

The next one seemed so much harder for some reason. Chris. Maybe because I knew how we had both felt sitting on the beach in Barcelona or because, in a weird way, he had been the first healing piece of my complicated European puzzle. What I did know is that

I had meant what I said to Jacob standing in the Barcelona club: *I genuinely like you both and want to be friends with you guys.* And that meant being honest about my newly realized feelings.

Me: Hey, you. Thank you for the call yesterday. I've been in a really bad place this last week and yesterday decided to just put my phone away. Sorry for not answering. It's just been a lot.

Chris: Damn, that's awful. No worries about missing the call. I know that feeling. If you want to talk about it, feel free to call whenever. Did anything in particular happen in AZ?

He wasn't dumb—and even if his trip to LA wasn't all I had imagined, the real shift from me came once I went to Arizona to film.

Me: Yeah, the part I was doing was weirdly similar to a lot of the bullshit with Javier. After the divorce, I was really strict with myself on going to the gym and not drinking, cause whenever I don't physically feel good it makes whatever else I'm going through worse...and after Europe I didn't go back to doing that. It's all kind of caught up with me and then that shoot just ripped it open. I'm just a mess.

Chris: Ah, that makes sense. I'm glad you're realizing it and taking the time you need.

Me: I'm sorry. I just need to fix myself right now.

Chris: I get it, Gabs. And I'm here if you need anything.

He could clearly see how my mental health was suffering and that I was in no shape to be in a relationship. Want to know how you're really messed up? Walk away from an awesome guy that all your readers fell in love with. Still, I felt a sense of relief knowing I didn't have to continue through a maze with anyone when I knew the center wouldn't be worth fighting to get to.

That Thursday Tyler had asked if he could take me to dinner for my birthday. Although I recognized that he was devastatingly handsome, nothing had gone down that made me feel he was pushing for anything beyond a friendship. So I said yes because it was another commitment that would get me out of the house, out of my head, and hopefully ultimately out of this funk.

Jess was over and, as I hopped out of the shower to dry off, I heard her voice from my bedroom.

"Wait, so is this, like, a date?" she yelled through the open bathroom door.

"No! I've known him for like ten years. He played my older brother," I shouted back.

"Well, what if he thinks it's a date?" she asked.

"He doesn't. He looks at me like his little sister."

"What are you going to wear?" Jess asked excitedly.

"Clothes," I responded. "Seriously, Jess, I'm not even wearing makeup."

"Where are you guys going?"

"Some place called Café Bizou. I've never been," I answered as she began typing it into her phone.

"Oh my God, Gabs, it's like romantic!" she squealed.

"It is not!" I rolled my eyes and grabbed her phone. "Oh, shit."

"See! It's totally a date." She snatched it back from me.

An hour later, I headed to the front door right when my mom was coming home.

"Where are you off to?" she asked.

"Dinner," I responded.

"A date?"

"No!" I shouted on the way to my car. It was just two old friends going to dinner to catch up. That's not a date. It was totally *not* a date.

I arrived at the admittedly very romantic restaurant and found Tyler sitting at the bar with some type of alcohol on the rocks that only older super cool men seem to be able to drink without puking—I'll never understand it.

"Hey, you!" He stood up and wrapped me in his giant arms that immediately made me feel like I had shrunk to a size extra small.

"Hi!" I took a deep breath, letting go of a small bit of the anxiety I had been feeling constantly weighed down by.

"What are you drinking?" he asked.

"Wine, please." He handed me the wine list.

Before everyone points out the fact that I had just told Chris I needed to stop drinking and focus solely on my mental health, let me do it for you. I'm aware that I needed to get back to my no drinking self-care formula of life—however this week was about getting back out into life, celebrating my birthday properly, and dinner with this (obnoxiously attractive) old friend. Could drinking be left out of all of the above? Yes, of course—but baby steps, people. Baby steps.

After a drink at the bar, we sat down for dinner at a very cute and cozy table under the dim lighting of the restaurant. Do you want to know how much I *didn't* consider this a date? The entire fucking time, I sat across from this totally eligible bachelor, blabbing on about my ex-husband, divorce, heartbreak, Javier, and what a complete and utter mess I was—because that's what friends who once played brother and sister, who are not on a date, do.

"Enough about my shit-show saga. What the hell have you been doing with your life?" I asked. The last I knew he was married with a child and living life happily ever after. Oh, social media.

"Christine and I separated a little over two years ago. It just wasn't working, and I was so unhappy. We figured it was better to do it when Blue was a baby than to stretch it out until its inevitable demise." He chuckled.

"Yeah, I can understand that." I listened.

"We're still waiting to do all the paperwork and be officially divorced," he said.

"We have that in common." We laughed.

"When I saw your post about the divorce the day you left for Europe, it really hit me. I really felt for you. It's amazing that you're writing a book and making something out of it all," he said as our food arrived.

"Thank you. It's been the best form of therapy I could have given myself. Who would have thought, divorced by twenty-nine," I scoffed.

"About as much as I would have thought I'd be divorced with a kid by forty-four." He smiled. Something about Tyler's energy just made me feel...safe. He had a calming, soul-touching presence about him—and he was fucking charming as hell.

After I'd lost the battle over contributing to the check, Tyler walked me to my car.

"So, I'll see you soon?" he said, again wrapping me up in a hug.

"Yes. This was so great. Thank you again for dinner."

"You're most welcome. Drive safe." He opened my car door and waited for me to get situated.

"You too." I smiled and he gently shut my door.

As he walked away to his car, he looked over his shoulder and flashed his deathly baby blue eyes that I was 95% certain had given him way too much leniency in life. I had successfully gotten out of my house, laughed, and had a genuinely good time—but still, it totally *wasn't* a date...was it?

The Ridiculous Misadventures
of...
THE UNICORN

Two days later it was time to slap makeup on my face for the first time in God knows how long, get my shit together, put my happy face on, and celebrate my birthday. As we sat at one my favorite restaurants in LA, sipped on wine, and scarfed down food, I couldn't help but feel...sad. There was just something that was making me dread going dancing. I just wanted to be home. Me not wanting to dance is like the Real Housewives not wanting to attend a Botox party. However, I had committed to climbing out of the deep hellhole of depression and was determined to somehow make the best of it. When we were waiting for our Uber, my phone went off.

Tyler: PEANUT! Are you guys still going tonight?

My one glass of wine assisted with my response.

Me: Yes, sir, just leaving dinner. Come cheer me up.

Tyler: Done and done. See you there. Keep smiling...you're amazing in so many ways, and these last few dudes shall think themselves accursed that they didn't just cherish the ground you walk on. True idiots. Love ya, kid. See you soon.

While I looked at my phone, trying to dissect what the hell he was talking about, another text came in.

Tyler: You get a prize if you can tell me what that is quoted from…WITHOUT GOOGLING IT.

I mean…it sounded like dramatic lingo à la Romeo and Juliet, but I've never been a huge Shakespeare fan (gasp…so kill me.) But you see, everyone? "Love ya, kid." It wasn't a date. This was safe territory, and I finally had a friend that made me feel safe and secure during this tornado of unhappiness.

Me, Jess, and a few of my other friends headed to the club. We got there early before it was too crowded and saw Tyler standing at the bar, chatting it up with one of the bartenders.

"Birthday girl!" He flashed his knee-weakening smile in the sexy dim lighting of the small club. I gave him a giant hug and immediately felt a little better about the night I had ahead of me.

After introductions and Jess reminding me how hot Tyler was, we all grabbed a drink and headed to our table for the night. There are benefits and drawbacks about knowing the bartenders on a personal level. On the bright side, you're not paying for drinks all night. We would end up spending roughly $30 each at the end of the night to pool together a big thank-you tip. If you're not from LA, that would normally cover a drink and a half. On the darker side…*you're not paying for drinks all night.* This means you are not only sucking down tequila and vodka like it's water, you're also drinking yourself into the zero-inhibitions state that is guaranteed to leave you with a massive hangover and regretting at least one thing. And because Tyler was a former employee, it was now like partying in our own big DJ-accompanied, open bar home.

"You never told me why you stopped working here," I shouted to Tyler while sitting next to him on the couch in our section.

"Too much partying. I was here until like 4 a.m. on the weekends. I love all the guys here and we're like family, but it wasn't healthy for me," he shouted back.

"Yeah and exhausting," I added.

"It was great while it lasted, and I was making insane money here, but I'm so over bartending. Shitty life of an actor that we have to always have a side hustle." He took a sip of his drink.

"I know it well." I laughed.

Too many drinks, a surprising amount of laughs, and more than a few deep conversations were had between Tyler and me. By 2:30 a.m. the club was cleared except for the employees, a few random friends, Tyler, Jess, and me. With the lights now turned fully up, Tyler laughed with his friends behind the bar as they counted their registers, and Jess and I took over the floor as our own personal stage while Beyoncé, Britney, and Missy Elliot played (all by our requests). There are some things you just can't beat and one of those things is drunkenly dancing as a DJ plays your own playlist, doing improv choreography like you are a fucking queen, and not giving two shits what anyone around thinks.

Finally, around 3 a.m., it was decided that we were all heading back to Tyler's place, a short ten-minute Uber ride away. No one was in any shape to be driving anywhere and, quite frankly, I didn't even have faith in Jess to make the ride as a passenger.

Tyler, Jess, one of the security guards, and I laughed and joked as annoying-ass drunk people tend to do at 3 a.m. in an Uber. When the car came to a stop, I looked around and realized we were in the parking lot of a liquor store.

"Oh my God, I cannot drink anymore." I looked at Tyler, deciding if I was disgusted or impressed with the fact that he wasn't tapped out.

"No, this is my place." He laughed.

"I'm sorry, what?" I asked as we all stumbled out of the Uber.

"You live at a liquor store!" Jess shouted with drunk excitement. Tyler laughed, humoring my intoxicated young friend.

"No, my entrance just shares a parking lot. Weird, I know. You'll see." He pulled out his keys and began to unlock a big wooden door that had a metal fence on each side.

"If I didn't know you, I would for sure think we were about to be murdered," I said.

"I mean, how well do you really know me?" He smirked as he pushed open the door.

It led into a small outside foyer. We walked through, and he unlocked a second door. I walked in and stopped. There were huge, vaulted ceilings, brightly colored adobe walls, and a huge piece of driftwood with industrial lights hanging from it as the main light source in the living room. Art like I had never seen before filled the sky-high walls all around us. It quite literally looked like an artist's dream home. I was awestruck.

"I'm sorry...this...this is where you *live*?" I asked as Jess and I gaped at the eclectic space.

"Yeah, ten years now." He tossed his keys down.

"How much do I have to pay you to leave?" I asked. Tyler laughed. "And this art...is just...incredible." I admired the different pieces on the walls.

"Thanks." He smiled.

There was a theme in many of the art pieces. A sorrow, an anguish, a darkness.

As Tyler made everyone some tea, I chatted with the security guard, and Jess drunkenly obsessed over the hot bartender that was still closing out the club.

"Can you call him? Is he coming?" she asked Tyler every five minutes.

"I texted him. I think he's coming by after he leaves." He'd laugh and smile at me.

"Sorry," I mouthed to him. He was being an awfully good sport wrangling the very drunk and equally horny twenty-three-year-old Jess.

"When are you gonna do my piece for me, Ty?" the security guard asked as he looked up at one of the paintings on the wall.

"Wait, I'm sorry, *you* did all of these?" I asked, shocked.

"Yeah, most of them," he said nonchalantly.

"Are you freaking kidding me? These are incredible! Why are you acting?" I spurted out. He laughed. "I mean, you know what I mean."

"I've only been doing it for like a year. I just had some stuff I needed to get out. I'm not an artist."

"Like fucking hell, you aren't. You have thousands and thousands of dollars hanging on your wall, idiot!"

"Well, thank you. I don't even sign them. It's just something I started messing with one day." He sipped his tea.

Just then, the hot bartender walked in, and Jess went from a drunken stupor to drunkenly energized and ready to have exactly what she had been waiting for.

After some awkward small talk with the rest of the group in the living room, they made their way upstairs just as the security guard was saying goodbye to head home. Tyler and I silently cracked up as the two stumbled up the stairs, and I repeatedly professed how sorry I was about my embarrassingly drunk and horny friend.

"It's fine, he's stoked." He laughed.

He refilled our tea, and we sat on the brightly colored couch in the living area.

"I can't believe you live here. This is like every artist's dream."

"Wanna hear the best part?"

"How can it get better?" I sipped my tea.

"It's rent controlled. I pay $1600 a month." I almost spit my tea out.

"ARE YOU FREAKING KIDDING ME?" I was legitimately offended. He laughed.

"I am not."

"You can't even get a shitty apartment for that in LA!"

"Well, it does come with its drawbacks," he said.

"Like what?"

"Well, I share my front yard with a rotating roster of homeless people and drunk Hollywood idiots."

"Bearable," I said.

"Sometimes there are freakishly large cockroaches seeking shelter from Hollywood Boulevard," he told me, waiting to see if I got squeamish.

"House guests that you have to murder. Manageable."

"There's no heat or air-conditioning."

"Definite deal breaker." We laughed.

I felt so comfortable with Tyler. It was like being with someone my soul had known for a very long time, and I remembered feeling that same way when we first met all those years ago on set. There

I was, totally drunk, obviously broken, and incredibly vulnerable, and he didn't for one second make me feel like he needed anything from me.

About thirty minutes later, the hot bartender came downstairs with a cowboy hat on (we didn't even think to ask at that point) and hung out with Tyler while I headed up to check on Jess.

There, strewn across the guest bed, fully clothed, snoring as if she had taken a sleeping pill, was my best friend. Oh, Jess, what would I do without you. I poked her a few times, shook her gently, but there was no use—it became glaringly obvious that we would not be leaving Tyler's house that night.

I tucked her in and headed back downstairs just as the bartender was leaving. He gave me a quick hug and headed out the door, leaving Tyler and I in the now-empty house. We stood there for a moment.

"So, Jess is passed out," I said.

"Well, you guys shouldn't be driving tonight."

"No! We were going to Uber home, but I can't even wake her ass up." I chuckled.

"You're more than welcome to stay here." He smiled sweetly.

"Are you sure?"

"Of course. Totally fine."

"I can sleep on the couch. She's knocked out, star-fished on the bed up there," I said.

"I have a king bed. You can have a whole side to yourself. Or I can take the couch," he offered.

"You are not giving up your bed for me." I thought about it for a moment. "It's fine, we can both sleep in your bed."

"Are you sure? I can sleep down here. Whatever you're comfortable with."

"Yeah, it's fine. It's just sleeping." I laughed.

We headed upstairs, and he gave me some sweatpants and a T-shirt. It was a huge relief to change into them after being in tight jeans and heels all night. I turned the light off, climbed into the king-sized bed next to Tyler, a good foot in between us, and took a deep breath.

"Thank you," I finally said, in the darkness.

"For what?"

"For not trying to fuck me."

"You're welcome." He chuckled.

"I don't think I've ever been in bed with a man who hasn't tried something with me. You're like a unicorn." I laughed.

"Gabrielle, whatever is going on here is cosmic—and that's way more important to me than a good time."

I lay there in the dark and realized that he was right. Every time I found myself around this person, it felt oddly spiritual—like something cosmic was happening. How *big* of a cosmic occurrence was about to happen in our lives? I don't think either of us had *any* fucking idea.

The Ridiculous Misadventures
of...
LATIN LOVERS ANONYMOUS

A few days after my birthday, on an afternoon that wasn't especially significant or noteworthy, I woke up knowing it was time. Time to do what I had been dreading since I had made the decision to write a book about my wild journey—it was time to finally sit down and write the chapter "Fuck Love." Boy, did that title seriously resonate with where I was currently at. While I had written the majority of *Eat, Pray, #FML* on my Europe trip, there were a few loose ends to finish before the book was complete. I had written all about the divorce (after being convinced by my girlfriends that it was imperative to include my version of CSI in detail), finished the sections about Mykonos that I had been partying too hard to complete, and put the final touches on the ending days in San Vito. But there was one section left that needed to be written: *how Javier and I fell in love.*

I begrudgingly sat on my bed, opened my laptop, and wished it was late enough to pour myself a giant glass of wine. Luckily, I wasn't writing in my journal anymore, so I was afforded the gift of the delete button. *We fell in love the way you fall off a fucking cliff— that ended with me dying.* Delete. *Because who wouldn't want to be whisked off on an Italian getaway with a new love before you get blindsided and slapped across the fucking face?* Delete. *And then, suddenly, all his feelings just disappeared, and I realized I was apparently dating a fucking magician.* DELETE.

Just start from the freaking beginning, Gabrielle. Once I got over the fact that I was going to have to revisit the five epic days where I thought I had met my Latin prince charming, whom I would obviously be having gorgeous babies and growing old with, it actually came sort of...easy. I got to a point where I needed to start inserting text messages from those early days, which meant scrolling way, way up to the very beginning of our correspondence. I began to read over them as I copied them into the manuscript.

Waking up to you this morning has been one of the best moments I've ever experienced.

I can't believe I get to be with you, I feel super lucky.

There are no rules in love. It happens when you least expect it, clearly.

Just then, staring at those text messages of false hope and short-lived happiness, my fucking phone rang. *It was him.* It was like he somehow felt my energy being focused on him and decided now was the perfect time to call. *What. The. Fuck.*

I picked my phone up, tossed it across my bed, and told myself it was just a weird coincidence and not some epic sign from the universe that our souls are connected (you know, what most women think when something like this takes place). But beyond the fact that it was eerily timed, it also made me really freaking irritated. I had told him I needed space. We had made the decision to take a break from each other, yet he had messaged me a few days later and was again calling me now. Hadn't not answering on my birthday sent a pretty clear freaking message?

Still, my trauma brain began to spiral. *What if he's calling me because something's wrong? What if he's not okay?* Luckily, I didn't have to ask Javier—I could ask his best friend.

Me: You've talked to him right? Like he's okay? He just called me again.

Manny: Yes talked to him yesterday. It's good. He asked me if I'm in contact with you.

Me: Okay. I wouldn't ever want to not be answering his calls if he wasn't okay.

Manny: He just doesn't get the damage that he makes. But he
is fine.

Not only did that make me feel fine about not picking up my
phone, I also recognized the truth in that statement. *He just doesn't
get the damage he causes.* Here I was, gasping for some fucking air
as I flailed around for a life vest while he was on a freaking cruise
ship living his dream.

Over the next few weeks I finished the chapters, which ended
up being the most difficult to write, and didn't answer one goddamn
message from Javier.

One early December evening, I was sitting on the couch at my
mother's home, wallowing in the fact that I was twenty-nine, depressed, and so very single. It had been about two months since I
had closed the door on my "friendship" with Javier. I had kept my
word and not answered any of the messages that had come from
Mexico City. *Stay strong, Gabrielle.* You don't need any more Latin
men in your life right now.

I rented a big blockbuster I hadn't seen and snuggled into my
not-so-sweet sorrow. A bunch of familiar A-list faces began to dance
across the screen, and then one I didn't recognize caught my eye.

Damn. Who the hell is that? I looked at the gorgeous Latin man
gracing my TV. *He's so hot.* I continued to watch the movie and became more and more intrigued about who this person was. I googled
him, only to discover he had been in dozens of big films, many of
which I had seen.

I opened my Instagram and typed in his name, easily finding
him because we live in an age where you can just click a button and
have someone's entire life posted before your very eyes. Rodolfo
González. I scrolled through his eclectic array of artistic photos, liking a few of them, and then realized what a freaking stalker I was
being. *Jesus, Gabrielle, put your damn phone down.* Besides, you,
my friend, are on a Latin detox.

I continued to watch the movie and a few minutes later my
phone lit up. It was Instagram notifications—*from Rodolfo.* I
opened my phone and saw that he was liking photos of mine—from

quite a long time ago. I went back to his page, liked a few more, as more notifications came through on my end. Then he followed me. I laughed to myself and followed him in return. Moments later, a message came through.

Rodolfo: Hola.

Me: Hola. Como estas?

Rodolfo: Bien y tu?

Me: Muy bien. Careful, that's about as far as my Spanish goes.

Rodolfo: Jajajaja. Do I know you? I think I would remember you.

Me: I don't believe so no…

Rodolfo: Where are you from?

Me: Los Angeles, born and raised. You?

Rodolfo: Mexico.

Of course, you are. *Run, Gabrielle.* Just, run. We continued to talk about basic things. All the while, Instagram notifications were still coming in.

Rodolfo: Let me take you for coffee before I leave for the holidays.

My depressed self thought about this—for, like, two seconds.

Me: Sure.

Okay, seriously? I just happened to be watching a film, thought this guy was sexy, decided to find him online, and now we were going on a fucking date. ONLY IN MY LIFE. I laughed as I sat texting back and forth with the person I was also watching on my screen, thinking about how incredibly ridiculous this all was. But, I mean—when depressed and living at your mother's house, right?

A few days later, I threw on a pair of tight jeans and a tank top and headed out to meet Rodolfo for lunch. I had never gone on a date with someone that I had never actually *met* before, but it was a public place, and he was a famous actor, so I figured the chances of me getting murdered were quite slim.

I pulled up to the casual lunch spot in Studio City, parked, and saw Rodolfo waiting out front, looking freakishly similar to Javier. I walked across the street, and he smiled as he stood up to greet me.

"Gabriella!" He opened his arms to hug me and kiss my cheek.

"Hi! Nice to meet you." I laughed.

"I know, this is so weird. I've never met someone from online like this."

"Neither have I, but welcome to LA." I smiled.

"I'm glad you could come. Let's sit." He spoke in a thick accent that, of course, made my knees slightly less stable.

We sat down and ordered on the outside patio. We chatted about him growing up in Mexico and moving to the States to pursue his acting career. He was very charming, and although he spoke good English, there were definitely moments he had to pause and think of the correct English word. We talked a lot about the industry we were both in, although he was on a totally different level than I had ever been.

After two hours and two cups of coffee each, we hugged goodbye and I headed to my car. It definitely wasn't the instant, connect-on-every-freaking-level, internal fireworks situation it had been with Javier—but he was sweet, talented, and *so* unfortunately my type. And it was a welcomed distraction from the ocean of depression that I was exhausted from treading. It was not lost on me how eerily similar Rodolfo was to Javier. He was the same age, Latin, a successful actor, and spoke a few different languages. Okay... maybe closer than I'd care to admit.

And so, I began to prepare for my first holiday alone in five years. But before I left on that trip, there would be one more surprise piece added to the ever-changing dating puzzle.

The Ridiculous Misadventures of...

DON'T RUN

In the three weeks since my wild birthday night that ended at Tyler's, we had been hanging out. I say hanging out because that's genuinely what it was. I would go to his awesome spot in Hollywood, and we would eat dinner, watch a movie, and talk about everything. We would lie on the couch and I would rest my head on his chest with his arm around me, but it never really felt like it was going anywhere beyond that—or that it needed to. I was so used to every man in my life being ready to take my clothes off the second I was in a horizontal position—this was totally new to me. And to be honest, it was really nice. I felt a level of comfort with Tyler that I had never felt with anyone before—male or female.

We had fallen into a very real, very comfortable friendship—one where we openly talked about the good, the bad, and the ugly.

"How often do you have Blue?" I asked one night when I was at his house for the fourth night in a row.

"Not often enough," he said somberly. "Right now, I only have her two days a week. Not even overnight."

I sat up and turned to face him.

"Why?" I asked.

"It's kind of heavy, dude. When Christine and I split, I went down a really dark road. I was partying a lot at the bars I was working at, being irresponsible, got into some drugs. I was never not being a good dad when I was with her. In fact, I was so hyperfocused that I was going over the top when I was with her—but I wasn't healthy. So Christine has her most of the time until I prove that I'm fully sober and okay."

"Then why the hell are you out drinking until all hours of the night?" I jabbed.

"I'm on top of it," he assured me.

"You're not on top of it if you're out drinking! I had no idea you were supposed to be refraining from all that."

"I'm not doing the heavy stuff that was causing a problem. But that is why I stopped working at the bar."

"I feel like an asshole. I wouldn't have dragged you out on my birthday if I had known that."

"Don't. I wanted to be there. I'm handling it all," he said as I heavily side-eyed him. "How's the book coming?"

"I'm almost finished." I begrudgingly allowed him to change the subject.

"Already? Jesus. I mean not that I know anything about writing a book but doesn't it usually take a long time?"

"I don't know. I've never written one." I laughed. "It's taken three months. Most of it I wrote in Europe."

"Can I read it?" He took me off guard with the question.

"I...uh...I mean...I guess? No one's read it yet."

"I can't wait." He smiled.

Every night that we hung out, we'd have another conversation that propelled our friendship, deepened our bond, and made me really thankful I had someone I felt at ease with.

"You have a wall up," he said one late night after a movie.

"What do you mean?" I asked, intrigued at what he had picked up over the past few weeks.

"I can just see it. You were broken so badly that there was nothing left to do but build a giant wall of protection around your spirit. Around your heart."

I was shocked at how accurate that statement was.

"Yeah. I've never had that. Even after my divorce, which was probably when it made sense to." I laughed.

"You're allowed to not be strong, you know. After everything you went through, you're allowed to be broken." I held back tears.

For some reason, hearing someone give me permission to not be okay made me feel like a giant boulder had been lifted off my chest.

"Thank you." My voice cracked.

"You're welcome. The right people will wait for you." Our eyes locked. And in that very moment, without me even realizing it, a tiny little crack was made in my giant wall. *By Tyler*.

There was something about his energy that just made me feel like everything was somehow okay. And every night, when he would walk me to my car, we would stand in each other's arms for a few moments too long.

Then one night, after three weeks of dinners, movies, deep conversations, and driving home from Hollywood at 2 a.m., it happened.

"I have to tell you something," he said as we were sitting on the couch.

"Oh God. Okay..." I waited with anxious anticipation.

"I don't know how much longer I'm going to be able to lie on this couch with you and not try to kiss you." There was a long pause as I thought of how the hell to respond to this unexpected statement.

"I don't...I don't want to ruin what this is," I said, looking at him.

"I know. It's different. I feel connected to you on some cosmic level—but I just needed to tell you, I don't know how much longer I can not kiss you for."

"Tyler. I'm a mess. You know that. I mean, I'm still in love with my ex," I said flat out.

"I know you are. And I'll wait. I just needed you to know."

"Okay," I said, putting my head back on his chest. He wrapped his big arm around me and turned the movie on, and I asked myself what I was actually feeling. I hadn't been dying to rip his clothes off—I hadn't even been hoping he would kiss me. I was genuinely comfortable and happy in this human's presence (and, fine, his arms) without any pressure or expectations—and because of that, I had been totally relaxed, goofy, makeup free, and 100% my true self around him. When you exist like that with someone for three weeks, without all the layers of bullshit society expects you to put forth, it's amazing how quickly you can bond.

We finished the movie, randomly stopping to talk throughout, but the kiss was never brought up again. It was now just simply known between the two of us.

He walked me to my car, gave me one of his hugs that made all the evil in the world melt away, brushed my hair behind my ear, and smiled.

"Text me when you get home, okay?"

"Okay." I smiled.

He wasn't going to kiss me. He was never going to kiss me until I let him know that it was okay. Finally, there was someone who respected my wishes—and respected my worth. This man was totally new territory for me. I drove home that night wondering if I should run the other direction—because I knew I wasn't healed. I knew that I wasn't ready to be responsible for someone else's feelings. I had just clearly learned that with Chris and Jake. But there was something deep, deep inside of me that ever so softly whispered...*don't run.*

*****

After the night Tyler confessed he wanted to kiss me, we had another week of dinners, movies, and talking. We would talk about his daughter and how he felt that he had totally lost his way when his time with her had been taken away. How difficult it was navigating the tension between him and Christine, and that, although he'd always wanted to be a father, he'd never imagined it would look the way it currently did. We would talk about the catastrophe of the last few months of 2017 and how I could not wait for this year to be over.

There were so many parts of Tyler that mirrored me. He had lost his mother at a young age and, like me, had been the one who found her lying on the floor.

"Do you think your life would have been different if she hadn't died?" I asked.

"In some ways. It definitely made me grow up faster than intended. I probably wouldn't have had as much displaced anger."

"Yeah, I feel that way too. Good old abandonment wounds."

"I know them all too well. Pretty messed up that the men in your life ripped those wide open," he pointed out.

"Wide fucking open." I laughed.

"I promise you I'll never touch those triggers. I know how real they are." I looked at him, feeling more seen than ever before. I had never felt more understood, acknowledged, and protected by someone else's words—and it caused yet another crack to break in my hardened wall.

Then one night while we were lying on the couch, he looked at me.

"I can't wait anymore," he said, looking into my eyes. I took a few moments as I looked back at him.

"Okay," I finally said.

"I mean, I can. I will. I just don't want to."

"Okay." I smiled.

And there, on the couch we had spent a month on, watching movies, learning about each other's hearts and weak spots, cuddling, and laughing, Tyler kissed me. A massive explosion of fireworks didn't go off inside of me to make me realize I would obviously be jumping into a relationship with this person—it was just a really good, connected kiss. It's one experience to kiss someone you barely know at the end of a first or second date. It's an entirely different experience to kiss someone you've spent a good amount of time building a foundation of friendship with. And as I lay on the couch, wrapped in his arms, kissing him, I didn't feel like I wanted to tear his clothes off—it felt like my heart was finally safe.

"I swear to God if you freak out on me and mess up whatever this is that we have, I will kill you," was the first thing he heard from my mouth after I pulled away from our first kiss. He laughed.

"I will never not be here, Peanut."

There was more kissing, more laughter, and the same comforting energy I had cherished as my safe haven for the past month. When it was way past my bedtime, he walked me to my car.

"Do you have plans Saturday?" I asked.

"No. Why? What's up?"

"Like...as a friend...do you want to come to my mom's tree trimming party?"

He looked at me and tried to hide the smile on his face. "I would love to come to your mom's tree trimming party...as a friend."

"Good. I'll see you Saturday." Now I was the one trying to hide my smile.

"Great. I look forward to meeting your mother."

"Oh, stop it!" I playfully smacked his chest as we both laughed.

"Text me when you get home," he said as he hugged me tightly.

"Yes, Jacky."

I got in my car and hopped on the freeway with thoughts swirling around in my head. Had I just crossed a massively bad line? Was this going to totally ruin whatever this amazing bond was that Tyler and I had? Was I completely falling back into old habits?

When I got home, I texted Tyler, as requested.

Me: I'm home. Thank you for having me. Again. Lol.

Tyler: You're welcome. Glad you made it home safe. Are you totally regretting everything and spinning into a downward spiral of panic yet?

How the fuck does he already know me so well?

Me: Just a bit.
Me: Kidding.
Me: But...let's not be kissing at the tree trimming party.

Tyler: Why would we be kissing? We're just friends, Gabrielle. God.

Me: Goodnight, idiot.

Tyler: Goodnight.

Saturday rolled around, and my mother's annual tree trimming party was ready to begin in my childhood home. Every year, she would get a big Christmas tree, and people would bring a dish or a bottle for the table. We would drink, eat, laugh, and decorate the tree. She'd been doing it since I was in diapers, and it was always the highlight of her December.

"My friend Tyler is coming tonight," I told her in the kitchen as we set up the liquor table.

"Oh?" she asked with all the motherly connotation that tiny word could hold.

"We did that film together in Michigan forever ago."

"Ah, yes! I remember. He's the one you've been hanging out with the past few weeks?"

"Yes. But we're just friends. He's great, you'll love him. But we're just friends," I repeated.

"Okay. Well, you know any of your friends are welcome. Is Jess coming?"

"Yes." I set the ice bucket on the table.

"Great!" she squealed with her holiday cheer in full swing.

As friends, family, and newcomers arrived, the house began to bustle with Christmas spirit. As I was shoving a massive bite of my aunt's famous shepherd's pie into my mouth, I glanced over to the front door just as Tyler walked in—with two bouquets of flowers.

I sat my plate of food down and headed over to greet him, mildly shocked that he 1) looked so dashingly handsome in his jeans and sweater, and 2) was holding two huge bouquets of beautiful flowers.

"Hi!" I swallowed as I walked over to him.

"Hey! These are for you." He handed me one of the bouquets.

"You so did not need to do this." I gave him a look that said *Just freaking friends, dude, remember?* "But they're beautiful, thank you."

We turned and walked into the kitchen where my mom, my once-nanny-turned-good-friend Kristen, and our other dear family friend Angie were all chatting.

"Mom, this is Tyler." I introduced him as he handed my mom the other bouquet.

"So nice to meet you. Thank you for having me." He went in to give her a hug.

I saw it from the very first moment. My mom was absolutely overjoyed with the charming, good-looking older man her daughter had brought home. God help me.

"These are absolutely beautiful! Thank you so much, Tyler. Welcome to the party!"

As I introduced him to Kristen and Angie, my mother looked at me and mouthed, *Oh my God.* I rolled my eyes and waved her off with my hand.

Tyler did not try to kiss me that night—or even get too close to me, for that matter. In fact, he floated around the party like a social fucking butterfly, talking to anyone and everyone. At one point, I walked through the house to look for him, and found him on a ladder behind the tree, hanging lights with the other men in the living room. More than a few people had cornered me to inquire if the new handsome addition to the party was my new flame.

"Who on earth is that handsome man I was just chatting with?" one of my mom's friends asked me, keeping her eyes locked on Tyler as she sipped her wine.

"We're just friends."

"Why? He's absolutely wonderful!" she persisted.

"Because I'm still working through my life falling apart. Twice." I laughed.

"Well, maybe once you're ready. He's so charming." She winked as she sauntered off.

I sipped my glass of wine as Jess came up beside me with a massive plate of food.

"Gabs, he's so hot." We both looked as he stood on the ladder, hanging lights and laughing like he'd known all these people for years. I grabbed a piece of cheese off her plate.

"Yeah, I know. But we're just friends."

"Right. Have you seen the way he looks at you?" she scoffed, knowing all too well what was brewing under the surface with us.

"I don't want to be in a relationship right now. I'm still in love with the asshole that broke my fucking heart a few months ago." More wine. More cheese.

"Yeah, and screw Javier for that cause Tyler is amazing."

"Would you just go decorate the tree. I'm getting more wine. I'll meet you in there." I rolled my eyes, and she waved me off and headed into the living room.

I walked into the kitchen where I thought I would be safe from the newly formed Tyler fan club. I was so very wrong. My mother, Kristen, and Angie were all huddled in the kitchen like a freaking pow wow of the Ya-Ya Sisterhood. They immediately became hushed when I entered. I side-eyed them as I headed to the liquor table.

"So, uh, we have a question," Kristen said.

Damnit, Gabrielle. Walked right into the lion's den. I turned and looked at them, waiting for whatever they'd felt the need to huddle up about.

"Why aren't we dating him?" Angie asked as they all looked at me, waiting for an answer.

"We? We're suddenly an entity now?" I laughed.

"Seriously, Gabrielle, he's smitten with you," she continued.

"Oh, please, not you guys too. We're just friends." I now officially sounded like a broken record.

"But he's so wonderful!" Kristen chimed in.

"He's also forty-four with a five-year-old," I shot back. "Deanna, would you please back me up here?" I folded my arms and looked to my mother to agree with me. She then responded with the most shockingly unexpected answer I could have ever dreamed of coming out of her mouth at that moment.

"So?" She looked at me, siding with the other Ya-Yas.

I scoffed as I looked at the three most prominent women in my life, who were now urging me to fall, yet again, face fucking first into a relationship. Like, hello, didn't you all just witness my freaking epic face-plant from my last failed attempt?

"Because I need to be single and heal," I said.

"Of course. Right. I agree. We just really like him," Angie recovered.

"Why has the entire party asked me about him? We haven't even been in the same room half the night, much less flirty," I asked, genuinely curious.

"You just look like you guys go together," my mom said casually as she picked up a tray of food and wafted out of the kitchen.

My mouth hung open as I tried to figure out how, in a mere two hours, Tyler had charmed the entire party, my closest friends, and my freaking mother into thinking I should ride off into the sunset with him.

I rejoined the party in the living room where everyone was adding ornaments to the tree. My mom and Tyler laughed as he used his 6'3" height and long arms to reach the higher areas. He looked over at me, smiled his charming smile, and the glow of the tree lights twinkled off his baby blues as he winked at me.

After a long night filled with much-needed laughter and happiness, I hugged Tyler goodbye.

"Seems you were quite the hit here tonight." I folded my arms and looked at him skeptically.

"You and your mom have amazing friends and family." He smiled as he put his coat on. "And your mom is incredible. Thank you for inviting me."

"Thank you for coming. And for the flowers." I smiled back.

"I'll see you this week?"

"Yes."

"Good." He gave me another hug, and I stood in his arms, realizing I was suddenly dying for him to kiss me. Well, what a turn of events this was.

He left without kissing me that night. As I cleaned up around the house, I replayed all the conversations I'd had throughout the night with people wanting to know if this interesting, charming new person was someone special in my life. But I was scared. I had been a brick wall to Jake and a sad disappointment to Chris, and I really, truly did not want to lose what I had found with this man. Besides, we had both decided that this was *solely* a friendship. Just then, a text message snapped me out of my thoughts.

Tyler: I have feelings for you.

Well...*shit.*

The *Ridiculous Misadventures* of...

HAPPY FUCKING NEW YEAR

My feet touched down in the Tennessee snow—it was Christmastime with my family. Every year we head to either Pennsylvania or Tennessee so we can all be together. LA has happened occasionally over the years but since it's just my mom and I, we're usually the ones traveling back to the mess of kids that have now taken my spot as the youngest in the family.

I was so excited to see my cousins. I needed time away. Time to be with my family after the wild ride the last few months had taken me on—and to finish my book.

As I got settled in the room my mother and I would be sharing for the next week, a text came in. It was a photo of Rodolfo, sticking his tongue out at the camera in the back of a car, somewhere on the outskirts of Guadalajara. He had become my safety net. I needed some insurance so I didn't fall into a relationship with Tyler—and the actor from my TV was it.

The week was filled with many laughs, more than a few drinks, and way beyond an appropriate number of calories. Of course, they all had questions about Daniel, whom they had all spent three Christmases with and whose lies they had listened to on our wedding day. There was even a photo from our wedding in one of the photo collages in my cousin's house. Over Daniel's face was a sticker of a piece of cartoon bacon.

"Why bacon?" I laughed.

"Cause he's a fucking pig!" my eldest cousin shouted from the other room. Couldn't argue with the sticker decision.

It was almost comical to me—everyone wanted to know about the sociopathic ex-husband that I was truthfully grateful to. He'd made it so incredibly easy for me to walk away. Without that, I don't know how long I would have stayed in an unhappy marriage, trying to make things work. What no one seemed to realize, other than my mother, who was still too angry to broach the subject, was that the only person in this fucked-up equation that actually mattered to me was Javier. He'd broken my heart in a way my ex-husband never could have. Maybe it was because no one could fully grasp the feelings we'd shared in those two whirlwind months or because they didn't know him and hadn't seen the roller-coaster ride that ensued. Either way, it really felt like no one truly understood the scar this man had so carelessly left on my heart.

When I was settling into bed for the night, I got a notification that one of my older Instagram posts had been liked by Tyler, who was currently back in San Francisco to visit family and friends.

Me: You're supposed to be out with friends not creeping on my Instagram.

Tyler: HAHAHAHA. Someone wanted to see you...I showed you...I thought you'd surely be asleep by now.

Me: Oh no, you're showing them what a giant mess of a woman you've been dealing with?!

Tyler: Haha you know it sucka. You're my happy mess.

A few hours later, another text came in just as I was about to drift off into dreamland.

Tyler: Yikes. I'm reading chapter three of your book now. I hope you're not freaking out that I'm showing my friends a picture of you like Javier did.

Me: Oh, don't be silly, lol.

Me: …the panic started weeks ago.

Tyler: LOL.

Me: Kidding. I'm fine. Sleep tight.

The next morning while at the breakfast table eating—what else—more carbs, my mother decided to not-so-slyly drop Tyler's name into the conversation. Of course, my entire family then asked about the dashingly handsome man that had won over my mother's entire Christmas party.

"You would actually love him," I said to my twin cousins and their significant others. "But we're just friends." I continued to try and convince myself.

It was true. My whole family would totally love Tyler and I knew that. He would fit in perfectly with my cousins. To be honest, he would fit really perfectly in just about every aspect of my life.

Tyler: Good morning, Unicorn. Midway through chapter four. Loving it thus far. You really are a fantastic writer.

Me: I'm so happy to hear that. And really appreciate you taking the time to read it and give me feedback. Seriously means a lot to me.

It was not lost on me that this man, who had now openly told me he had feelings for me, was not only doing a deep dive into every trigger, wound, and scar in my life, but also seeing the inner workings of my most personal moments—all while attempting to court me.

Tyler was also in the middle of trying to handle a very angry ex-wife and a daughter he wasn't getting to see nearly enough. Obviously, he had made the bed he was currently lying in, but it was still hard to watch him try his best to keep the peace only to be met with anger. He had successfully scheduled a lunch for his dad to see his granddaughter, and I was anxiously waiting to hear if the restaurant was still standing.

"I'm ready to freaking bury 2017." He breathed a heavy exhale from the day into the phone.

"Dude, look who you're talking to." I scoffed.

"Yeah, I hear you. We both have a lot to put behind us. The choices I've made starting in 2015 and culminating in 2017 have been heavy. Ready to move forward with the lessons."

We stayed on the phone that night for almost two hours. It was so easy to get lost in Tyler. He had the type of energy that you just wanted to constantly be a part of.

"How's Tyler?" my mom asked as I snuck into the room at 1 a.m.

"Fine. Good," I whispered back.

"I like him," she said under the glow of the nightlight.

"Yes, Mother, I know." I laughed as I crawled into bed.

The next afternoon, I spent a few hours writing and sipping tea on the wooden deck that overlooked my cousin's beautiful property. There were tall trees dusted with snow, a large barn with horses to the left, and clear skies in front of me. I felt like I was in a little slice of heaven.

When I returned inside to defrost my frozen fingers, I walked into the living room and heard an oddly familiar voice. It was Rodolfo. *On the TV screen.*

Yes, there, in the Knoxville, Tennessee, living area, was the hot Latin guy I had been texting over the last several days—acting opposite of the biggest names in Hollywood. I let out an audible laugh.

"What?" my aunt asked.

"Nothing." I laughed.

"Have you seen this?" my cousin asked. "It's such a good movie."

"I haven't." I was having trouble wiping the smile off my face.

"What on earth is so funny, Gabrielle?" My mother looked at me, amused.

"That's the guy I went on a date with before we left," I said.

"YOU WENT ON A DATE WITH CHRIS PRATT?!" my younger niece shrieked.

"No! Him!" I pointed at the screen.

"THAT'S who you went on a date with?" my mother exclaimed.

"I told you he was an actor!" I laughed.

"Well, yeah, but..." My mother stared at the screen as she approvingly shrugged at the smoldering face staring back at her.

I snapped a photo of the TV and sent it to Rodolfo.

Me: Just walked into the living room and my family is watching TV...

Rodolfo: Jajajajaja.
Rodolfo: When are you back?

Rodolfo had very easily become the man I was able to flirt with and feel totally wanted by—and because I was subconsciously running away from my growing feelings for Tyler, I figured...why the fuck not?

The following evening, my family, with ages that spanned from twenty-eight to seventy-six, and I were belly laughing in the middle of a game of Cards Against Humanity. As happy tears of laughter streamed down my face, I, for a fleeting moment, totally forgot about how utterly sad I had been the last two months. In fact, I almost—*almost*—felt happy. My phone buzzed.

Tyler: I'm having the greatest night I've had in the last few years with my dad and my brother.

Me: That's amazing.

Tyler: I do know one way it could be better.

Me: Dropping another gem there, dude.

Tyler: Damn...I'm that predictable? This Javier character totally stole my game. I have no chance. Oh right...this isn't the Tempest. This is Romeo and Juliet.

I had to give it to him. Total mic drop text.

Tyler: Points for me. That last text deserves an award.

Christmas came and went, and more snow fell from the sky in chilly Tennessee. I soaked in the time with my family as I mentally prepared to return to Los Angeles for the final day of what had undoubtedly been the longest year of my life.

The morning I was headed back to sunny Los Angeles, I awoke with a very distinct feeling—and instead of keeping it to myself this time, I decided to share it.

Me: Good morning. Well, I woke up missing you. And then I said to myself, "No, Gabrielle, don't text him that. It's too mushy and confusing." And then I heard your voice in my head saying, "Stop being such a weirdo," so I decided to send it to you anyway. Sincerely, what the fuck is wrong with me?

My mom and I headed to the airport while it was still dark back in LA. Unlike when I left Europe, I was actually excited to get home—for maybe more reasons than one. As we were settling in for takeoff, my phone buzzed.

Tyler: Peanut…I just opened my eyes. This is the very first thing I have seen today. I've read it probably six times. I have no idea what it says past "I woke up missing you." I'm super glad you listened to my voice in your head. Pretty happy that I'm bringing in the New Year with you.

Me: In a not committed and serious type of way…I am too.

Tyler: Totally not committed and serious at all. Promise.

Me: Liar.
Me. Kidding.
Me: Kind of.

I shut my phone off and smiled.

"Tyler?" My mother couldn't help but smile herself.

"Yes, Mother. Just friends."

"Uh-huh...sure." She smirked.

I popped my headphones in and looked out the airplane window. I was so ready to say the fuck goodbye to 2017.

*****

New Year's Eve had arrived. I sat in my bedroom in my mother's house and thought of what a different place I had been in 365 days prior. For one, I'd been married. In fact, at the time, I thought I was happily married. Me, Daniel, and another couple all went to the Four Seasons for massages and a day at the pool before a fancy dinner to ring in the New Year. Yes, the same Four Seasons Daniel ended up taking Laurel to, only a mile away from our then home. Looking back on it now, I realize that the stomach-ache Daniel had been mentioning when we returned home to freshen up for dinner was simply an excuse to run to the bathroom for lengthy periods of time to text the girl he was having an affair with. Even after kissing me, yelling "Happy New Year!" and clinking glasses with our little group, he'd rushed off to the bathroom for fifteen minutes. All the while, I was feeling bad for him that he wasn't feeling good on the first moments of our 2017—oh, the irony.

Apart from the fact that I was no longer married (well, not technically, but for all other purposes), living at my mother's house, and single again, I had really transformed into a totally different person after my Europe trip. I'd had my heart broken for the first time, I'd learned how to finally be okay by myself, I'd found a new deep passion for travel and adventure, and I had *officially* finished writing a book about it all.

Most of all, I was really excited to see Tyler. It had been about a week and a half since we'd seen each other after a month of consistently hanging out. It felt nice to be looking forward to something after so many weeks of forcing myself to get out of bed.

I walked out of my room and into the entryway just as Tyler was handing my mom a gorgeous bouquet of roses. As she beamed at him and stood on her tippy toes to give him a hug, he looked at me over her shoulder and winked.

"Hi." I smiled and crossed my arms, pretending like the flowers were too much.

"Don't worry, I brought you some too." He stepped forward and put his arms around me, holding the second bouquet in his hand. I took a deep breath and inhaled whatever delicious cologne he was wearing and let myself linger in the safety of his arms for a moment.

"You look stunning," he said as he stepped back and handed me the flowers.

"Thank you. You clean up pretty good too, Jacky D."

We celebrated, laughed, and brought in the New Year together. And per usual, everybody absolutely *loved* Tyler.

When the champagne ran out and the guests had said goodbye, Tyler and I fell into my bed as he kissed me. After fifteen minutes of heavy making out, I realized that I did most definitely want to tear his clothes off this time. I pulled away and looked at him.

"It's okay." I smiled.

"I don't want you to think that's why I'm here. I want so much more than just this," he said back to me. My heart melted a little bit. I took his hand, placed it where it needed to be, and whispered to him.

"I know. I trust you." He kissed me, deeply.

For the first time that night, Tyler and I did a little more than just kiss. And although it was clear we were waiting to sleep together, the passion that came from the emotional bond we had built was something I had never experienced before. It was a perfect last night of 2017.

As I lay there, wrapped in Tyler's arms, I let out a sigh of relief. Because the year that had exploded my marriage, demolished my trust, broken my heart, and damn near killed me...was finally over. And although that didn't mean all the hurt was gone, or the problems were magically fixed, for that one moment, in Tyler's arms, I felt a glimmer of hope. Hope that the depression would fade, that the stars were beginning to realign, and that I finally had the optimism I so desperately needed to begin this new year. But as the psychic in the New York bar had warned me...I hadn't seen the last of Javier.

The Ridiculous Misadventures of...

HE'S WORTH IT

The first weekend of January, I sat in one of my girlfriend's living rooms, magazines and clippings littering the floor, as we put together our vision boards. If you just squealed, *"Oh my God, I do that!"* then high-five. If you just rolled your eyes, don't knock it till you try it. That shit works.

As I cut and pasted my goals and dreams for the year, the women in the room were dishing on the men they were or weren't sleeping with.

"What about you, Gabrielle? What's going on in your post-divorce, post-Europe love life?" my girlfriend asked.

"You mean besides seeing my ex's face plastered on billboards all around town? I'm fine. Totally fine," I joked as we all laughed. Seriously, it was like a sick joke from the universe. *Oh, you're trying to go no contact and heal, Gabrielle? Cool, here's Javier's face on this random bus stop. Have a nice day!* Fuck my life.

"Why do we ever date actors?" one girl chimed in. "Anyone new in your life?"

"I've kind of been talking to two people, but I don't think I'm ready for anything serious," I said.

"Spill!" another girl shouted from the other end of the couch.

"One of them is amazing and ready to run away together, and the other is just super hot." I laughed. "Well, I mean, they're both super hot."

"Who are they? What do they do?" The girls all waited.

I pulled out my phone to show photos of Rodolfo and Tyler. The phone was passed around so they could all see the two current candidates. I pasted a photo of Bali on my vision board.

"DAMN GIRL! These men are in LA? Why can't I find men that look like this in LA?" We laughed.

"This one is definitely a fuck my brains out and throw me around," one of them said about Rodolfo.

"Yeah, but this one is like get it out of your system and then marry him before I take him," another commented about Tyler.

"So you see my predicament?" I laughed. "He's like the best guy too. I just don't know if I'm ready to be in another relationship."

I mean, in all fairness, it had only been four months since my heart had been shattered and I'd been thrust onto a solo trip of a lifetime—and only three months since I had returned home and *really* begun to heal. And while my self-love cocktail had successfully begun to pull me back from the dark beyond and into the beautiful light, I was terrified of venturing into another relationship—especially as I noticed my feelings for Tyler growing.

It was probably because of this that I had continued to entertain the pointless (yet oddly satisfying) flirtation with Rodolfo. So, when he asked me on a proper dinner date, I figured, what better way than to make sure I don't fall into a relationship with Tyler?

I met him at a romantic Italian restaurant that was tucked away on one of my favorite artsy streets—which also happened to be about a mile away from Tyler's place. *Seriously, Gabrielle, you're going to hell.* In my defense, I had been brutally up front that I was not looking for a relationship, and we had not had any kind of exclusivity talk. And, Jesus, it was just a date.

"Gabriella!" He stood up from the table to greet me with kisses on the cheek. He pulled out my chair as the owner, whom he was apparently on a first-name basis with, brought us two menus and a bottle of red.

"How was Mexico?" I sipped my wine as he told me about the time with his family on their ranch.

"You have to come one day. It's beautiful." He smiled. What is it with these Latin men ready to whisk me away to some foreign country? Sorry, dude, I know how this story ends—with me, on a plane by myself, wondering if I'll survive a night of salsa dancing or get kidnapped by the cartel. I'll pass.

"I keep seeing you post about the book you're writing," he said in his thick accent. "What is it about?"

I took a breath as I began to tell him what a tornado my life had been the last few months. He sat there, listening, and was more shocked by the fact my ex-husband had chosen tonsil hockey with a barely legal blonde over the woman that was sitting in front of him than he was about the whole Javier fiasco.

"You're actually oddly similar to him—I wouldn't be surprised if you guys went out for the same roles," I said.

"Who is he?" he asked, curious.

"Javier Alvarez." He paused for a moment.

"Nope. Don't know who he is." He took a bite of his food. "I was married too, actually."

For a moment I had a slight wave of fear wash over me.

"You're...you're not *still* married, right?" I asked, realizing I had accepted a date from a stranger after we'd stalked each other on Instagram and really didn't know a damn thing about him.

He laughed. "No! No, we divorced a few years ago."

I breathed a sigh of relief. Rodolfo was intelligent, artistic, and interesting—but if I'm being honest, in the back of my mind, I was wondering what Tyler was doing.

After dinner, we took the rest of the wine back to his place. We snuggled on the couch and watched *The Shape of Water*, which then led to a fantastic conversation about the brilliance of Mexican filmmaker Guillermo del Toro. While I was passionately ranting on about the cinematography in the film, he smiled, leaned over, and kissed me mid-sentence.

Kissing Rodolfo was like eating a really good dessert—it just tasted good. It didn't matter if you were interested in taking the entire cake home or learning the recipe, you were just content devouring the piece in front of you. We had a hot and heavy make-out session, but every time he tried to take it further, I declined. Maybe it was because I was still trying to decide if I wanted to actually date him—or maybe it was because my feelings for someone else were stronger than I realized.

That weekend, I was having coffee with my girlfriend who had hosted the vision boarding night when a text from Tyler came in.

Tyler: Dinner tonight, pretty one?

A smile instantly appeared on my lips.

"What are you so smitten about?" She caught me. "The fuck your brains out guy or the marry guy?"

"The marry guy." I laughed, although that word made me want to projectile vomit my coffee like *The Exorcist*.

"Seems like you've made a decision," she suggested.

"It's never been a decision between the two. It's just the decision of getting back into a relationship. I can only play the *I'm damaged and healing from my asshole exes* for so long with him."

"Well, maybe it's not the right time." She paused. "Unless, you know, he's worth it."

"Right." I smiled.

That night I met Tyler at a famous diner by his house. After an hour of laughter and stuffing our faces, things took a turn.

"Can I ask you something?" I said, turning to face him in the booth.

"Uh-oh. Okay." He chuckled.

"Have you been with anyone since we've been hanging out?" I asked. I don't even really know where the hell the question came from. Maybe the poorly repressed guilt I was holding after seeing Rodolfo. But whatever prompted it, I was so *not* expecting his answer. He let out a defeated sigh.

"Oh. Oh, you have..." I came to the realization on my own.

"It was a mistake. But yeah, I have. Once," he admitted.

"Hey, I get it. We're not together, and I've been the one holding you at arm's length."

"It was over Christmas," he said. I mean, I couldn't be mad when I'd been sexting with Rodolfo.

"Oh. Someone in San Francisco?" I asked.

"Actually...it was with Christine."

My heart literally dropped out of my ass. I suddenly felt the surge, big time, in a way I didn't know was possible with Tyler—and because of that, my mouth blurted out something before my brain could catch up.

"YOU SLEPT WITH YOUR FUCKING EX-WIFE?" The shock on my face must have been pretty apparent—maybe because it was the last person on earth I was expecting him to say, especially after all of the things I'd heard about their relationship.

"It just sort of happened. Right after, I thought, *What the hell did I just do?* On the ride back to LA, it started a big fight because I basically said there was nothing to talk about and it never should have happened."

I sat there, mouth inadvertently hanging open, not sure how to process this information.

"I...I don't know what to say. I'm like in shock," I said.

"Well...I mean we hadn't decided what this was, and I was never planning on telling you about it. Or anyone for that matter."

"Then why did you tell me?!" I asked.

"Because you asked!" I could see he was immediately scared I was going to run.

"I just thought it would be a random girl or someone you used to hook up with. Not, you know, your freaking ex-wife."

"I can assure you she's the last person you ever have to worry about. We've known each other forever—it was just a very weird mistake." He grabbed my hand.

It was in that moment I realized how much I actually cared about the person sitting in front of me. More than that, I realized I didn't want him to be with anyone else. It suddenly didn't matter if I wanted more time—or that I was scared of stepping into commitment again—because in that moment, *I realized he was worth it.*

"I've been talking to a guy named Rodolfo. We had coffee before I went to Tennessee, I got dinner with him on Monday night. We hooked up. We didn't have sex. I don't want to be with him. And I don't want you to be with anyone else." A flash of anger flickered in his eyes, but it was quickly pushed aside by the smile that came from hearing my final words. He grabbed my face, looked past my eyes, into my soul, and kissed me.

"I don't want to be with anyone else," he said, our noses still touching.

And just like that, the wall that had kept out Jake, redirected Chris, and had made me feel like fucking Rapunzel, whom Javier had locked up in a castle, came crashing down. Well...it had at least broken down to a big-ass pile of debris Tyler could begin to make his way through.

It was there, that night, in the plastic booth of the little diner, that I made the leap. The leap to being open to a relationship with this person. The leap to saying yes to what the universe had put in front of me. Would I fall flat on my fucking face again? Well...*we're only about halfway through the story.*

The Ridiculous Misadventures
of...
72 HOURS

The next morning, I woke up in Tyler's arms after a more peaceful sleep than I'd had in quite a long time. I reveled in the experience we'd had the night before. Whenever you have sex with someone for the first time, it usually goes one of two ways. You either awkwardly bump and move around because you're nervous and don't know the other person's rhythms and style, or you have crazy wild and passionate sex that you know will be damn near impossible to recreate because you're putting on a performance to be what you think the other person likes. We had climbed into his bed with the intention of having sex—and ended up making love. It was romantic, passionate, connected, and above all, felt so incredibly right. *I don't want you to be with anyone else*, I had whispered breathlessly as he stared deep into my eyes. *I only want you*, he'd whispered back, kissing me.

I stretched out in bed and rolled over to face him, the sounds of Hollywood waking up on Saturday morning coming through his second-story bedroom door.

"I don't want to leave. All day." I smiled at him, still just as good-looking in the morning.

"Then we won't leave." He smiled back.

And we didn't. We stayed in bed until 5 p.m. that day, Tyler only leaving to fetch us bowls of cereal from downstairs.

"About this whole not wanting to be with anyone else thing." He looked at me.

"Yeah..."

"Do you really feel that way?"

"I do. I just have some fear around the whole title thing."

He laughed. "I would expect you to after what you've been through. We don't have to have a title."

"Okay." I smiled.

"But I will eventually make you my girlfriend. Just so you know." He smiled back.

"Is there anyone else you have to, um...cut out?" I asked, bracing myself.

"Actually, yes. Nothing serious. She's a woman I've known for a while and basically proposed a friends-with-benefits type of situation. I haven't seen her since I've been hanging with you, but she's messaged me. I'll need to tell her," he explained.

The familiar yet long forgotten surge of jealousy burned inside my chest.

"Who is she?" I asked, trying not to sound like I was peeing on him to mark my newly claimed territory. He laughed, seeing the attempted pee.

"Just a woman I went on a few dates with and wasn't really interested in. It's nothing. Really. Just a courtesy call." He leaned over and kissed me. "And you?"

"Just Rodolfo. But it was never moving in a serious direction. Just a courtesy text." I smiled. A pause.

"Why do you think you're scared of commitment?" he asked, point-blank.

I was a bit taken aback. Not because it wasn't a totally fair question, but because in my twenty-nine years, that had never been me. I had never been the girl who was scared of commitment or who guarded her heart. I mean, hello, if there was ever a time to do so, wouldn't it have been after finding out my husband was shooting our unborn children down the throat of his Instagram model girlfriend? Instead, I openly fell into the arms of Javier, which sent me (or, rather, shot me out of a fucking cannon) on a trip that changed my life. So why was I suddenly freaked out about a stupid title, and more importantly, commitment? I thought about it for a moment.

"Honestly, it's not because I got my heart broken. There are a few reasons."

"Okay. Tell me."

"For one, I never want to make someone feel the way Javier made me feel. I don't ever want to be responsible for making someone's heart hurt that way," I explained.

"I get that. But you've been nothing but open and transparent with me—even when it's been hard to hear. That's really all you can do. The other person makes their choices from there."

"I know. It's still a fear. But more than that, I'm terrified to be trapped the way I was in my marriage. I would have been so miserable trying to stay and fix things. And marriage is the ultimate commitment. If I'm carrying any baggage from my divorce, it's that—the fear of being trapped again."

"That makes a lot of sense. It's not like what you went through was some normal experience. It also happened so back-to-back. I'm sure there's a lot to sift through. Wouldn't mind meeting either of them in a dark alley." He smirked.

"They wouldn't want to see you in a dark alley." I laughed.

"I'm sure thankful for them though. Their stupid mistakes gave me a chance to be with you. I can't imagine having you and ever letting you go."

"I don't think either of them view it as losing me." I scoffed.

"They might not now. But they will."

We laughed, made love, cuddled in each other's arms, and played twenty questions. Around 5 p.m., we ordered Chinese food and ate it straight out of the boxes, with chopsticks, while sitting in the bed we hadn't moved from the entire day. It was, more or less, heaven.

"This song makes me think of you," Tyler said, turning the volume on the speaker up.

"Is this "Linger"? By The Cranberries?

"Yes." He smiled.

"Have you listened to the lyrics of this song? It's like...someone being tortured by love." I laughed.

"Well, not in a literal sense, just like, you know, the chorus."

I laughed but then blushed as the lyrics played. *I'm in so deep. You know I'm such a fool for you. You've got me wrapped around your finger.*

"Thank you," I said out of the blue, taking a bite of my eggroll.

"For what?"

"How patient you've been with me. You've been really imperative for me during the past few months."

"I meant what I told you that first night. Whatever is happening here is different. Unicorns," he said, looking handsome as ever in the dim lighting of his bedroom.

"Unicorns." I smiled. "What do you think your biggest fear is?" I asked. He thought about it for a moment.

"Not being able to protect the people I love. And something happening to my kid." A dark flash traveled across his face as he pulled himself out of the terrifying thought. "Ever since my mom died, I've felt the need to protect people," he said. "What about you?"

"The people I love dying. Definitely have a big fear of abandonment."

"I know that from reading your book." He brushed my hair back with his hand and pulled me in to kiss me. "I will *never* abandon you."

I, of course, scoffed, because it is so very easy to say that to someone. Especially during the honeymoon stage.

"You can laugh it off if you want. I'll just prove it to you." He smiled.

It was so interesting to me—we had both lost a parent in a tragic way. For my little six-year-old self, that had instilled a fear of abandonment in me—*when I love someone, they die.* For thirteen-year-old Tyler, it had also instilled a fear of abandonment, only causing a slightly different belief—*I can't let anyone I love die.* And here we were, our two biggest fears being mirrored back to each other. At that exact moment, lying blissfully in Tyler's bed, having deep conversations that allowed us to fall in love with each other's souls, I had no concept of the type of intense healing this relationship was going to bring. Turns out, we as humans attract people and relationships into our lives that will not only mirror unhealed trauma we need to address, but also that demonstrate attributes we witnessed growing up. So was it any surprise that here I was with a man who had also lost a parent, had developed similar wounds, had a daughter who would soon be the age I was when I lost my father, and had an essence so similar to the man I called dad?

The following day we decided to venture from his bed to eat brunch down the street at a quaint outdoor café. As we sat and smiled at each other, holding hands, he yet again surprised me.

"As much as I like you, I'm not going to rush this."

I looked at him, trying to make my face muscles hide my smile. "Because you think I'll panic and run?" I laughed.

"No. Because you're healing. And Javier didn't give you space to do that." My smile faded into a surprised look. It was not the answer I was expecting.

"It must be weird reading the details of what led me to my commitment issues."

"It's been hard at times. But mostly it's made me see what an incredible chance I have. To help redefine what those men messed up for you. In whatever way you'll let me."

It almost took my breath away. I had never felt so clearly seen by someone—so understood and so valued. Tyler was unknowingly chipping away at the pile from the broken wall—one brick at a time.

That was the only time we ventured out of his house that weekend. We spent the rest of the time in his bed. And when we made love, it wasn't followed by confusing feelings or questionable decisions like it had been with anyone else the past few months. It was followed by deep conversations, intimacy like I had never truly experienced, and, as much as I didn't want to admit it, the early stages of love. It was quite possibly the most blissful and content seventy-two hours of my life—without the hurt from reckless men, the exhaustion of unending depression, or the fears from the world's challenges. For that brief moment, the scars of my marriage and the heartbreak of the man after seemed to just magically melt away. Still, a big question remained: *Was I ready for this magic to truly be enough?*

The Ridiculous Misadventures
of...
FALLING IN LOVE

Things really became solidified during that seventy-two-hour period when Tyler and I didn't move from his bed. We just saw each other's souls. It had really been like that our entire friendship. Only now, after I finally stopped fighting what I had been feeling for the past month, it had become a relationship. A few weeks later, during dinner on Valentine's Day, something important happened. We sat there, that annoying couple, looking into each other's eyes and unable to keep our hands off each other—and I saw it. That same look I'd seen dance across Jake's face that night. The same look I'd seen in men before that had broken me. The same look that had totally made me panic. Only this time, to my surprise, I held Tyler's gaze, and that same look danced right back across my own face. *And my heart smiled*—because in that moment, I realized something. However it had happened, through the month of deep conversations, or the way he waited while I worked through so much bullshit, it had somehow snuck up on me—I was totally in love with this man. But not the type of love you've seen in fairy tales, watched in movies, or, you know, read about in my last book. It was a slow-developing love, built on a soul connection, which was a new feeling for me. And because of that newness, for some reason, I questioned it.

The following month, we booked a trip to the Big Island of Hawaii, where Tyler's family owned a home. We had three incredible, romantic, adventurous days together before my mom and her boyfriend arrived to join us. We made love, cooked dinners, sipped wine, watched sunsets, and laughed until our cheeks hurt. Tyler had meant what he said that morning we went to brunch. He gave me space. He didn't constantly ask for things to progress or demand a title. He never made me feel like I needed to fix myself for him. And because of that, on the third night in Hawaii, watching the beautiful sunset from the balcony, things took another step forward.

"I'm ready," I said, out of nowhere.

"For what? A cocktail?"

"No." I laughed. "To be your girlfriend."

He looked at me in that way that made my heart feel safe but my knees feel weak, smiled, and kissed me. Finally, I had someone in my life that heard what I needed—*and then gave me exactly that.*

On the seventh day, I woke up to an email that allowed me to breathe a huge sigh of relief. Daniel had finally, after ten months of pouring money into lawyers, fighting every little detail, and even having the audacity to ask for the ring back...*signed the fucking papers.* I had sunk over twenty-thousand dollars into the process—*and didn't get a dime from him.* What I did get is something that money can't buy. *Freedom.*

We all took a shot of tequila at 9 a.m. that day.

It was during that trip that I felt like it was time. Tyler and I had been officially together for three months, and I had been silent about it on social media. Some may roll their eyes at that notion, but when you're in a relationship with someone who is very active and open on social media and they don't mention you, I'm sure it can bring up all types of insecurity. Was I nervous? Of course. Everyone had seen my marriage fail and then watched me splash Javier across my page because we were obviously going to end up together. You could say I had more than a little anxiety about announcing I was venturing into another relationship—but I loved Tyler and wanted him to know that I wasn't hiding him, even with all the fear I was still attempting to move through. So, after a magical day on one of the whitest, emptiest beaches I have ever been on, I posted a photo of Tyler and me. It simply read: *Found a unicorn on the Island.*

On our way home, we walked through town. While devouring coconut ice cream, we stumbled into a gemstone store. As you know from Europe, I love getting rocks with meanings behind them. I picked up a beautiful green one that I was immediately drawn to. *To heal broken hearts*, the card read. Oh, how appropriate.

One night while Tyler was inside cooking, my mom and I sat on the patio, watching the sunset.

"He's amazing, Gabrielle. You two seem so happy." She beamed.

"Yeah." I sipped my wine.

"What is it?" her motherly intuition asked.

"I'm just...scared, I guess," I admitted.

"Of what? The same thing that happened with Daniel or Javier?"

"No, actually." I paused because it was almost too scary to say out loud. "I'm scared of him dying." I finally breathed life into the words that had been sitting at the pit of my stomach.

"What? Why?" she asked, taken aback.

"He's older. It reminds me of you and Dad. And I don't want to go through that. I don't want my kids to go through that." My voice cracked. I was expecting her to become emotional. To feel the weight of how the tragedy we had endured had manifested. But being my mother, she surprised me yet again.

"Gabrielle. You could get hit by a bus tomorrow and die. We never know when we're going to go. You can't live your life in fear of what you can't control." She pulled me in and wrapped me in her arms, which now seemed much smaller than when I was a child. "He's not Daddy, baby," she whispered to me.

On our final evening, Tyler and I walked along the beach with the beautiful Hawaiian sunset overhead. An elderly couple passed us, holding hands.

"God, life is so short," Tyler said.

"Depends on how you look at it."

"I feel like the time I have left with my dad is getting more and more real. Like it's just around the corner." I looked over at him, walking next to me. I knew from growing up with only one parent how incredibly important the remaining one was.

"I wouldn't say just around the corner. But I know what you mean," I said. This topic always made such a familiar grief resurface. "At least you have people left. You have Blue and your brother. When my mom goes it'll just be me. I'll be alone." He stopped walking and pulled me to face him.

"You won't be alone. I'm your family."

In that moment, my whole heart completely let go of the fears that had been keeping me from allowing this relationship to truly take off. And for the first time, I picked up a giant piece of brick and moved it out of my own damn way in order to walk further toward this man. In that moment, standing there, I knew that Tyler would be in my life forever. What I didn't realize was how many massive fears he was subconsciously bringing to the surface. Or how deeply those fears would affect my soul.

The Ridiculous Misadventures

of...

SOCIOPATHS

The week after I returned home from Hawaii, I had plans to meet two of my best friends, Tess and Elizabeth, for a much-needed catch-up session. Tess and Elizabeth had both been close friends of mine since high school. They were the ones who had whisked me away to Santa Barbara when Daniel left on his work trip that turned out to be the beginning of the end. Elizabeth had moved in with me when my high school sweetheart passed—and never left my side. Even when I was in the shower, she was sitting on the bathroom floor, talking to me the entire time, because she knew I wasn't strong enough to be by myself. Tess and I had managed to keep our friendship strong through different colleges in different cities. She was the maid of honor at my wedding and was always there with sound advice and more compassion than I felt deserving of. They were my tribe.

Before heading to dinner with them, I stopped to get my car washed. I was still driving the car I had leased from Daniel's friend back when we were married and, coincidentally, the car wash was right across from that dealership.

I pulled out of the lot in my newly cleaned car and headed to the freeway to go meet the girls. All of a sudden, my car started to make weird noises. I soon realized it was the locking and unlocking of my doors. Slightly confused, I kept driving.

I hopped on the freeway and my phone started to ring. I picked it up and saw the last name I was expecting to see. *Daniel Paul.*

"What the...What the fuck?" I literally said out loud in my car. "What the fuck?"

Just then, I glanced over my left shoulder and saw my ex-husband driving next to me, pointing at his phone and mouthing: *Pick up!*

Now, if you're reading this thinking, *What? Come on, that's like out of a freaking movie*, then good, you're exactly in the mental head space that I was in. Begrudgingly—because what the hell else I was going to do—I answered.

"Hello?" I said in the most *what the fuck, this is so creepy* tone possible.

"Hey! I have your spare key! I was just at the dealership turning my car in, and I somehow have your key instead of mine. It's super expensive if you don't turn it in. If you want to pull over, I can give it to you," he said as we drove alongside each other.

"Uh...Okay," I said, still not fully comprehending that this was real life.

I took the next exit and turned into a gas station parking lot that was just off the freeway. I hadn't seen Daniel since I'd run into him and Laurel at the gym months before. Want to know how you're *really* over someone? Have a random run-in, with zero makeup on, wearing elephant pants and some shitty old tank top that shows you probably didn't shower that day. *Couldn't, have cared, less.*

I got out of the car as Daniel parked his shiny new BMW X5 a few feet away. I couldn't help but look at the expensive car and think about some of the ridiculous emails I had received from his attorney over the past months. He'd claimed that I was responsible for half of the $60,000 worth of debt he had apparently racked up on his business account and that he had no money to pay any type of spousal support. And, finally, he'd demanded my engagement ring back.

There is only one thing I regret not including in *Eat, Pray, #FML*—and since I am here with you all yet again, I figured I would take this time to clear it up. When Daniel and I split, the divorce financially devastated me. Daniel made what should have been a simple settlement into months of attorney fees (that I was the only one paying for, since he had hired a family friend). I learned that some people (who, might I say, are probably *not* reading this book) assumed that I was rich enough to go take some lavish vacation in Europe for a month. Do I *need* to address this? Of course not—but if you know me in the slightest after reading what you have, you know I love a good clapback. Not only did I barely have *any* savings after my divorce, I had to live on what I did have and try to get back on my feet (and out of my poor mother's home). How did I manage to go to Europe then, you ask? *I SOLD MY FUCKING ENGAGEMENT RING.* Yes, five-thousand for the engagement ring and one-thousand for my wedding band. Guess how much I spent on that "lavish" Europe trip? About $5k. So, I would like to take this time to say, *"Stop judging people on your own assumptions."* Okay, rant over. Back to the movie scene that was currently taking place in my life.

"Hey!" he said, overly chipper as he walked up and handed me the key.

"Hi..." I said skeptically.

"I know, most random thing ever right?" He chuckled.

"Yeah." I did not. "Nice car," I added.

"Oh, thanks," he said. Then he hit me with something even more surprising. "So, look...I uh, wanted to really apologize for how everything went down. You're such an amazing person with a good heart, and I never wanted to hurt you. I didn't think I would ever be the type of person to do something like that—and it really weighs on me. Actually, I've wanted to email your mom a few times..."

"Oh. Don't," I assured him. She hated Daniel more than all of my friends combined.

"Yeah...so I just wanted to say I'm really sorry. I know we used to talk about if anything ever happened, we would still be friends after."

I'm sorry, did he actually just say that? Is this really taking place right now? Am I on drugs?

"I know we're really far away from that happening, but I hope one day we might be able to. You've always been such a homie."

Oh, okay, I *am* on drugs—because that is the *ONLY* explanation for why my cheating ex-husband just referred to me as a "homie."

"Look, dude, everything happens for a reason. I'm a lot happier now, and I wish nothing bad on you and Laurel," I said truthfully.

"Oh...yeah, well," he said in a tone insinuating they weren't in a full-on relationship. I mean, come on, man, at least be proud of your twenty-year-old girlfriend. After all, she *is* an Instagram model with *a lot* of followers.

"And thank you for finally signing the papers," I added.

"Yeah, sorry it took so long. It took me forever to get my attorney to explain it to me the right way."

"Maybe because you weren't paying him."

"And I see you have a boyfriend now. That's great, you look really good." He flashed his car salesman smile.

Okay. So now you're admitting to stalking my social media and pretending that it's totally normal? I have officially entered the twilight zone.

"Yep. Things are good." I realized this conversation had gone on entirely too long. "Thanks for the key, and I appreciate the apology."

He took a step toward me and put his arms around me. After the shock of having my bubble invaded wore off, I patted his back with one of my hands and took a step back to head to my car.

"Good to see you. Take care," he said.

"Yeah. You too," I said as I got back into my car.

What the actual fuck just happened? I thought to myself as I drove to tell my girlfriends the far-fetched reason I was late. I left that random run-in feeling surprisingly—guilty. Not because I knew that I was totally over this person and didn't even really hate him anymore, but because I knew what was going to be published in the not-so-distant future. And for a *split second*, his random and shocking apology made me remember the person I'd married. But that's the brilliance of a sociopath—they can always make you forget they're a wolf in sheep's clothing.

The Ridiculous Misadventures
of...
OLD FLAMES DIE HARD

I had been putting it off. Putting it off, dreading it, yet all the while knowing that it was freaking inevitable—*I had to talk to Javier*. It had been seven months since we'd last spoken. Seven months of obnoxious signs from the universe that constantly reminded me of him. Seven months of burying the feelings of my broken heart, which was still confused without the closure it so desperately yearned for. And seven months of wondering how this conversation was going to go. The website was launching, and the book was coming. Out of respect for him and peace of mind for myself, it was time to have that talk.

I had been open with Tyler from the very beginning, sitting on his couch and telling him (maybe too openly) that I was still in love with my ex. There had been days I had broken down in tears and he'd held me, knowing deep down I was crying about Javier. I was desperately trying to move on, to allow myself to freely fall deeper in love with this new man—to finally fucking heal. But if anyone can tell you, it's me—healing isn't linear, and it most definitely isn't on your own fucking schedule.

"I think I'm going to reach out to Javier to talk." I finally breached the subject, nerves rumbling in my stomach.

"Okay." He was calm but uneasy.

"Since the website is launching and I'm going to start promoting the book soon...I just think I need to have a conversation with him out of respect for his privacy," I explained.

"I think that's really big of you. I can't say it doesn't make me nervous."

"Nervous how?"

"Nervous that you'll see him and have all these feelings rush back," he admitted.

"That's not going to happen. I haven't spoken to him in seven months for a reason. And I'm happy, with you. I don't want you to be nervous about it."

"Okay. I hope it goes well." He offered a half-hearted smile. Even when he was dying on the inside, he never failed to support me.

Ugh. Okay, Gabrielle. Here goes nothing.

Me: Hey, Veto. Not sure if you're in town or not but wanted to see if you wanted to grab coffee at some point.

Sent. The seven-month clock was now officially back at zero. I waited.

He quickly responded and, after a few pleasantries, he suggested we meet at the same pier we had met at when we first reconnected. Looking back on it after the initial shock wore off, it probably wasn't the best idea to meet this particular man at the same spot where our story originally began.

As I drove through the canyon to the same beach I had met him at a full year earlier, it dawned on me how much had changed—*how much I had changed.* I'd gone from a blindsided divorcée to falling madly in love. A brokenhearted woman to a fearless badass. As depressed as I had been when I came home from Europe, one thing was for certain: I was a different freaking human in all the best ways. That trip had changed me. 2017 had changed me—and Javier didn't really know me anymore.

I parked on the highway and took a deep breath. I didn't know what the hell to expect, or what I was walking into. I picked up my phone, called Tyler, and told him I loved him and that I would call him as soon as I left.

Shit. It was really happening. *Okay, heart. Keep it together.* You haven't done all this fucking work for nothing. He's just a man. *Just a scared, broken, unhealed man.*

I grabbed my purse and walked across the road to the entrance, where I saw Javier casually leaning on the railing outside of the pier's entrance. As I walked toward him, he smiled and stood up to greet me.

"Hey!" I smiled as he opened his arms to hug me.

"Hola! What do you say, for old time's sake?" He motioned to the pier where we'd walked the first time we'd met at the beach.

"Sure," I agreed.

We began to walk down the pier toward the coffee shop that was at the end, overlooking the Pacific Ocean.

"You look great," he said as we strolled.

"Thank you. How have you been?"

"I've been good. Was back in town for a while, leaving on Saturday for a month on a new film."

As we caught up on all the unimportant things of life, I tried to figure out how to go about having this conversation. It all seemed so surreal. We were back at the spot where we'd thought our lives were going in a much different direction with each other—and it was so very different now.

We grabbed coffees and walked upstairs to the rooftop seating that overlooked the ocean. He told me about his time shooting in Mexico and what a crazy experience it was going straight into it after all that had taken place in our lives.

"What about you? How's your child of an ex-husband?"

"Well...I am 100% officially divorced!" I told him.

"Hell yes!" He put his hand up and we high-fived. Then he paused and looked at me. "You know, I tried calling you on your birthday."

"Yeah, I know. I was going through a lot once we came home from Europe. Probably more than you realize. I needed some time to get through it all."

"Yeah, I understand."

"Also, I turned twenty-nine, asshole." I smacked his arm.

"Oh my God, you took that seriously? I was joking! I always teased you that thirty was coming up quick. I know how old you are!"

I gave him a questioning side eye.

"I can't believe you couldn't tell I was joking. Did you forget my sense of humor that quickly?" He laughed.

"I guess it was the state I was in at the time." I smirked. "I just needed some time without you in my life. I wasn't healing."

"Yeah, I understand. I've really been doing a lot to take steps to fix some things in my life."

"Like what?" I sipped my iced tea.

"Therapy. Talking a lot about you and what happened and why I handled it the way I did. I learned a lot from it all."

"Good. I'm glad. That makes me really happy," I said, honestly.

"I've really been reflecting on my mistakes and how I could have done a lot of things differently. I'm really sorry, Gabs." He looked down to his hands.

"It all happened for a reason." I smiled.

"Right. I mean you're going to have a best-seller from it!" he joked.

"Yeah, that's actually one of the reasons I needed to talk to you." *Just rip the Band-Aid off, Gabrielle.*

"How's it going? It seems like it's gaining traction already."

"It's really...wait, how do you know that?" I asked.

"Gabs, I look at your Instagram at least once a day," he said matter-of-factly. I let out a weird noise that was something between a surprised scoff and a chuckle.

"What are you talking about?"

"I care about you, and I always wanted to make sure you were okay. Even when we weren't talking, I would always ask Manny how you were doing when he spoke to you."

"I...wow. I didn't think..." My brain tried to wrap itself around this information.

"What? That I cared? Of course, I care. I think about you all the time," he said, directly. "I still feel really connected to you—that's never changed. There were days when I was in Mexico and I would just feel it. Like, oh, today isn't a good day for her."

"Yeah, I've had those days too." I paused. "I did want to talk to you about the book." I tried to get the conversation back on track. "I'm launching the website this week, and I'll be posting about it more, and I wanted to give you the opportunity to delete whatever you may need to. You know, like all our Instagram photos," I explained.

"Why would I need to delete anything?"

"So people can't figure out who you are."

"Honestly, Gabs...if anyone ever asks me if I'm the person from the book, I'd say yes I am and I hope they learned something from it. I don't want to delete anything."

I looked at him, almost in disbelief. "Just think about it. Okay?"

"I don't know what there is to think about. But okay. I'm so excited for you. It's going to be amazing and I can't wait to read it." His support really meant more to me than he knew. I had enough anxiety putting my entire life out for the world to read—and he never once added to that.

"So how are you and the new guy?" he asked out of left field. I froze.

"How do you...oh, right. Instagram."

"He seems like a great guy." He sipped his coffee.

If he only knew what a truly great guy he was. "He is. He's amazing. We're good. It's just been a lot."

"How so?"

"I mean he came into my life pretty quickly after Europe. I was still considerably fucked up when he entered the picture," I said, feeling the guilt creeping up.

"But it's better now?"

"Yeah, it's good now. He's been amazing. He's one of the best humans I've ever known. But I don't know...I don't really trust myself or my decisions after 2017." I laughed, although it was so very true and not funny at all.

"I can understand that. I feel that way too," he agreed.

"And I'm terrified to ever hurt someone the way you hurt me," I blurted out, momentarily forgetting who I was sitting across from. "Sorry."

"Don't be. I deserve it. And I get it. I don't ever want to make anyone feel that way again either."

Two hours flew by like it always did with us. Through all of the pain, heartache, uncomfortable conversations, and potentially awkward situations, it was as if no time had passed at all. We always seemed to fall into the ease of being around each other—for better or worse.

We continued to talk as we walked along the pier, back to my car.

"So, I bought a house," he said. I stopped dead in my tracks.

"You what?" I shrieked.

"I did!" He smiled.

This was a particularly huge deal for Javier because, when his brother passed, he had sold his home and had quite literally run away to a different country to bury himself in work. Since then, he'd never felt comfortable enough to call Los Angeles home again—until now.

"That's amazing! I can't believe it."

"Yeah, it's been pretty great. I love it and I finally feel like I've put down roots again. I would love for you to come see it one day," he said, momentarily forgetting that I was me, the woman whose heart he'd shattered, who now was in a relationship with someone who wasn't him.

"I'm really happy for you." I smiled, disregarding the last sentence completely. We reached my car.

"Thank you. I'm so glad I got to see you, Gabs. Thank you for calling. I've missed you. And I'm so happy you're doing well." He put his arms around me, hugging me as he had that very first day by the beach, a little too long and a little too tight.

"It was good seeing you too." I took a step back out of his familiar yet forgotten arms.

"Be well, okay?" He smiled and kissed my cheek.

"You too."

As I drove along the coast, attempting to process what had just taken place over the past two hours, I called Tyler.

"How'd it go?" he asked. I can't imagine what he must have been going through while he counted the minutes.

"It was fine. We caught up, I talked to him about the book, we talked about you." I told him everything we had spoken about. I told him I loved him. I told him I couldn't wait to see him later that evening—all of which was completely true. What I didn't tell him was that, deep down, in the depths of my soul, a little spark was ignited that day. Perhaps I didn't tell him because, at that time, even I wasn't aware of its flickering ember. But you know what they say—*old flames die hard.*

The Ridiculous Misadventures

of...

THAT...I WILL FUCKING FIGHT FOR

I carried on with life the same way I had before seeing Javier—nothing had changed. Well, except for the fact that I now knew he was looking at my social media on the daily, thinking about me more often than not, and was totally okay screaming from the rooftops (well...the bookshelves) that he was the man that had shattered my heart.

A few months earlier, I had started seeing a new therapist. I've been in and out of therapy my entire life. When you walk in and find your father lying on the floor dead, it's kind of a prerequisite in order to transition into a life with any type of normalcy. I personally think everyone should go to therapy, even when nothing is remotely wrong. If everyone was required to, maybe so many of us wouldn't end up in therapy talking about the things that were done to us by the people who should have been in therapy in the first place.

Her name was Arna. She had very long brown hair, a soul that believed in many different realms, and she looked like she owned a crystal shop in Sedona. She was clinical, yet just as much spiritual—and it was exactly what my soul needed.

I had been consistently going, ripping open every ounce of my wounded heart and putting in some serious work on myself. Even things I thought weren't issues at all came up.

"Take me to the very first time you felt abandoned," she said to me as I lay there with my eyes closed.

"My dad dying."

"What do you wish you could say to him?" I took a breath as tears cascaded off my cheeks.

"I wish you wouldn't have left. I know you had to. I know it wasn't your fault. But I wish I would've had more time with you. I wish you could have seen me grow up. I wish you could have been at my wedding, see my films, read my book. I wish you could have been proud of me." I pushed my cracking voice out. She walked me through the scenes of my life until I felt complete with the person it involved. Next was my high school sweetheart.

"I'm so sorry. I'm so sorry you died. I'm so sorry you didn't get to live the rest of your life. I wish you were still here to be my friend." I felt all of the sadness I feel every time I have the cold realization that an actual life was lost so very young—a boyfriend, a friend, a brother...*a child*.

"Let's move to the next time you felt truly abandoned. Where are you?" she guided.

"Standing in the empty bedroom of my old home," I answered. The home I had found out about the affair in. The home where I packed up my life and moved on. The home where my world changed.

"And what do you want to say to Daniel? Because you never really had an honest conversation with this man you shared your life with."

"I don't hate you. I don't miss you. But I am so disappointed in you. Because you took my biggest trigger and used it against me. You lied to everyone. And you really are just such an asshole." I laughed through the tears that hadn't subsided through the entire process. And then, we arrived at the last one—the most recent time I'd felt abandoned.

"Where are you?" she asked. The surge. More tears.

"I'm sitting on my bed in my room at my mom's house."

"And what is happening?"

"I just found out I'm going to Europe alone."

"How are you feeling?"

"Like my heart has been ripped out of my chest." These tears felt different—they weren't sad, angry, or bitter tears. They were just pure, wet pain.

"What do you want to say to Javier?" *Ugh. So many things.*

"I get why it had to happen. I understand you were going through things. But I'm so angry at you. I'm angry because, after my divorce, I was fine. *I was fine.* And now, after what you did, I am not fine. I am not okay. You broke me and left me to put myself back together. I hate that I still love you. I hate that I still protect you. And I hate that I know all of it had to happen."

Therapy with Arna was no joke—but with each and every session, I felt like I was moving a little bit further through the thick quicksand I had found myself in after Europe, and my heart felt it gained another repairing stitch each time.

*****

I had been out of town for two weeks filming a movie and was so ready to come home to Tyler. Every day we spent together, it felt more and more like I had known this person my whole life. The way he looked at me, cared for me, supported me—it made me feel like I could finally breathe again.

The night I got back, I drove straight to his house to wait for him to get home from a bartending gig he'd picked up. I walked in to greet his dog, Charles Bronson, who welcomed me with a wagging tail like a living stuffed animal. I headed up to Tyler's room to get changed and found a beautiful bouquet of flowers with an envelope that read "Peanut." I smiled as I read the beautiful card and felt butterflies in my stomach that I would soon get to be in this man's arms again.

I clicked the power button for the TV, tossed the remote on the bed, and headed toward the bathroom to wash my face when I *froze.* A voice was suddenly in the room with me. A very familiar voice. *Javier's voice.*

I turned around and walked back into the bedroom, seeing none other than my ex-boyfriend staring back at me through the TV screen. *I swear to God, I will never date an actor again,* I said to myself, realizing that I was currently in a relationship with one. Seriously, out of all the channels, and all the times, it just happened to be a rerun of a show he was in, on his scene, where he was speaking. *Welcome to my life.*

Tyler arrived back home, and I quickly forgot about the random resurgence of my ex.

"You taste like alcohol," I laughed, as we lay there, kissing in bed.

"I had two drinks while I was working."

"Anything else?" I asked, knowing he was back in the environment that had been his downfall more than once before.

"No. Of course not."

We fell asleep that night in each other's arms, where I was totally content with the way my heart felt beating next to his. Even with all the healing, surges, and obstacles in my world, life with Tyler had been pretty blissful and amazing. *Until it wasn't.*

I can't really tell you when exactly it started, but somewhere along the way, Tyler got frustrated—and rightfully so. While I had been transparent and honest with him about where I was in my life and my brokenhearted journey, it didn't make it easier to know that many times when he saw me cry, it was about another man. Or that the therapy I was going to was to heal from how that man had broken me. So, after months of love, compassion, understanding, and care, I started to see little glimpses of resentment, anger, and helplessness.

Tyler and I *rarely* fought. And when we did, we only fought about two things—Javier...and alcohol. Tyler had been honest that his past had been tainted with spurts of addiction stemming from the anger of a little boy who had tragically lost his mother. I knew the story and the wounds all too well—except instead of managing mine with substances, I managed mine with men. When I came into Tyler's life, he wasn't using, unhealthy, or still in the dark place of addiction that had taken his daughter from him. But he will always have that genetic predisposition that leaves him vulnerable if he makes a bad choice. And that week, we had all the elements for a disastrous cocktail.

"Have you heard from Javier since you met at the pier?" he asked out of the blue one day.

"No, why?" I always felt like I was back in middle school at the principal's office when we spoke about Javier.

"Just wondering. Weird feeling, I guess."

"Well, no, I would tell you if I had."

There had been more than a few conversations between Tyler and me that were similar: He would try and be there for me emotionally while I was dealing with residual hurt and anger. Then, somewhere in the conversation, his human side would inevitably come forward and make a jab at Javier. Sometimes he would say that what Javier had done was a cop-out. Other times it would be, "Funny how he left you right after you finally slept together." But the one that always caused the conversation to take a turn was simply, "God, you guys were only together for a freaking month and a half." Of course, all of those statements were not only true, they were also valid—especially coming from a man who was very much in love with me and tired of seeing my heart hurt.

Whenever that statement was made, I immediately felt the need to defend not only my relationship but myself. It felt like he was invalidating the feelings I knew to be true, the experience that followed, and ultimately, the person I had now become. And that? *That I would fucking fight for.*

Earlier that month, Tyler had confessed to me that he had slipped up. Not only had he slipped up, he'd flat-out lied to me about it. Believe it or not, I didn't carry many wounds with me from my epic explosion of a marriage. What I did most definitely have an issue with? *Lying.* So when he finally came clean that the night I had returned from my shoot and pointed out that he tasted like alcohol, he had in fact been snorting cocaine with the other bartenders, who knew damn well his well-being and parental rights were at stake, I was pretty livid.

Tyler is one of the most genuine humans you will ever meet. If he cares about you, he has your back *fiercely*—almost to a fault. He was caring, deeply sensitive, and loving. But like all human beings, there was another side—and Tyler's other side *was dark*. It was rarely seen and often needed to be provoked to rear its ugly head. It was a deep rage that he'd held close to his heart from the moment his mother hit the floor when he was thirteen. It sat there, festering, not having an outlet or any idea how to heal itself, until his loving yet still very Persian father decided that the three males left behind would *"no longer be sad anymore."*

Over the years, he'd tried to heal that pain—first, in high school, with marijuana, football, and rugby and then in college with fist-fights and alcohol. A tide had turned when he'd met Christine and they'd had Blue. But the unhappiness he found himself in within his marriage and the failure he felt as it inevitably crumbled led him back to numbing the all-too-familiar unhealed trauma.

The slipup, the uncovered lie, and the fight that then ensued was the appetizer for a truly ugly main course I was in no way prepared for. Thinking about that night still makes me want to cry.

What made this night so sad was that the bulk of it was absolutely amazing. There's nothing worse than a magical memory being tainted and ruined by some huge catastrophe. And because we only ever fought about two things, they were, of course, what ended up being our downfall.

Tyler had bought us tickets to go see the Gipsy Kings at the Greek Theatre in Los Angeles. We both got all dressed up, I splashed on bright red lipstick, and we headed out for a night with some of our favorite music.

At dinner, we got lost in incredible conversation and each other's eyes. We shared oysters and sipped on overpriced yet delicious mixology cocktails and laughed until our cheeks hurt. From there we Ubered to the outdoor theatre, where we ended up being two rows from the stage. We took a photo before the show began, looking like the happiest couple in the entire world, reveling in the energy of new love, live music, and the warm California air. This is where we made our first mistake—*we kept drinking.*

We danced, smiled, sweat, and had one of the best nights I could have imagined. It was so freeing, and dancing to the pulsating Latin beats ignited my soul. What I don't think either of us realized during the fun of it all was the amount of alcohol that was being consumed—especially by Tyler.

After the concert ended and the encore was over, we walked the mile back to Tyler's place. We laughed, highlighting our favorite moments from the show. Then, without either of us intending to, it happened.

"That one guitar player was so fun to watch!" I said.

"Yeah, I have to be careful bringing you around Latin men," he joked.

"Very funny." I rolled my eyes.

"One wrong step and you'll be calling up Javier."

"Careful. You need to pull it back, right now," I said, glaring at him in a way that said, *I know where it leads when you drink too much and you're teetering dangerously on the edge.*

That was all it took. Because in that moment, right then, on the streets of Los Angeles, I challenged Tyler. And one thing to never, ever do is challenge Tyler when he's been drinking.

We walked the remaining mile home arguing, stopping to scream at each other. There was full-blown crying in the middle of the sidewalk. I would throw a defensive jab and walk off yards ahead of him, waiting for him to wake up from his drunken stupor, realize that his intoxication was saying cruel and irreversible things, and apologize before serious damage was done—but that apology didn't come.

When we finally reached his house, shocked that the cops hadn't found us on the street to ask what the hell was going on, I grabbed my stuff from upstairs.

"What, so you're just going to fucking leave?" He followed me into the bedroom.

"I'm not going to stay here and be treated like this, Tyler. You shouted at me the whole fucking way home. You're drunk, clearly."

"I'm not even that drunk, Gabrielle, Jesus!" he snapped.

"I'm going home." I continued to cry harder, knowing there was no getting out of the downward spiral we were waist deep in. I headed out of the bedroom toward the stairs while he followed behind me.

"I've done nothing but be here for you while you heal from that fucking piece of shit who you were only with for a goddamn month!"

He looked at me—and even with the alcohol clouding his judgment, he knew he had just taken a serious misstep.

"STOP QUESTIONING MY FUCKING RELATIONSHIP, TYLER. IT ISN'T ANY OF YOUR FUCKING BUSINESS WHO I LOVED OR WHO BROKE ME," I shouted, startling even him with the power in my voice.

"I'm sorry, come here." He was in angry tears too as he reached to grab my arm.

"DON'T FUCKING TOUCH ME!" I screamed as I thrashed my arm violently away. I suddenly flashed back to standing in my old home with Daniel, yelling the very same words at him. And just like that—*I didn't feel safe anymore.*

"We are done. *I am done.*" My tear-filled eyes could have burned a hole right through him.

I walked out the door, leaving him crying at the top of the stairs. I Ubered home at 4 a.m., mascara and tear stains streaked across my face, my faith in mankind diminished even further. I had finally seen the dark side that was buried deep within Tyler—and it triggered me in so many ways. It reminded me of my uncle, a raging alcoholic who said unforgiveable things when he was drunk. Feeling trapped yet again, as I screamed the same words I had yelled at my then husband. The triggers were so great and the fear was so big that I knew what I was going to do. The old Gabrielle might have stayed to fight for the man she knew had a heart of gold. The Gabrielle who had been broken, lied to, and damaged? She was going to run. I had yet again felt invalidated about my past relationship and feelings. I felt like all that I had escaped and survived in 2017, that had become a part of my story, my truth, and my soul, was now being challenged. And that...*I would fucking fight for.*

The Ridiculous Misadventures of...

THIRTY

For some fucked-up reason, exes seem to have an internal alarm clock that goes off one of two times—either when everything is finally going smoothly in your life and you don't need them to rear their unwanted heads, or when you're super freaking vulnerable and will blindly look past all of their previous wrongdoings. This was the latter. *Ring ring*. Javier's alarm clock went off.

"I have to confess, I read some of the excerpts from your book on the website. It definitely made me a little jealous. But it was also really good. You're a great writer." I paused. Jealous? What could he possibly be jealous about?

"Thank you. I actually had a lot on my mind last night. Weird knowing you apparently did too...although why does that even surprise me anymore?" I chuckled.

"Yeah, I get that. I've had a lot on my mind as well."

"About?"

"Everything that went down with us and what the hell happened that made me lose it."

I waited to hear if this would be the moment I finally heard an honest explanation.

"And?" I asked.

"It's interesting. I remember how strongly I felt for you and I miss it. And I beat myself up for what happened."

"Yeah. I wonder how it'll be for you to read the book. I mean, if you do. It's intense every time I have to go through it."

"Obviously I'm going to read it, Gabs. It'll probably make me regret it all even more. I'm just really glad you don't hate me, and I still have you in my life in some way. And that you found this unapologetic badass version of yourself."

I scoffed. "For the record, I've always been a badass. But this all definitely made it reach a new level." I laughed. Then I paused, thinking. "Why did whatever you read make you feel jealous?" I asked out of sheer curiosity.

"It was the section where you were in Mykonos. It wasn't you sleeping with him that made me jealous but after, when you were lying with him by the pool and he was holding you."

"Okay..."

"I can remember being in that same moment with you. Maybe jealousy isn't the right word. Envy."

I was now pacing back and forth in the backyard as I had this very unexpected conversation.

"Well...not that I think you deserve to know this, but nothing with anyone on that trip meant what those five days in San Vito meant." I could feel his smile through the phone.

"I really appreciate you saying that. You're right, I don't deserve it. Those final five days we were there meant everything to me. And the fact that I still stalk your social media and think about you is really new for me."

By this time, my mouth was literally hanging open. For almost a year now, I had wanted nothing more than to hear the words I was currently listening to. Why had it taken him so long to realize this? And why the hell was he vocalizing it *now?* When he knew damn well I was in a relationship. *He* didn't know what had gone down between Tyler and me. Looking back on it now, I see just how manipulative those words really were.

"I guess I just had so much buried and didn't know how depressed I was. Everything that happened between us was so intense. I constantly regret how badly I handled it all."

Is anyone else waving their hands in the air and saying, "Oh my God, what the fuck is going on right now?" Not just me? Okay, cool.

"That was the hardest part and I think still is," I said. "That deep down I know and believe in what we experienced and other people don't. The people who matter to me. And it's such a no-brainer that I can't be with someone who can just wake up one day and feel differently. But there's still this tiny little obnoxious voice somewhere that's like...yeah, but what it could have been." I regretted the words as soon as they left my lips because it was all he needed to hear to know that, in some capacity, no matter how small, I hadn't *fully* moved on.

"I know. I felt things with you I'd never felt before. I'm a better man because of you. And I'm really just happy that you're happy. I feel lucky that I was once loved by you, and I wish I'd been able to accept it back then." His voice shook.

"Me too. I have to go." And just like that, Javier pushed the once-closed door back open.

*****

As if breaking up with Tyler wasn't gut-wrenching and complicated enough, in a few short weeks we would be filming a project I had written and was set to direct—with him as the lead. We had talked about the drinking, apologies were made, and I had worked hard to maintain a friendship with this person I had grown so close to. We somehow managed to not go a single day without speaking, and we both tried to pretend it was going to be easy transitioning into a friendship.

By the time the shoot rolled around, we had it pretty dialed in. At the end of the day, we're both professionals and I had written this piece specifically for him to star in. Not only was it the first project I would be solo directing, but my mother was playing the high-powered attorney, and Amy fucking Smart was playing Tyler's wife. It was a pretty big deal.

The entire script was centered around Tyler's character's toxic relationship with his alcoholic wife and the tragic outcome for their daughter. It was super heavy material for any actor to tackle—much less an actor who had personal mirrors in the material and was being directed by the woman who had recently broke his heart. *Oh, Hollywood.*

The shoot was flawless. It was so empowering walking onto a set of sixty people on a huge soundstage, knowing that I had made it all happen. Sixty percent of our team was female, including my right-hand line producer, who had done my first film with me, and it was an awesome moment for women in film. I was incredibly proud of the work Tyler did, as were his famous co-stars—especially knowing everything else that was currently going on.

After the last of the crew wrapped out on the final night of production, I offered to let Tyler crash for the night because I knew how deeply exhausted he was. We had been broken up for about a month, but were still talking daily and seeing each other often. It had been brutal—not because we were working together but because we so desperately missed each other. And the breakup had happened just as things were truly progressing in such a wonderful way. Every time I would stand in his presence, I would question if I had made a giant mistake. And that night, after he bared his soul on set and we remembered how great we were together, I fell into his arms—and, for a moment, forgot what I had been running away from in the first place.

Two weeks later, I finally moved out of my mom's. It had been a year since I'd found out my husband was becoming my ex-husband and that the place I called home was tainted with lies and probably numerous female fluids—*puke.* The divorce had left me broke and after a year in my childhood home, I was finally ready to get my own place. This was a particularly big step for me because, at the ripe age of twenty-nine, I had never lived alone. I'd moved out when I was eighteen, lived with roommates in college and my early twenties, and then moved in with Daniel right before we got engaged. Yes, before my FML trip, my abandonment fears had manifested in me never wanting to be alone—and that included living alone. But I had changed on that trip—and I was *so* fucking excited.

I'd found the cutest bungalow apartment, which was more like a little freestanding one-bedroom cottage. Plus, it was a lot closer to the city, away from the bubble of the valley that I had grown up in and was now constantly dodging my ex and his new girlfriend in.

Tyler helped me move, which was a godsend. Yes, I am a badass and put my entire king-sized bed together by myself, but I can't hang a TV to save my freaking life, and Tyler can do all that shit with his eyes closed. He joked that he was still doing all the boyfriend duties without actually being the boyfriend, but it had become pretty clear that we were on the road to rekindling the fire that had never truly been extinguished.

Then one afternoon, a few days before I was about to leave my twenties behind, the annoying-ass alarm clock went off once again. Only this time, it was the everything-is-going-smoothly-in-Gabrielle's-life alarm. I opened the phone to see Javier's face smiling at me.

"Gabs! How are you, how's it going?"

"Great. We wrapped filming, and I'm officially in my new place."

"Oh my God! That's incredible. I can't wait to see the film. I'm so glad you got a place. I think it's going to do amazing things for you to live on your own."

"I love it here. I never want to leave." I laughed.

"So happy for you." I looked at him on my phone screen.

"Where are you?"

"We're shooting out in Iceland now. Gorgeous, lots of adventurous stuff to do."

"So lucky to be doing what you love and all that on the side. Just got it all, don't ya?" I chuckled.

"Close."

"Oh, what's missing? An awesome person who understands your career and travel passion, who you can laugh with, go on adventures with, and be best friends with, who calls you on your bullshit, and never get bored of in bed?" I asked directly.

"How did you know?" He laughed.

"Don't be discouraged. You're still young...ish," I joked.

"You say it like it was just some easy choice for me."

I could tell he wasn't joking anymore. "I don't know what it was for you." I sighed, because that seemed to forever be the question.

"Amazing. Then incredibly painful. I couldn't process it all while struggling with the grief that surfaced," he concluded.

"Which begs the question, were you actually in love or just in love with the idea of it." I wasn't trying to sugarcoat it at this point—I was officially Javier-bullshit diabetic.

"I loved you. Very, very much, Gabrielle. That is the truth. I loved you so much that if I didn't deal with what I was going through, it would have been completely unfair to you." There was a long pause.

I had never had any real confirmation that he had, in fact, loved me. It was always just something he alluded to and a feeling that I knew without a doubt. And for some reason, to hear it finally be confirmed, just made it hurt all the more.

"I know," I finally said, because it was the truth. He looked at me for a moment.

"Do you think we're always going to have this pull toward each other?" he asked.

I thought about the heaviness, fear, and hurt that one simple question made me feel. "I don't know. I hope not," I said honestly. Because it just hurt too damn much.

"What are you doing for your birthday?" He changed the subject.

"I don't know yet. Wishing I was out of the country on an epic solo adventure. I really wanted to go to Asia, but it was between that or moving out of my mom's. So, here we are." I laughed.

"Good choice." He smiled. "Do you mind if I call you on your birthday?"

"Sure," I agreed, for the second year in a row.

*****

Over the next month leading up to my thirtieth birthday, two things happened. The first was falling in love with Tyler all over again. Every time I opened my new apartment door to see him holding flowers and staring at me with those deadly baby blues, my heart skipped a little beat. The second was realizing that this meant I had to walk away from the potentially damaging...*thing* that was going on with Javier. Because even though he had become such a big part of my life, it was clear there wasn't really a world that existed where we could define a friendship with boundaries strong enough to protect my relationship.

When I opened my eyes on the first day of my third decade, I felt something unexpected—pure and utter excitement. Excitement for what was to come, for the year ahead, and for the woman I could feel myself becoming. Perhaps it was the first little piece of intuition telling me what a massive year in my life this was going to be—but even then, I had no idea of the magnitude.

Tyler made a giant breakfast spread that rivaled a hotel buffet. We spent the whole day in our sweatpants, watching movies and reveling in our reconnection—and when Javier's call came in, just like the year prior, I declined.

"Are you ready for your gift?" Tyler asked.

"Yes!" I shouted from my bedroom, where he had sequestered me while he was bringing it in. I knew he was making me an art piece. I had been nagging him about it since the first day I walked into his home and saw all of his stunning work adorning the walls.

"Okay, you can come out," he shouted through the door.

I walked into the living room, not knowing what to expect— and immediately had happy tears come to my eyes. There, hanging before me, was by far the most meaningful, captivating, and truly beautiful gift I have ever received, even to this day.

Carved into the massive wood piece was the image of a map with a giant compass surrounding it. It was framed by tree-like branches he had burned into the wood. On the left, he had glued the rocks from my Europe trip as a forever reminder of my soul-defining journey. But it was the right side that really blew me away.

"Oh my God," I said, moving closer to examine a little heart-shaped rock surrounded by something.

"That's the rock you got in Hawaii. It broke, and then I found this heart-shaped rock...I dunno, I thought it looked cool." He timidly waited to see my response.

"It's perfect," I cried, overwhelmed with the care, love, and utter beauty that had just been given to me.

The small pieces surrounding the heart-shaped rock he had found were none other than the broken green pieces of the rock I had bought at the gemstone shop in Hawaii—*the one that was meant to heal broken hearts.* Tyler had no idea what the rock meant—or how perfect it was that it had shattered and he'd placed the fragments around a full, solid, healed heart.

Two days later I finally returned Javier's call. As it rang, I realized that, almost a full year later, we were about to have the same conversation we'd had in 2017 after we returned home from our trip.

"Hey!" His voice came through the other end.

"Hey! Sorry I missed your call."

"That's okay, I figured you were busy. How was your birthday?"

"It was really great. Everyone panics when they turn thirty. I'm, like, ready," I said.

"I love it. And how's the new place treating you?"

"It's amazing. I love it. I'm not leaving until I buy a house one day." I laughed.

"Great. I'm so happy for you, Gabs. And you and Tyler are good?"

"We are." I smiled.

"Good. He seems like a really good person and is so good to you."

I chuckled. "You can tell that all from my Instagram stories?"

"I can just tell how much he genuinely loves you."

"Yeah. He does. Everyone loves him." What a strange conversation to be having with this particular person.

"Probably a much-needed relief from everyone hating me." He laughed, although it was solely to cover up the hurt, which I still heard. "I feel like maybe we shouldn't talk anymore for a while. I want to respect your and Tyler's relationship and don't want to cause any harm to that," he finally said.

"Yeah. It's probably for the best," I agreed. Even though that had been the reason for the phone call in the first place, it still felt like someone was punching me in the gut.

It had needed to happen from the moment he'd cracked the door back open in the first place. Hell, it had probably needed to happen long before that. After Europe, it had been my decision to not talk—one which he hadn't been completely on board with. But now, a full year later, we had both finally decided that our lives were better without each other in them right now. To really remove Javier from my life, I needed three elements to come together. The first two, us both deciding it's what was best, had just been taken care of. The third? The universe keeping us apart. No more cosmic signs, too weird to be coincidences. I needed to be kept far away from this human so that I could focus on my relationship. Thank God he was in another country. So...*can you finally get on board, universe?*

The Ridiculous Misadventures
of...
THIS JUST ISN'T MY LIFE

I had been very adamant about one thing during my relationship with Tyler—I didn't want to meet his daughter too soon. I remembered what it was like when I (at the ripe age of eight-years-old) said to my mother, "You need to start dating. Because you need a husband and I need a daddy," and then waited to see which man ended up being the lucky chosen one. It was never a revolving door of men being carelessly introduced and then ripped away from me—my mother did it in the exact way you should—and I wanted to give that same care and respect to his daughter.

It wasn't until early December, after Tyler and I had been in each other's lives for a full year, that we both felt like it was time.

"Even if we don't end up together, you're never going to not be in my life, and therefore in Blue's," Tyler would tell me. I would be lying if I said I wasn't nervous—it was a huge step in any relationship, much less in one that had already broken up once—but I agreed, and off I went to meet the other most important woman in his life.

I walked into his house and saw him beaming from ear to ear, excited for the introduction he'd been waiting for from the first night we spent together. From behind his back, holding onto him tightly, popped a little head of purple hair and huge blue eyes. She was the epitome of an adorable kid, cute enough to be in every wholesome commercial on your TV, but with a punk rock edge that screamed, *Tyler Thomas is my dad, and we don't take shit from nobody.*

"Blue, this is my friend Gabrielle," Tyler said as she emerged from hiding behind her massive father.

"What's up, dude. I've heard a lot about you." I smiled at her.

"Hi," her little voice peeped.

"You can call her Peanut, if you want. That's what I call her." Tyler smiled.

"Why Peanut?" she asked.

"Cause she's small, like a Peanut," he said, making her giggle.

"Do you want to see the Christmas village Dad made?" she said, looking up at me.

"I would *love* to see that." I smiled at Tyler.

"I'm gonna run upstairs and get our coats. Are you good for a few?" he asked.

"We're fine!" I headed over to the Christmas town with Blue.

By the time Tyler came back downstairs, Blue and I were in the middle of a full-blown make-believe game where we would walk into the living room and pretend to be wildly shocked at all the decorations.

"Now pretend that we left the house, and it was normal, and we came home to all of this!" she squealed.

"WOW!" I exclaimed as I oohed and aahed.

"What is going on down here?" Tyler laughed as he walked in on us marveling at the sights of Christmas.

"Shhh. We're playing a game!" I whispered to him.

That night we went to see the massive Christmas tree at the nearby outdoor galleria. We strolled around as it snowed bubbles and watched Blue, wide-eyed with the magic of the holiday.

"Peanut, look!" She pointed at the giant tree that was lighting up in sync with the music. Grabbing my hand, she pulled me along to get a closer look. I picked her tiny body up so she could peer over the base to see all the fake presents and toys that were situated underneath the tree.

"Guys, look over here!" Tyler shouted.

We turned around, Blue sitting comfortably on my left hip, and smiled for a photo.

I could see how incredibly happy it made Tyler to finally see the two most important women in his life together for the first time. I fell in love with him a little more that night, seeing what a wonderful father he was. Blue was so sweet, and because Tyler hadn't introduced her to any other "friends," she quickly felt at ease with the idea of me coming around more and more.

It didn't take a therapist to see it—this relationship was poking at so many different fears and triggers of mine. Fear of losing Tyler, the way my mother lost my father. Fear that this relationship would end up the same way my last two did—in fucking flames. On top of all that, I was literally watching a father with his little girl at the exact same age I was when my entire world stopped spinning—the age I was when my own father dropped dead. And those fears and triggers began to subconsciously build inside me.

I will say, from the very first meeting, I felt a little bit of pressure. None that was placed on me by Tyler, or Blue, or anyone other than myself. I knew how tough it had been for this little girl in her short five years. A divorce, her dad going down a dark road and losing so much time with her, and her mother inevitably and understandably suffering because of it. I didn't want to be the next thing that became a wound on her little heart, and I carried that—*heavily*.

When Christmas rolled around, Tyler and I took another big step. We headed to Pennsylvania so he could meet my family. It was a pretty tall order for him, considering the last man they had met and accepted into the party that is my family ended up being a lying narcissist of a car salesman. Thankfully, Javier and I weren't even together long enough for him to meet them over a holiday—but they had of course heard the story. So, needless to say, Tyler was walking into the lion's den. Luckily, Tyler was a fucking bear.

He, of course, won them all over. It was true what I had said the year before, sitting in Tennessee with all of my cousins. *My whole family would love Tyler*. In fact, everyone in my life who had met Tyler instantly loved him. A new joking slogan had even begun circulating in my friend group—#TeamTy.

There was one incident that happened over Christmas that poked at the unfortunate but very real trigger that I had developed around Tyler. Over the year, we had experienced a handful of nights that were tainted by alcohol and scarred with words not meant, and they had reminded me of the all-too-familiar wound I had acquired that awful night of the concert. My family has a long history of alcoholics. That's partly why my mom sticks to one glass of wine, two if she's feeling like a wild child. Seriously, that woman can have one shot of tequila and be dancing on tabletops—it's a gift I'm jealous of. When you come from a family with alcohol issues, you can go one of two ways—you either have a serious problem, or you err on the side of caution. I had been lucky that my unhealthy drinking years never resulted in any type of addiction. My cousins definitely like to party but know what the line is. And then there are my uncles. My mom's older brother I wouldn't necessarily call an alcoholic—he drinks enough to damage his health but not in a way that is destructive to those around him. Her younger brother? Full-blown, raging alcoholic. He was a danger to himself and others, a true example of addiction. It had been sad to watch my poor aunt try to navigate it all over the years and hold on to the amazing soul we all knew existed within him. Either way, when we all get together for Christmas, there is a table made into a makeshift bar. And one night, after my cousins and their spouses decided to induct Tyler into the family with shots and a joint, I saw flickers of the Tyler I so desperately never wanted to see again. Flickers of the night we had first fallen apart, and I had seen the monstrous face of addiction he had been working so hard to mask. I saw the addiction. I saw my uncle.

It wasn't a massive fight or an unrecoverable misstep—it was simply a trigger that was poked at just enough for me to be back on the defensive, waiting for the other shoe to drop. And when New Year's arrived, it did.

We had gone to a cabin in Big Bear with Tyler's father, his wife, their daughter, and Blue. The dynamic between Tyler and his dad's wife probably set us up for failure before we even arrived. And although it was all in all a pretty fun trip, especially for the two kids, and it was great to spend time with Tyler's dad, that is where the first bit of pressure that I had pushed down the first night I'd met Blue turned into a burning, bubbling panic inside of me. It wasn't

Blue—it wasn't even my relationship with Tyler. But as I sat there, with two kids screaming and playing on New Year's Day, and the awkward tension between Tyler and his dad's wife, I felt a voice—a scream—from deep inside my soul. That voice started my downward spiral of questioning, hesitating, and unaddressed panic within me. It simply said: *this just isn't my life.*

Half of my heart was saying, *"This is the man I'm supposed to be with forever."* The other half, however, was screaming that it didn't want to be trapped again. Trapped in a relationship the way I was trapped in my marriage. Trapped by the responsibility of a child and ex-wife and all that both of those things encompassed. If I had accumulated any scars from my marriage, it wasn't not to trust men or look through their phones—it was a fear of entrapment from commitment. And that scar was freaking deep.

A few days later, I sat on my bedroom floor and cried like I hadn't cried in a long time—perhaps since I'd learned I'd be going to Europe alone. I cried as I wrote a five-page letter to Tyler. It hurt—badly. Why was this so devastating for my heart? Save me Thought Onion. Superficial?

• Welcome back to the world of abandonment, Gabrielle. You're about to be alone again.

Well, yes. But I was the one walking away, choosing to leave. Still, my abandonment wounds ran so deep that even when I was the one running the other way, I subconsciously felt I was abandoning myself. And what's the scariest trigger of abandonment? *Being alone.* Authentic?

• What if you're walking away from something magical?

That fear was real for me. What if Tyler had just come into my life at the wrong time? Before I'd had time to collect the debris from the explosion of 2017. Subconscious?

• You're about to break Tyler's heart just as badly as Javier broke yours.

Fucking. Devastating. The greatest fear that I had taken from my relationship imploding with Javier was now manifesting right in front of my fucking face. What made it so much worse was that, no matter the few toxic fights that had taken place or the glimpses of his addiction that had so clearly triggered me, one thing was true—*I really did love this man.* And to walk away from someone you love, no matter the reason, is one of the hardest and most soul-crushing things you can experience as a human.

I folded up the tear-stained letter and got in the car to drive to Tyler's house. After a few hours, many tears, and more awful feelings than I could manage, I drove away from the man I loved. And unbeknownst to me, a piece of me broke that night. It was a fracture that was small enough to go unnoticed, buried deep under the surface, where all the pain sat fresh. But uncared for fractures will eventually break under pressure—and it was now only a matter of time.

The Ridiculous Misadventures of...

THE INEVITABLE

This was the second time Tyler and I had broken up. The second time I had now broken this amazing man's heart—and the second time I was now feeling like I'd lost my best friend. I was, for lack of better words, really fucking sad. There was something inside of me that wasn't ready—something that would not allow me to push past all the fears Tyler brought up in me. And one March evening, after many weeks of trying to sort through the conflicting feelings that my brain and heart found themselves constantly arguing over, I agreed to go dancing in an attempt to get out of my self-pitying funk.

Manny and I had developed a friendship over the past year, and he had really been there for me in a different way than anyone else really could—because he was Javier's best friend. That being said, like Javier's mother, he didn't just blindly agree with everything Javier did and, because of that, we had many interesting discussions, my occasional drunk dial at 3 a.m., and a handful of very fun dance nights.

Me: Are you going tonight?

Manny: Yes, I'm gonna be there. Come over, it's a lot of friends coming.

In an attempt to pull myself out of the pit of sadness and guilt I was wallowing in, I threw on jeans and some fiery red heels and headed over to the club to meet Yeseña. Yeseña and I had met at the bar Tyler had worked at and had developed a pretty strong friendship over the last few months. She was a fiery Cuban who was also inherently shy, which at first made her seem like she absolutely hated you. After a few nights of dancing and me pouring my love life out to her, she'd finally begun to let down the massive wall the world had taught her to build strongly around her heart—and we became best friends.

Manny came out to greet us and ushered us inside.

"You ready for a good night?" he asked in his thick accent as he smiled at me.

"YES. I so need to dance," I replied.

It was always so dark inside the club that it took a few minutes for your eyes to adjust. On top of that, I'm blind as a freaking bat and didn't have my glasses on. He guided us all over to the area that his group always had reserved. I began to see familiar faces and smiled, greeting people with hugs and kisses on each cheek. Then I glanced over my right shoulder and my entire body *froze*. Seriously, the people around me must have thought I'd seen a fucking ghost—and to be honest, in my world, I kind of had. There, standing a few yards away from me, was Javier.

Between the dark lighting and my grandma-grade vision, I didn't know if what I was seeing was actually real, and all I could think was *Thank GOD I look fucking hot tonight.*

I looked at Manny, who was smiling, fully knowing that he had purposefully not mentioned that the "friends" that would be there tonight included his best friend, my ex, and the person who had more or less been infiltrating my life without even really being in it for the last year and a half. I looked back at Javier. I hadn't seen him in person since that day on the pier. Everything seemed like it does in the movies where things move in slow motion. I took a few steps toward him.

"Hi," was all that ended up coming out of my shocked mouth.

"Hey, Gabs," he said in a tone that was less surprised, which told me he had known I was coming. He put his arms around me to give me a hug, and we stood there, in the middle of a packed nightclub, for a full minute, squeezing tightly. I can only imagine what

Manny, Yeseña, and random club patrons must have thought of this weird sight that lasted entirely too long. When I finally took a step back and let my arms fall, I looked at this person that I hadn't seen face-to-face for eight months—and hadn't spoken to since November.

"I didn't know you were back," I shouted over the loud music.

"I got home a few days ago," he shouted back, smiling. "It's so good to see you."

"I...yeah..." I still must have looked like a deer in headlights.

"You look like you've seen a ghost." He laughed. Why was he not shocked to see me at *his* spot with *his* friends?

"I mean...did you know I was going to be here?" I asked.

"Yeah, Manny told me. I told him to tell you I was gonna be here..." I turned and looked at Manny, who was laughing.

"Seriously?! You're so sneaky!" I yelled over to him. I turned back to Javier. "Are you sure it's okay that I'm here?"

"What do you mean? Of course it is."

"Well, it's your spot with your friends. I didn't know you were back."

"Gabs, it's great to see you. I'm glad you're here. Have fun." He smiled. Just then, Yeseña came up behind me with a shot of tequila.

"Yeseña, this is Javier."

She side-eyed him and waved.

"Hey, nice to meet you," Javier responded. There was an awkward beat.

"Okay! Let's go dance," I said to my girlfriend. I headed to the table to set my purse down, leaving Javier to join some of his friends.

"That's...*the* Javier?" Yeseña asked. I still didn't even feel like I was in my body.

"Yep!" I replied in disbelief. Or denial. Whatever.

"Oh, shit." She laughed.

We headed to the dance floor as one of my favorite songs came on. I playfully scolded Manny with a slap on the arm and started dancing. Something in my soul comes *alive* when I'm able to dance to music I love. I don't know if there's anything else in life that really does what dancing is able to do for me. I could feel Javier's eyes on me at different times, and I tried to ignore it. After a good amount of dancing, I headed back to the table for water and to place myself under the air vent, so I didn't look like a drowned rat. Seriously, I *hate* people that can dance all night and just be delicately glistening like they barely lifted a finger. Yeseña is like that—and it's *so* unfair.

Javier came over as I was chugging a bottle of water.

"Wanna dance?" he asked with that annoying charm that no one can escape. *Oh sure, because nothing bad ever came from us dancing before...*

I grabbed the hand that he offered, and we headed back out to a small clearing in the packed club. I instantly forgot every basic salsa step I knew and felt like I was playing Hungry Hungry Hippos with my feet.

"How's your mom doing?" he asked as we took a seat back at the table.

"She's good! Busy as always. And yours?"

"She's doing well. But you know that."

He smiled, knowing that we still kept in touch. "Have you heard anything from your asshole ex?"

"Just the usual embarrassing videos people send to me of him being a social media star." I laughed. I then went on to tell him the story of the run-in I'd had with Daniel off the side of the freeway.

"You're kidding me," he said, laughing. "That would only happen to you. Good riddance. Sometimes I look at their Instagrams just to laugh. Like, you were married to him!" he teased.

"Okay, okay, in my defense, he didn't look like James Franco from *Spring Breakers* when I was with him." We both laughed. There was a lull in the conversation—and I knew what was coming.

"How are you and Tyler?" he asked. He didn't know that we had broken up—and I was still very much hurting around the entire situation.

"We're good," I lied. I was not about to have *this* conversation with *this* man in a loud-ass club when it was still so fresh. Before he could question me further, Yeseña came up behind me.

"I'm gonna head home," she said as she hugged me.

"What?! What time is it?" I asked, surprised, since we had only been there for about an hour and a half.

"I kind of have a headache." I questioned her with my eyes. She leaned in and lowered her voice. "Also, it's so obvious. He hasn't let you out of his sight." That was the problem. As much as I tried to pretend it didn't exist, that it wasn't really *a thing*—it was. And it was totally apparent to anyone in the same room as us.

"Oh, stop it! We're all here as a group, don't leave. My car is like two blocks away. You think I'm going to walk in these heels in downtown by myself?" I said.

"I'll take you to your car," Javier interjected.

I gave Yeseña a death stare, which she laughed at.

"Text me when you get home," Yeseña said, glaring over at Javier.

More dancing and lots of sweating later, my feet were totally shot, and everyone was ready to call it a night. I said goodbye to Manny, whom I had grown to adore, and headed for the exit.

"My car is at valet. I'll drive you," Javier said as he put his jacket over my shoulders.

"Okay," I said, trying to remind myself that it wasn't my fault I had run into my ex-boyfriend and was now being driven to my car by him.

We got in the same pickup truck he had picked me up in on our first date. Only so very much had happened since then. I crossed my legs and put my feet up on the dashboard. Let me try and explain the subtext of what this next conversation actually meant.

Javier: Aren't those the shoes you wore in Vegas?
Aren't those the shoes you had on when we had wild sex our last night in Vegas?

Me: Yes.
And I know that's all you're thinking about right now.

Javier: I remember them well.
I remember having you bent over with them still on. And now that's all I'm thinking about.

Me: I'm sure you do.
Yeah. Idiot.

I showed him where to pull in to drop me off at my car. I reached down to grab my purse as he came around to open my door. I hopped out and handed him his jacket.

"Thank you," I said.

"Of course. Will you text me when you get home?" he asked.

"I haven't even had anything to drink." I laughed.

"I know, but just so I know you made it home safe."

I rolled my eyes. "Okay."

He put his arms around me, and we again found ourselves stuck in the same frozen squeeze that was a little too tight and definitely too long.

"Goodnight," I said as I turned and headed to my car.

"Drive safe. It was really amazing to see you tonight, Gabs."

As I drove home, I felt a total mix of emotions. Weird guilt— mostly because of the fact that Tyler and I had fallen apart not so long ago. Confusion—as to what the actual fuck had just happened. But the worst? The one I didn't even want to admit to myself? Butterflies. Isn't time supposed to make those fuckers die or at least fly away and ruin somebody else's life? Not cool, heart. *Not, cool.*

I got home and could hear his voice in my head. *It was really amazing to see you tonight, Gabs.* Yeah—and it won't be happening again anytime soon. Because I have moved on. Because we all know where this road leads. *Because he doesn't deserve to have any more time with you, Gabrielle...*

Because we all know it most *definitely* will happen again. Fuck.

The Ridiculous Misadventures
of...
SUICIDE

I t was definitely not lost on me that the man the New York psychic had told me would be popping back in had just abracadabra'd his way back into my world. I attempted to not put too much energy on the fact that we fatefully had run into each other. Besides, I was busy shooting a film that I had booked, deep in the editing process on my book, and trying to navigate this new road with Tyler. It was actually really fucked up—I had totally broken this man's heart, the one thing I had been terrified of doing to anyone, *especially* him. What made it more ridiculous? We were so close and he had been my other half for the better part of a year now, so I couldn't fathom not having him in my life. And what happens when you break up but feel the need to keep that person in your life? Well, you attempt to become best friends, of course. *SOUND FAMILIAR?* I was quite literally in the opposite shoes of the same situation that had happened to me in 2017—and it fucking sucked.

But when I awoke that morning for an 8 a.m. call time on set, I had no idea how my seemingly complicated problems were about to become so very insignificant.

I groggily rolled over to shut my alarm off and saw that I had a missed call and voicemail from my aunt who lived in Kansas City. She's always been one of my favorite people, and was married to my uncle Damon, the alcoholic.

"Gaby," her frazzled yet controlled voice came through the phone. "Can you call me as soon as you get this please."

It was six in the morning—something was very wrong.

I called her back immediately.

"Hey." I heard her holding back tears as she answered.

"What's wrong?" I asked, my heart rate quickening as I waited for the answer.

"Damon killed himself last night."

Everything just...*stopped*.

"What? How? Are you okay?" The shock ran over me like ice.

"No. I mean I am, but...I wanted to call and tell you before I called your mom."

Oh my God, my mother. I instantly went on autopilot—all that mattered once I hung up the phone was that I get to my mom's house so I was there when she got the news. What made all of this ten times worse? My uncle had taken his life in the same exact way that their father had—a gunshot to the head.

I sat frozen on my bed. I didn't know how to even process what was going on in that moment. Without thinking, I scrolled through my phone and called Javier—because if anyone knew how I felt in that moment, it was him. It rang and went to voicemail. I hung up and dialed Tyler.

"Hello?" His groggy voice came through the phone.

"Hi," I said. He could hear it all in my voice.

"Peanut, what's wrong?" He was immediately alert.

As I cried and told him the news I had gotten, I began to get dressed without feeling like I was even in my body.

"Should I come meet you at your mom's?" he asked.

"No, we're supposed to be on set in an hour. But thank you. My mom is going to lose it." My voice cracked, knowing that the loss I had dealt with in life didn't nearly compare to hers.

"I know. Okay, I'm here. Call me anytime you need today. Or if you need me to come over after."

"Thanks, Jacky." My heart ached with a mixture of grief and longing for the comfort of Tyler's presence.

I grabbed my set bag and jumped into my car. I don't even think I brushed my teeth. I flew down the empty freeway to my mom's house. She, too, was supposed to be on set that day at 8 a.m.

When I made it to my childhood home, I found her in the entryway, getting her things ready to leave. It was clear she hadn't spoken to anyone in the family yet, but what the hell do you say in a moment like this.

"What are you doing here?" She smiled, surprised to see me.

"I need to tell you something."

"What?" She immediately realized this was not a good surprise.

I grabbed her hands in mine, knowing there were no right words in a situation like this.

"Uncle Damon killed himself last night," I told her.

I watched as the shock fell over her—she took a step, almost losing her balance, and then fell into my arms.

We sat in her living room for twenty minutes and spoke to my aunt, her older brother, and the rest of our family. We all cried that this human was no longer on this plane.

"In a weird way, it's a relief—that he isn't here suffering anymore," she said to my aunt, who, through tears, agreed.

My uncle had been an alcoholic for as long as I could remember—the majority of my memories of him involved him being some level of intoxicated. It had worsened after the Hurricane Katrina relief effort, where he'd been waist-deep in water, passing by floating bodies, and then again when he was forced to retire from Homeland Security and felt he no longer had a purpose. He had talked about taking his life when he was drunk numerous times. But no matter how many times someone tried to help, or my mother paid for rehab, nothing ever changed.

After my mom hung up with my aunt, she looked at me, and I nodded in tears. We were going to do what we always did when trauma hit—what I had watched her do when my dad died—*keep, fucking, going.* We made it to set that day at 8:02 a.m.

My castmates and crew were so supportive and gracious that day. I had already formed a bond with my fellow co-stars, but this was the day that really solidified that our friendships would span beyond the final scene of this film.

As I sat in my trailer, my phone rang. It was Javier.

I picked up. "Hey."

"Hey! Did you mean to call me this morning? I was sleeping."

"Yeah, I did." I paused, trying not to cry and ruin the makeup that was now on my face.

"Gabs, what's wrong?" he asked.

I took a deep sigh to try and control my breath. "My uncle killed himself last night," I finally said. It was as if all the air was instantly sucked out of both of our rooms. It took about fifteen seconds for him to speak.

"Oh, Gabs..." His voice trailed off. It was a devastating thing to experience—hearing his heart break because he knew what a different kind of grief suicide brought. And in that moment, I experienced a small glimmer of what Javier must have gone through when he lost his brother. It was one thing to lose an uncle that way. A brother who you spent every day with? I cannot even imagine.

"I know there's nothing I can say. Is there anything you need? Anything I can do?" he asked.

"Honestly, I don't even really know why I called you," I said.

"I'm glad you did. I'm so sorry."

"The most fucked-up part is that he did it exactly how my grandpa did. And at home...for my aunt to find him." My heart was heavy for my aunt, who I knew would have that violent image burned into her memory forever, and for my mother, who shouldn't have to deal with losing anyone else ever again.

I sat in my trailer, flooded with memories of Tyler and I walking down the streets of Hollywood that awful night of our fight. The things that were said, the feelings that were hurt—God, I fucking hate what alcohol can do to people. Tyler's history of addiction was a massive fear of mine. And this, this was exactly why.

A few months later, our family met to spread Damon's ashes in Estes Park, Colorado, and it finally hit me in a way that I was able to put into words. It hadn't really felt like he was gone because we lived in different states and Christmastime hadn't rolled around yet. But standing there in Colorado, it was very clear what I was feeling—anger. I was angry at him. For the way that it happened. For how he treated the people that I loved when he wasn't sober. That so many memories of mine were tainted with his disease. You see, the thing about grief is, no matter how much you want to control it, predict it, fix it...*you can't*. You just have to let yourself feel it. Because once the anger subsides and the sadness comes, all you're really left with is how you choose to move forward. So, here's to you, cool Uncle Damey—I now choose to remember the laughs, the love, and the legacy you left behind.

The Ridiculous Misadventures of...

PANDORA'S BOX

It had been about three months since I had broken up with Tyler—three months that I had been officially single, not gone on any dates, nor hooked up with anyone. During those three months, a little tiny seed was planted deep in my subconscious. It had happened that night I ran into Javier at the club—and it had been covertly getting watered anytime I saw him out. However, I knew very well that crossing a certain line with him physically would open up a whole can of fucking worms—no, it would open up Pandora's box.

That night, some of my new friends from the film had made plans to go dancing. It was going to be like any other fun night out—except I had casually invited Javier.

The good and bad thing about hanging out with newer friends? They won't smack you in the face the way your best friends would and say, "Gabrielle what the fuck are you thinking?" They all knew about Tyler, but they also knew I was writing a book and about the man who was the catalyst to the whole damn thing. I had run into Javier two other times at the same club. Both times we had found ourselves spending too much time talking in the corner and sharing the occasional dance that would come dangerously close to being flat-out inappropriate. He even won over one of my closest friends—Jess. Yes, in a mere three hours in a dark nightclub, accompanied by tequila, Javier had taken my best friend from *Fuck this fool, I don't want anything to do with him* all the way to (and I quote) *"Oh my God, Gabs, I totally see why you love him. He's so much fun and so funny!"*

That Saturday night, we all met for a drink before heading to a dance spot about a mile away.

"So, um..." I questioned how to even break the news that I'd invited *that guy* who I had, you know, written a fucking book about.

"Oh God, what?" Katy, my co-star asked.

"Javier is coming tonight." I took a giant gulp of my drink.

"Shut the fuck up," one of the guys responded. Everyone had a weird look of bewilderment and excitement on their faces.

"Like, *the* Javier?" Sully, our very flamboyant and fabulous hair stylist, said with epic dramatic attitude.

"Yes. We've seen each other a few times, we're friends. It's just dancing," I explained.

"Honey, in no world is dancing with a hot piece of Latin ass just dancing," Sully said as he looked me up and down. I tried to not smile because I did in fact know exactly what us dancing together looked like. But this was the first time we had ever really *made* plans, and I honestly had no freaking idea what to expect of this night.

"It's fine! He's a good time. You guys will like him." I laughed to cover up my nervousness. We all finished our drinks and headed out.

After a short walk (which is never *really* short when you're in freaking heels, let's be honest), we arrived at the club. Javier was standing out front waiting for us. Sully came up behind me and whispered as we walked up to meet him.

"Oh, girl, you're in trouble. He's yummy." I elbowed him as I laughed. Thankfully the two pre-club cocktails distracted my brain from what a big and potentially dangerous night was ahead of me.

"Hola!" Javier put his arms around me and gave me a kiss on the cheek. "Wow, you look great." He looked me up and down.

"I'm a little drunk."

"Oh God, here we go." He chuckled.

I introduced him to everyone as we paid and headed upstairs. It was my ideal type of place. Not super crowded, tons of room to dance, and a fun group of people who were all ready to have a good time.

Sully had quickly become one of my favorite humans. We'd instantly connected on set, and he was so much fun to go out and dance with. He was a fabulous mix of Thai and Salvadorian and could salsa dance like a fucking pro. He kept giving me looks of "Oh girl" as we all danced because, I can assure you, he wanted to hop into bed with Javier just as much as I did.

It only took about fifteen minutes and a few sips of my drink for Javier to get the balls to grab me to dance. We're always the pair that is either busting out moves in the middle of a circle like we're in one of those awful dance battle movies, or off to the side having to remind ourselves that we're not having sex with our clothes on—there's really no in-between. As he held me tightly against his body, I could feel him breathing on my neck—and it was the type of breathing I knew all too well. I turned around to face him and we danced with our lips only a few centimeters apart. After a few moments, I dropped down, looked up at him, and danced back up to stand face-to-face.

"Shit," he said as he bit his lip.

I laughed as I backed away to go dance with the girls. Katy pulled me outside for some much-needed fresh air and girl chat. As I fanned my damp neck, Katy grilled me.

"Girl."

"What?" I asked, knowing exactly what she was about to say.

"It's so freaking obvious you can cut the sexual tension with a fucking plastic spoon."

"We're just dancing! I can't cross that line. I *cannot* cross that line," my tipsy self repeated, more for my own brain than to her.

"Are you sure about that?" She laughed.

"I mean...I can't, right?" I hoped she would burn the dangerous thought out of my brain.

"It depends on why you're doing it. If you think you're gonna re-break your heart and get stuck in all these feelings again, then no. But if you need closure and want to have one final epic fuck, I fully support that. Everyone needs that on their own terms with the guy that broke them." She laughed.

"Right. I mean, I'm single...I can totally do that. One time." I worked it all through in my brain.

The Ridiculous Misadventures

"ONLY if you can wipe your hands and be done with it after. If it's just sex," she reiterated.

I'm fully aware that half of you reading this right now are saying, "Yeah, right, she cannot just have sex with Javier. That is the worst possible road you could walk down, Gabrielle. Don't do it. Don't do it." And the other half are saying, "Hell, yes, drive down that fucking road with the top down. Go have your dominance moment and show him what the fuck he is missing, Gabrielle!"

As I contemplated the two different paths in my head, I finished the last sip of my drink and headed back inside to the rest of our group and my dangerous decision.

Once we were all danced out and the club was nearing its closing time, we decided to call it a night. Standing out front, everyone began to say their goodbyes.

"I can take you home, Gabs. My truck is right across the street," Javier offered.

I thought about it—for like two seconds.

"Yeah, sure," I said as I moved to say goodbye to my friends. I hugged Sully.

"Girl, go get yours." He drunkenly smacked my ass. God, I love gay men.

"Are you sure? I can totally walk home with you," Katy offered, giving me a final chance to take the road of fewer epically bad complications. I smiled and gave her a hug.

"It's fine, I'm good." She hugged me and looked at me.

"One. Time. Closure," she said.

"He's just taking me home," I insisted.

I turned back around, away from my friends, away from the safety, away from the smart decisions, and headed over to Javier's truck with him.

It took us three minutes to get back to my little apartment.

"My feet are killing me," I said. The four drinks over the course of the night were not enough to block out the pain of dancing in heels for three hours straight.

"That was such a fun night. Your friends are great," he responded.

"Yeah, they're a fun group."

"I love Sully. He's amazing."

"He is." A pause as we sat on the quiet street at 2 a.m.

"So am I dropping you off or coming in?" he finally asked. Another pause. Okay, Gabrielle, which road is it going to be?

"You can come in if you want. I can make us some tea." I left the ball in his court, although I knew exactly what he wanted to do with it.

"You're sure?" he asked.

"Javier, it's just tea." I laughed.

"Okay," he said as we hopped out of his truck and walked inside.

"Wow, what a great place, Gabs!" he said as I flipped on the lights and immediately threw off my heels.

"Thanks, I love it here."

"Give me the tour," he demanded.

As we walked from room to room, it dawned on me that Javier was in my house. The only man that had ever been in this house in a more-than-friend capacity was Tyler—and this wasn't just any man, it was *that* man.

He sat down on the couch as I made us some tea.

"I can't believe I'm in your house," he said as I handed him his tea and took a seat beside him. At least both of us were understanding the weird gravity of the current situation.

"Weird, right?" I said.

"Weird but good. I missed you. It's been good being able to see you."

"Yeah, it has."

"How's the book coming?"

"It's coming. Finishing up the final edits. Should be out by next month."

"I'm so excited for you. I can't believe you wrote a fucking book. Like, you're an author."

"Wild right? I really do appreciate you signing the release."

"Of course. You know I'm proud of you. It was the least I could do." He sipped his tea.

"I'll give you that one." I laughed.

"How many things am I going to read about that make me want to crawl under a rock?" he asked.

"Things about you or about my trip?"

"I know what's in there about me. I lived it with you. I mean other things."

"What, like who I slept with?" I asked.

"Yeah. I mean I read the sample on your website, and I know you had something with that guy in Barcelona."

"Four. Including you," I answered matter-of-factly. I watched to see if he would even care as he digested this information.

"Okay, I can't lie. It hurts a little bit, but obviously I asked for it," he said honestly.

"Yeah, but I get it." I looked at him, unsure if I wanted to ask my next question. "And you?"

"Me?" He seemed surprised I was asking.

"Yeah." I waited. He took a long pause.

"There were two other girls," he finally said.

I genuinely thought I was going to feel a massive surge—but as I waited to feel the deep pain in my chest that I now associated with this man, I realized it wasn't coming. In fact, there was...*nothing*. My mouth, however, did drop open.

"I am so glad you didn't tell me that until now," I finally said.

"I would never."

"That would have killed me, and I would have hated you."

I'm sure some of you are thinking, *Well, Gabrielle, you can't really be mad, you slept with other people too*...which is totally correct. However, I wasn't the one who had broken up with the person I was in love with, blamed it on needing to be alone and grieve, and then decided to go have sex with some random people in Europe. There's a different type of sting when the person who isn't picking the pieces of their shattered heart off the floor does something—and I knew if I would have learned about it all after the trip or before I had done some healing of my own, it would have absolutely broken me.

"It was awful. Honestly, I felt like I was cheating on you," he told me.

"What cities?" I asked, with a shocked yet amused expression. A mild look of dread came across his face, and I knew he'd been hoping I wouldn't ask that. He sighed.

"One in Naples...one in Rome," he finally said, with regret.

"ROME?!" I exclaimed, taken aback. "That was like the first five days!" I laughed.

"I know." He didn't return the laugh. In fact, all I saw on his face was guilt and shame. "I was so sad and needed some type of connection. It felt like glorified masturbation, honestly. I felt so gross after. And I thought about you both times."

"Yeah, I know all about that," I admitted.

"I felt so guilty," he said.

"Well, don't, we weren't together. Although I'm super hardcore judging you right now." I laughed.

"I'll take it." He, too, finally let out a laugh.

After twenty minutes of talking on the couch and drinking tea, he finally decided to take the ball I had left in his court and figure out if he was allowed to shoot.

"So what do you think about me being here?" he asked—and I knew exactly what he meant.

"You mean do I think it's a good idea that we sleep together?" I decided to not dance around the subject.

"Yeah. I mean, you know what I want, but I want you to be comfortable, and I don't want you to ever feel any type of hurt because of me ever again." I thought about this for a moment. Then, in true Gabrielle fashion, I made a plan. One that would give me exactly what I needed—and wanted.

"Here's the thing. I've needed to get you out of my system for a very long time—but if I'm going to cross that line, I really need to *fully* get you out of my system," I explained.

"Okay, what do you have in mind?" he asked, intrigued.

"Something along the lines of locking ourselves in a house for twenty-four hours and letting me *really, fully* get you out of my system."

His eyes lit up. "That sounds like a really logical and fair plan. Like next weekend?" He smiled. "But Gabs are you really sure? I don't ever want to do anything to hurt you, ever again."

I stood up and set my now empty cup of tea down.

"I'm going to take a shower. You're welcome to head home or you can get in my bed," I said. He stared at me, surprised by my directness, as I headed to the bathroom.

When I got out of the shower, I wrapped a towel around myself and walked into my room. Javier was sitting on my bed. He smiled.

"Can I rinse off?" he asked.

"Sure." I handed him a towel.

I dried off, lit a few candles, and hopped into my bed. A few minutes later, Javier opened my door and walked in—completely naked.

He walked over to his jeans on the floor and pulled out his wallet.

"Shit," he said.

"What?" I asked from under the covers.

"I don't have a condom." He looked at me.

"You're the king of condoms. How is that possible?" I asked.

"I'll run to the liquor store really quick."

"You're literally naked and it's two in the morning." I laughed.

"So, do you just want to...I mean I just got tested last week," he said. For those of you rolling your eyes, yes, I believed him. He was notorious for using protection and legitimately thought every woman wanted to trap him into a relationship by getting pregnant.

"Well, I've been with the same person for the past year so...it's fine with me," I said. Again, let me take this time to state that I do *not* recommend or promote unprotected sex—it is something I have done with very few people over my lifetime, and only those I trusted with my body. Think what you want about Javier, but he would never put me in danger in that (or any type) of way.

"Is this really about to happen?" He looked at me, clearly realizing the weight of this massive line we were about to blatantly cross. Here we were, almost a full year after a whirlwind romance, massive heartbreak, and six months of not speaking. So much had happened and in that moment, I realized something. He wasn't just *that guy* for me—I was *that girl* for him.

Without me having to answer, he walked forward and climbed into my bed. The bed that had only ever had Tyler next to me in it. And in that moment, before it all began with the man who had devastated my soul, broken my heart, and flipped my world upside down, I felt pure and utter *sadness*. Because I knew the decision I was about to make would be the nail in the coffin for the man who loved me beyond this realm. I knew once I crossed this line, there was no going back to Tyler, and for a split second, I almost stood up. I don't really know how to explain it. It was as if something inside me whispered, *Don't worry, it will all lead you to where you need to be.* And with that, I touched my lips to the man who had captured, played with, and broken my heart.

We were in my bed for three hours that night. Some of it was filled with passionate, intense, lovemaking, some with animalistic, wild sex. At times we would stop and lie there breathless, covered in sweat, and talk and laugh about the insanity of it all. About an hour in, I looked over at him—he never took this long to climax with me.

"What's wrong?" I asked, out of breath.

"I'm nervous," he admitted.

"Nervous? Why?" I laughed as I sat up on my elbow.

"I was always nervous having sex with you."

"What on earth are you talking about?" I was totally shocked and confused by this information. This was coming from the man who walked around like he was a freaking sex God and had more partners to practice with than I cared to think about.

"You've always made me nervous, Gabrielle. I had such intense feelings for you, so I always wanted to make sure I was good enough."

"But you're like...you. You know you have no problem in that department," I said, still surprised.

"Yeah, but a lot of the people I've slept with I didn't care as much. I didn't feel the way I felt about you. It's different. And now, after everything we've been through, I'm just, I don't know, really nervous."

I stared at him, appreciating his honesty but also totally basking in the fact that I, this girl he had emotionally ruined, made *him* nervous.

"Well, you don't need to be. Relax." I put my hand on his chest.

I thought about if I wanted to bring this next part up. Then I figured, hello, we're having sex to get shit out of my system, not to make *him* happy.

"So you know how I told you I have two types of orgasms?" I said.

"Yeah..." He waited.

"Let me teach you how to give me the bigger ones." I smiled. It's notoriously difficult to, well, get me there. Don't get me wrong, the sex with Javier had always been so passionate and intense it never really mattered that I didn't *fully* get there. Only three men have ever mastered giving me an orgasm and it wasn't until I was *super* comfortable with them. If you've slept with me and you're reading this, it's probably not you. Don't take it personally; I'm a great actress.

"Please!" he said eagerly, like a schoolboy ready to ace his science final.

After I gave him the ever-complicated lesson on how to do what I required in bed, we rolled over and realized there was light coming through my windows. I looked at my phone to see it was 5:30 in the morning.

"So next weekend. Twenty-four hours?" He smiled.

"Yep. That should do it." I smirked.

"Any special requests?" he asked as he kissed my neck.

"I'll send you a list."

"I want to stay and sleep with you, but the dog's been alone for almost twelve hours," he said with his hands still on me.

"Who said you were invited to stay?" I laughed.

"Right, I'll just grab my pants and leave now," he joked.

We dragged ourselves out of my beyond disheveled bed and got dressed. I walked him to the door, where the early morning light poured in.

"This was amazing," he said, kissing me. "I'll see you next weekend?"

"I will see you next weekend."

"Okay." He smiled.

"Okay."

I shut my door, leaned up against it, exhaled deeply, and slid down to the floor. I had just spent the entire night with *that* guy. I'd just rolled around my bed for three hours with *that* guy. I'd looked at a massively important line and deliberately chosen to cross it, like the third trip back to the all-you-can-eat-buffet when you already have one button undone. So now the real test begins, Gabrielle: can you *really* have sex with this man and not have a flash flood of feelings come rushing back in to drown your ass? Jesus Christ, Gabrielle—you just opened up Pandora's fucking box.

The Ridiculous Misadventures
of...
24 HOURS

L ater that morning, after a meaningless three hours of sleep, I awoke to a text from my ex-boyfriend. Which one you ask? The one that had just left my bed a few hours before, not the one who wanted to love me to the ends of the earth. *Fail.*

We decided that the following Saturday would be our twenty-four hours of what I liked to refer to as *fucking my ex out of my system*. And in an effort to keep my emotions out of it, I approached it like I was going for one last meal and I would order exactly what I damn pleased.

I went about my week the way I would go about any other week in my life—except I could not stop thinking of all the things I would be doing that Saturday night. I decided that I didn't need to feel guilty about this. After all, I deserved to have some type of closure with this fucking man after everything I had been through—and I was single. This one time, I was going to allow myself to *just freaking let go*. No baggage of a broken heart, no concern about what people might think. I was just going to do what the hell I pleased... for twenty-four hours at least.

That Friday I had plans to go salsa dancing with a few friends, but we decided not to go at the last minute. I was planning on having a relaxing night in with me, myself, a glass of wine, and my TV, when my phone rang.

"Yes?" I laughed, answering the call from Javier.

"If you end up salsa dancing tonight, you can just come stay at my place so you don't have to drive all the way back tomorrow."

I looked at my unopened bottle of wine and laughed.

"If you want me an extra night you can just say so."

"I do. I'm saying so."

I sat there, pondering the two options I now had on my Friday night. I could make him sit at home wanting me for the next twelve hours or I could pack a bag and go have mind-blowing sex. Before this insane plan had even begun, it had gone from twenty-four hours to forty-eight. *Fuck it.* It was the final hoorah of my sexual escapades with Javier. My unopened wine could wait.

Standing in Javier's bedroom for the first time, moonlight pouring in from the windowed balcony, I took a moment to really think logically about this plan I had created for myself. Superficial thought?

• You fucking deserve this Gabrielle. *Go, get, yours, girl.*

I mean...yeah. Moving on. Authentic thought?

• You really need to protect your heart.

This was definitely not lost on me. I was in dangerous fucking territory, quite literally in the lion's den. Don't let yourself be torn apart like a piece of meat, Gabrielle. So, what's at the core?

• This man is like a drug.

It really was just that. The exact thing the New York psychic had so precisely told me. I knew damn well this wasn't healthy. I could stick my nose up and cross my arms all I wanted to, but I knew deep down that this road was not going to lead anywhere good. This was the man that had broken me—and here I was, taking my super-glued heart and putting it on a silver platter. But for whatever reason, my heart was telling me that this path, albeit fucking crazy, was going to take me somewhere I needed to be. And if you don't allow yourself to act with your heart, how will your brain ever catch up?

After the high of hearing him lose himself as he collapsed on top of me, I caught my breath, lying in the arms of the one man I had never thought I would be with again.

Once he was fast asleep, I rolled over and stared up at the ceiling, lost in thought. When Daniel and I split, he was quick to tell everyone that the main reason we'd broken up was because he wasn't getting enough sex. He even went as far as to say I had intimacy issues. Not knowing I was being gaslit by a narcissist, I actually started to believe that it might be true. *What if I have some huge sex issue? What if I'm broken?* Even with how busy we both were at the time, Daniel and I were having sex two to three times a week. He just wanted it twice a day, *Fifty Shades of Grey* style. I don't care if you're fucking Brad Pitt from the nineties, dude, that shit ain't happening. But I had slowly started to wonder if there was some truth to that—because even when Daniel and I did have sex, I didn't enjoy it. In fact, it was always a chore. There were very few times I could remember being truly turned on and really into it with him, and it usually involved some type of alcohol assistance. Then came my Europe trip where I discovered that I had been using sex to protect myself from my abandonment issues. For the past two years, those two elements had built up in my brain and made me question...*shit...do I really have intimacy issues?*

But lying in Javier's bed that night, after an exhausting, passionate, *Fifty Shades of Grey* experience—I realized something. Daniel was *fucking wrong.* I just needed to find someone that ignited that passion within me. So, whether it was an epically bad decision or a dangerously toxic situation, crossing this line with Javier had given me one, massively empowering answer: I don't have a fucking problem. *I just wasn't in love with my husband.*

The following morning, I woke up to breakfast, coffee, and Javier doting on me like this whole situation was totally normal. As I rolled around on the floor with his dog, he casually shouted to me from the kitchen.

"How are you feeling about everything with Tyler?" he asked. Even hearing his name roll off Javier's lips was a bitter reminder that I had crossed a line I would never be able to recover from—and that made my heart hurt.

"Trying to be friends," I said somberly. "I just miss him a lot. It really sucks."

"Can I be honest with you?" he said.

"Always."

"I knew it wasn't going to last. I could just feel it when I saw the things you posted on social media. It felt like you were forcing it." I immediately felt the surge—but not the normal surge. No, this was the *if you talk about that person in any negative way, I will punch you in the fucking face* surge.

"That's hilarious coming from the guy who plastered me on his Instagram three days into knowing me." I scoffed. He immediately knew he'd hit a nerve.

"Fair enough. I learned a big lesson from that," he admitted.

"I don't know how you could assume that from what you saw on social media."

"It just seemed like you weren't happy, I guess. I know how much you cared about him."

"Care," I corrected him.

"Right. I know you do, I can see that."

"Yeah." I so needed to get out of this conversation topic. It just hurt too much. "Let's go upstairs."

"Now?" he asked, surprised.

"Yes. I mean, hello, what do you think I'm here for?" I laughed. He smiled and stood up to follow me up to the bedroom.

"Oh, wait..." He walked into the kitchen and returned with a bottle of whipped cream. "As requested." He smiled.

He tossed me on the bed, and I watched him undress. He then proceeded to put whipped cream on every part of my body he wanted to lick.

"I don't think I've ever known someone else's body the way I know yours," he said.

By the time we were done, we were both a mess of sweat and sticky sugar. We showered and he rinsed my body off just as deliberately as he had licked it all moments earlier. I stared out of the shower door at his fish tank that sat just outside the window.

"Did you name them?" I asked, washing my hair.

"The fish? Of course. I call them the Fantastic Eight." I let out a laugh. "What? Haven't you seen the movie?"

"Yeah. I kind of dated one of the guys from it when I came back from Europe."

He looked at me, mildly shocked.

"Who?"

"Rodolfo González." I laughed.

"Are you kidding me? You dated him? I compete with him for roles like...all the time."

"Yeah, you guys are definitely the same type."

"I have to fucking change the fish's names now." He laughed. "I can't believe you went out with him."

After dinner that night, while lying in bed, a rather unexpected conversation took place.

"What do you think was missing with you and Tyler?" he asked.

"I don't really know how to explain it. I think my relationship with him brought up a lot of fears. But hurting him was seriously devastating for me."

"You were as up front with him as you could have been the whole time, Gabs," he said, trying to make me feel better—and failing. "You're actually the reason I'm so up front with women now."

"What do you mean?"

"I don't ever want to make the same mistake I made with you ever again. Like the girl I dated while I was shooting in Canada. I was bluntly honest in telling her that what we had was never going to go anywhere."

I sat up on my elbow. "Why do you think you were never able to do that with me?" I asked.

He looked down. "I just didn't want to hurt you because I loved you."

"But you ended up hurting me so much more." I stared into his eyes. He looked away, ashamed. "So now that we're here, let me give you the opportunity to finally just be direct with me."

"Okay." He waited.

"What the hell really happened?" I asked, waiting for the answer I'd been searching for since September 4th, 2017.

"A big part of it was all the grief I was feeling. But to be honest, I panicked. We were making all these plans and it was getting so serious, I just...freaked out. And I know I was the one initiating all of that—which is why I felt so awful."

"Thank you," I simply said. "For finally giving that to me." A pause. Then I let out a small chuckle.

"What?" he asked.

"You're just never going to be the guy that shows up for me," I said, looking at him. He looked back at me, unsure of what to say.

"No," he finally uttered.

It was this moment—this simple moment, lying in his bed, having a seemingly straightforward conversation—that absolutely changed *everything*. Because in that moment, the gray storm clouds parted, the sun shone through, and I heard the stupid fucking angels sing from the heavens above. He was *never* going to be the man that showed up for me. He was *never* going to be the man that I deserved. He was quite simply not capable of being the man I had once built him up to be. Thank you, forty-eight hours—because that massive realization *set me fucking free*.

The Ridiculous Misadventures of...

THAT MAN

I t was a normal evening much like any other—except for the fact that I had been sick the night before. Not the "I don't feel good so I should go to bed" kind of sick but the "waking up to puke, lying on the bathroom floor because it's cold and you're feverishly sweating, I feel like I'm fucking *dying*" kind of sick.

After a miserable night, I finally passed out in my bed and stayed there most of the day. Luckily, it was Sunday and all that was required of me was catching up on trashy reality TV.

I did, however, have plans to see Javier the next night. We had completely disregarded the twenty-four-hour rule and had fallen into a full-on friends-with-benefits situation. It was ridiculous. I would go to his house, and we would swim, watch movies, have dinner, laugh, and talk about anything and everything—and then proceed to have wild sex. It was pretty simple, actually: in the bedroom, it was like we were the only people that existed in each other's worlds. When we were anywhere else, we were friends. Don't ask me how, but it was working. The revelation I'd had in his bed, when my heart finally realized he would never be the man who showed up for me, truly allowed me to take a step back from the residual feelings I had for this man—and it became purely physical. But when 7 p.m. rolled around and I wasn't exactly feeling like the healthy sex goddess he was expecting to waltz into his house the following day, I called him to tell him that I didn't think I'd be able to make it.

"I mean, I feel better, but I was, like, violently sick dude. Like exorcist shit," I said into the phone.

"I hate when you call me dude." He laughed.

"I don't want to get you sick tomorrow."

"I never get sick, we'll be fine," he responded, with such a typical *dude* answer.

"Right, Mr. Invincible. I don't know. Let me see how I feel in the morning."

"Fine. But get some sleep. I want to see you. And I need you rested." I could feel his sexual smirk through the phone.

I hung up the phone, unmuted the TV, and headed into the bathroom to pee. As I sat there, zoning out on the toilet that I had been praying to the night before, my eyes landed on the box of tampons on my toiletry shelf. *Huh. Tampons. Wait...*

I leapt off the toilet, ran to my room, tore through my purse, and opened my birth control. *No. No, there's no way.* I counted the empty pill slots in my head as I looked at the calendar on my phone. *Oh...shit.*

As I tried to convince myself not to panic, that it was totally plausible that I just happened to be a week and a half late after having more than a little bit of unprotected sex with who, at this point, might very well be the most fertile Argentinian bachelor who ever lived, my stomach suddenly didn't feel sick anymore. Instead, it felt like the moment you wake up way past your alarm, or, you know, find out your husband has been jetting off to Miami with girls that are still in their teens. I recounted my birth control pills and recalculated the date. I then thought back to the previous month. My period had come, but it was—weird. I hadn't thought anything of it. There's no way...I mean...right? *SHIT.*

Me: Okay so...
Me: Don't freak out.

Of course, my phone rang.

"I hate when you do this. What's wrong?" he asked, looking at me over FaceTime. *Oh, dude, this is potentially so much worse than me being upset with you.*

"I was supposed to get my period last week and the time before it was supposed to come it was like...I dunno not really normal." I waited for him to say something, then uneasily started rambling. "But I don't feel like anything. I'm sure it's fine. My boobs don't hurt. I don't feel weird. I'm sure it's fine." I realized I was now panic reasoning, trying to convince myself that it was, in fact, *fine.*

"I mean, Gabs, don't you think you should take a pregnancy test?" Hearing the words *pregnancy* come out of his mouth made me feel like I was about to throw up—again. "At least to be sure?" *This cannot fucking be happening right now.*

"Yeah, I guess." I was attempting to not tailspin as he started typing on his computer. "Seriously, I'm sure it's fine," I repeated.

"I don't want to freak you out, but I just googled signs of pregnancy and everything you said you went through with being sick last night is on the list."

The panic in the pit of my stomach started to bubble like a pot of boiling water.

"This can't be possible," I said to myself yet out loud into the phone.

"Of course, it is, Gabs, we had unprotected sex multiple—"

"YES, OBVIOUSLY I KNOW IT'S POSSIBLE."

He seemed weirdly calm about the entire situation. Why was he not in pre-panic mode like I was?

"Are you home?" he asked.

"Am I what?" I was no longer in my body, apparently.

"Are you home?"

"Yes, why?"

"I'm coming over. I don't want you to have to take a test by yourself."

"It's almost 11 p.m. You don't have to do that."

"Yes, I do. You shouldn't have to do that alone. And I'll stay with you tonight."

"What about the dog?" I asked, still somewhere in between panic and shock.

"I'll bring him. I'm leaving here in five minutes. I'll see you soon."

It was in this exact moment that I realized two things. One, that this man, with all of his flaws, everything he had put me through, all of the "cop-outs" and back and forth roller-coaster rides of bull-shit—really did care about me. Not only did he really care about me, *he was my friend*—and he knew I needed him. The second thing I realized? I was *so not* fucking ready to be a mother.

As if on autopilot, I grabbed my keys, got in the car, drove to CVS, and walked to the aisle you never really want to walk to unless it's planned. I stood there, staring at all the different options, and all I wanted to do was burst into tears. The worst part? All I could think of was wanting to be safely back in Tyler's arms—and how this would *absolutely crush him*. I knew how disappointed he would be in me. How disappointed my mother would be in me. How disappointed *I* would be with me.

"Do you need anything?" I was snapped out of my wormhole by an employee walking by.

"Uh, no, thanks," I managed to get out.

I grabbed whatever test looked most familiar to me from those god-awful commercials that run way too often on TV and always make it sound like a wonderful happy-go-lucky fucking process.

As I stood in line, knowing all too well that the cashier was not going to assume that I was out buying a pregnancy test at 11:13 p.m. on a Sunday night because my significant other and I had been planning to celebrate with balloons and fucking confetti, my phone rang.

"I'm about to get off the freeway. Are you okay?" Javier asked on the other end.

"No, I'm hyperventilating in line at a CVS, waiting for this cashier to judge me about who my potential baby daddy is."

"It's going to be fine, Gabs. Wait for me. I'll be there soon."

I grabbed a pack of gum (as if that would somehow hide the giant pregnancy test box) and paid the cashier, who did his best to act like I was buying some skin care essentials. Bless him.

Once I was back at my apartment, I sat on my couch, took a deep breath, and thought about the gravity of the situation. My mind was racing to a million different places—so I tried to focus it on a Thought Onion. Superficial thought?

• WHAT THE FUCK IS WRONG WITH YOU, GABRIELLE?

Yeah. Well. Moving on. Authentic?

- I am so irresponsible for even putting myself into this situation in the first place.

It was more than just the fact that I wasn't ready to bring a child into this world, or the fact that I wasn't in a relationship with the person who would be the father. It was the fact that, if I'm being brutally honest, I knew I wouldn't be able to keep a child under all of these circumstances—and that made me feel like a terrible fucking human. So terrible, I didn't even want to see what the subconscious thought might have in store, lurking beneath the surface.

- What if I can't do it?

That really was the biggest fear in all of this. The fact that this was all happening with the man I, at one point, so desperately loved. The man I so clearly saw a future with—someone I wanted to have kids with, had vividly imagined a family with. How on earth would I be able to end what I had once wanted with all of my heart. *Why.* Why did it have to be *him*?

Knock, knock, knock.

Shit. Here we go.

I opened the door, and his large dog stumbled into my small apartment. My panicked face looked at his, although he was hiding his much more effectively. He opened his arms and put them around me. I stood there for only a moment, because standing still for too long made me panic even more.

We sat down on the couch—the same couch we had sat on only a few months earlier when we had made the decision to open up Pandora's box. My heart felt like it was literally going to leap out of my chest.

"How are you feeling?" he asked.

"How are YOU feeling?" I quickly shot back.

"I'm fine," he said, way calmer than anyone should be in this situation.

"HOW ON EARTH ARE YOU FINE?"

"Because it's you. It's us. We'll figure it out either way. Thank God it isn't someone else."

I was a bit taken aback. The very thing that was allowing him to somehow be calm about the situation was the thing that was making me feel like I couldn't fucking *breathe*. Because if this was all real, if this was all actually happening, deep, *deep* down I didn't know what the hell I would do—and that was fucking terrifying.

"Have you thought about what you would want to do?" He snapped me out of the tailspin that was currently happening inside my brain.

"I don't know. I mean, I don't want to have a child with someone who doesn't want to be with me. When I'm not in a relationship and in love," I said. "I know you want to be a dad, but not like this."

He didn't agree or object—he didn't attempt to sway me one way or another. In fact, it became very clear in that moment that he would in no way be telling me what I should do with my body.

"I just don't know how I'd be able to go through with that, knowing it was something I once thought we'd be doing together. Like…I wanted that with you at one time," I shared.

"Yeah, I know," he said solemnly.

We sat there for a moment in silence.

"Really wish you wouldn't have Google diagnosed me," I finally said with a laugh.

"As opposed to you just thinking you were eating too much a few months from now?" He laughed back and I playfully smacked his arm.

"Okay. Let's pee on a stick." I stood up to head to the bathroom.

"Should I wait here or…?" He stood too, unsure of what to do.

"No, idiot, I don't need you to come pee with me. It takes a few minutes before it tells you." I laughed.

I went into the bathroom and read the directions. They are so simple but for some reason we feel like we have to re-read them five times like we're about to disable a fucking nuclear bomb. As I sat there, peeing on this stupid stick, I thought about how insane this all was. I was about to release *Eat, Pray, #FML* into the world in a few weeks. I was already doing interviews about the man who tore my heart out and sent me brokenhearted on a journey across the world. This was *that* man. And here I was, peeing on a stick, waiting to see if we were about to be tethered to each other by much more than the eternal words in a book.

I set the stick down on my sink and looked at myself in the mirror. Two minutes and counting.

I came out of the bathroom and sat beside him on the bed.

"Two minutes," I told him. He grabbed my shaking hand.

"It's going to be okay either way," he said.

We sat there for what seemed like a fucking eternity. Finally, when we knew enough time had passed, I stood up and took a step toward the bathroom.

"I can't look. Can you do it?" I felt deep, complete, and utter panic—and I knew right then that this was something *I did not want*. It was the moment you feel as if you're out of your body and you start praying to God that you'll never do another stupid thing ever again if he can just give you a pass this one time. *Please, God.*

"Yes." He stood up. "What am I looking for?"

"One line is negative, and two lines is positive."

"Okay." He turned back to me. "It's going to be fine," he repeated.

He left the room, the stillness so overwhelming I could hear my heart thumping against my chest. Please, God. *Please.*

"Gabs…" he said from the bathroom. Tears instantly came to my eyes.

"Don't fuck with me," I shouted. He walked into my room and looked at me.

"It's negative," he said with a smile.

I let out the deepest breath and threw my arms around him. We stood there for a minute just holding on tightly, knowing we had somehow escaped what could have been a life-altering change for us both.

When I finally stepped back from his embrace, I looked at him and wiped the one tear that had fallen from my eye.

"It's negative," I said, smiling.

"It's negative," he repeated. "What a twist in book two this would have been!" We both laughed.

We high-fived and vowed to *never* not use condoms again. That night, I fell asleep in *that* man's arms. And while I realized he wasn't anywhere near perfect, or my knight in shining armor, he hadn't let me down. This one time, he didn't run. He didn't hide. He showed up for me in the way I'd always wished he'd been capable of—and I will never forget that.

The Ridiculous Misadventures
of...
DIVINE INTERVENTION

Tyler had been out of town working on a movie for the past month, and though we had been talking in some small way almost every day, it was the first time I really felt the distance in our breakup. I can't say I wasn't triggered thinking about him with the many different attractive women I knew were on that film set (ah, thank you, social media,) but here I was in an all-out friends-with-benefits situation with the Achilles' heel of his existence...so who the fuck was I to talk?

On June 22nd, 2019, my life officially changed. Not the drastic change that happens when you find out your husband had been juggling enough women to impress a circus crowd or when you find out your new love is in fact nowhere near ready for the relationship he started, but the type of change that started as a planted seed and had now broken through the earth with its first bloom of the season—it was the day that *Eat, Pray, #FML* was released.

Ironically enough, on the biggest day of my new career path, I was in an Uber on my way to see none other than the man who was the catalyst for the entire thing—Javier.

"Oh my God, Gabrielle! It just hit number-one best new release on Amazon!" Yeseña squealed in the back of the car as she showed me her phone.

My heart was so full. The whole day I had been flooded with messages, social media posts, and true support from so many people. Part of me wanted to jump up and down, screaming and shouting from the rooftops. The other part of me wanted to burst into tears—because it was officially *all* out for the entire world to judge.

We'd been invited to an event Javier was putting on, where I not only saw his parents again, but finally met his sister, Sophia. It was so strange that I'd had a legitimate relationship with her that happened entirely over text and FaceTime—we'd never actually met in person.

"Wow, you look stunning," Javier secretly whispered to me as he greeted Yeseña and I.

"Uh, hello, it's a big day! We're celebrating!" Yeseña said.

"What do you mean?" he asked, confused.

"Her fucking book came out today!" she shouted, forever my cheerleader.

"What?! Oh my God, you didn't tell me!" He pulled out his phone.

"Yeah, it's kind of been a busy day." I laughed.

"Ordered. I'm so freaking proud of you, Gabs." He smiled at me.

"Thank you. Couldn't have done it without you...literally."

The show that night was awesome. Yeseña and I danced with Manny and Cesar, another friend of Javier's, as we all laughed and celebrated. After saying goodbye to his family, I handed him a card I had brought with me.

"What's this?" he asked.

"Just a thank-you."

It was a final thank-you that I had written for the support he'd shown me around the book. He didn't *have* to sign the release. He didn't have to be excited and supportive that I was about to put so much of his personal life out there. And I will forever be grateful for that.

Just as I arrived home that night, a voice note came in from him.

"Gabs...I am so proud of you. I am so happy for you. I am so amazed by you, inspired by you. I am beyond grateful to you. You were the catalyst for my healing to begin. I will never ever ever ever forget how hard and strong you held me on my brother's birthday when we were in San Vito. Those are the moments, the connections, that I value in life. Nothing else matters. You have always been there for me, and I have always felt that I had your love, your support, your compassion, your understanding, and your patience more than anything. You are one of the most incredible and important people in my life—I'm always, always, always going to be one of your many guardians...and I love you very, very, very much. Thank you for making me a better person."

It had all come so weirdly full circle. Here I was, releasing this new piece of me into the world, doing interviews and podcasts, and constantly being asked the question I would soon learn would plague my very existence for years to come—*do you still talk to Javier?* As I danced around the answer, knowing I not only spoke to him, but was actively being intimate with him, I became worried. Worried that people would find out I had let the man that broke me back in. Worried that it somehow meant I was letting all of my readers down. Worried that I hadn't learned my goddamn lesson the first time. And that night, when our story was officially released into the world, we both knew it was time. Time to take a step back from the tangled web of friendship sex we had woven and gotten all too comfortable in. And so we did.

A few weeks was all it took for me to detox from the drug known as Javier. We were naturally not talking nearly as often and hadn't seen each other since the night of his event. I had been spending my time engrossed in the early success of my book. Hearing how it was resonating with people and helping them heal suddenly gave my life a whole new purpose and meaning. I was spending my time with my girlfriends, salsa dancing until my feet couldn't anymore, and enjoying another LA summer. Tyler and I seemed to be finding our footing in a friendship and were able to talk with a little less hurt after he came back from filming. However, I didn't yet realize *why* he had been able to make the shift in his heartache toward me in the last month. Not yet, at least.

One day I was out with my new group of friends from the film I had done in April. I was in my *no drinking, self-love cocktail the shit out of myself* phase, so I was DD for the day. They had all met both Tyler and Javier on different occasions, and as they sipped on margaritas and we laughed our asses off, Katy brought up Tyler.

"We're friends! I *want* him to date. I *want* him to find all the happiness he deserves," I said to the group. I could tell they were not entirely convinced.

"I don't know, I've always been team Ty. Just saying," one of the other girls chimed in.

"Same. I mean Javier is great and exotic and all but, honey, that was until I saw that Greek God of yours!" Sully added.

"Okay, first of all, he's Persian and Irish, and second of all, he's not mine anymore." I laughed.

Tyler and I had been texting most of the day. He was headed to a comedy show with some of the people from the film he'd just done.

Me: Have fun on your date!

Tyler: Not going on a date, idiot. Going to a comedy show.

Me: Oh fun! To see the big-breasted blonde.
Me: Lol. Fucking with you.

Tyler: Jesus Christ. Lol. She's married by the way.

Me: I'm kidding.

Tyler: I know.

He sent me a picture of himself flipping off the camera.

Me: Rudeeeee! Send that to Daniel.

Tyler: Already did. And Javier. Fuck 'em all.

I was cracking up in the middle of the restaurant while the rest of the group continued to consume tequila.

Tyler: You better tell the next sucker that he'll have to answer to me if he fucks around.
Tyler: Kidding. Not kidding.

Me: Not kidding. But then again, I'll fucking cut a bitch so...

By the time I had dropped each drunk friend off at their respective homes, Tyler was done at his comedy show, and we decided that we wanted to grab a bite to eat and catch up. We hadn't seen each other since he'd been back. When all the craziness, heartache, and back and forth was said and done, one thing remained: *we freaking missed each other.*

We ate crepes on the patio of Crave café at 11 p.m. and laughed as if no time had passed at all.

"I missed you, idiot," he said, smiling at me across the table.

"I missed you too. Three weeks is too long."

"How's the response on the book been?"

"Amazing so far." I smiled.

"Has Javier read it?" My smile faded. I *hated* talking about Javier with Tyler. It was such a sore subject that never led to anything good.

"I don't think so yet...I'm not sure."

"I'd love to hear what he thinks about it all," he said. I could tell he was getting upset just thinking about it. I took a bite of my food.

"And there he fucking is," Tyler said as he threw down his fork.

"What?" I asked, confused. Seeing the look on his face, I turned around. And there—at 11:30 p.m., randomly sitting on a restaurant patio—I saw none other than Javier walking through the front door. *Seriously, only in my freaking life.*

Our lighthearted, fun mood immediately shifted. Tyler had never seen the man that in some way kept me from fully being his until this moment—on a night we weren't even supposed to see each other, had contemplated ordering Postmates, and just so happened to be in the exact same place at the exact moment Javier walked in. What the actual fuck, universe?

My entire body immediately went into fight-or-flight mode and the innate need to do damage control began.

"Please don't say anything to him, Tyler," I begged, seeing the fury building inside of him toward the man who had hurt me.

"I'm not going to say anything to him, Gabrielle."

I let out a sigh of relief. "Let's just go," I offered.

"No, we're going to sit here and finish our food," he demanded.

For the next twenty minutes, I prayed Javier didn't walk back out and see us, because, knowing him, he would come right on over to say hello and hug me. When we finished eating, Tyler and I got into the car and headed back, unscathed by the potentially catastrophic run-in I was *so* not mentally prepared for.

"I wish I would have said something," he said as I handed him tea, sitting on my couch.

"Why? What would that have done?" I asked.

"Not like that—just introduced myself and said hi."

"I'm sure he would have been super nice, and it would have been fine," I said.

"I just wasn't prepared to see the person who has been the biggest obstacle in getting the one thing I wanted so badly and care so much about. But I would have been able to at least humanize him and take away some of that power he holds," he explained.

"He doesn't hold any of that power. He's just a man."

"Yeah..." He looked down solemnly.

We changed the subject, and after twenty minutes of laughter and remembering why we so enjoyed being together, and more than a few moments of reignited chemistry, I realized something: *I freaking missed this human.* In a way that I had never really missed anyone before. It had felt like a part of my soul had been missing for the past few months that Tyler wasn't there—a part that even Javier wasn't able to fill. Looking at how my life had unfolded the past few months, it almost felt as if Tyler reentering my life was divine intervention. Not only to pull me away from a toxic love but to re-instill in me what it is I truly and undoubtedly deserve. I looked at him longingly.

"What?" he asked, seeing the look on my face.

"Nothing..." I said.

"No, tell me."

"I just really missed spending time with you."

"And?" He knew there was more.

"I don't want you to leave," I said with a sadness on my lips.

"Then I won't leave."

"It's not that simple."

"It is. We don't have to cross that line. I know where you stand and how you feel. I can just hold you," he said, clearly seeing all that I had been going through emotionally and knowing exactly what my heart needed.

I can just hold you. It seems like such a simple statement—yet it held so much weight in my little heart. So many men over the course of my life had disregarded what I had needed. Had seen my fragility and chosen to cross the line if I didn't flat out say no. This man knew me. He knew my deepest wounds, my biggest fears, and the purest parts of my soul.

"I don't want to confuse anything," I finally said.

"It's not confusing. I'll stay."

We fell asleep that night in each other's arms—and I slept deeper than I had in months. Because I knew that, for at least the next eight hours, I was totally and completely safe. But in the morning, I would learn the real reason why Tyler had been able to step away from his heartbreak—and divine intervention or not, it was something I was definitely *not* prepared for.

The Ridiculous Misadventures

of...

FEAR OF ABANDONMENT

I woke up with Tyler's arms still around me. Normally, we would cuddle for ten minutes until we were both like *Okay, get the fuck off me now,* roll over, starfish, and go to sleep. But after a few months apart, it was like neither of us wanted to move in fear one of us would disappear. I always felt safe in his arms—like nothing in the entire world could ever harm me. I had missed that feeling.

He stirred awake and squeezed me tightly before rolling over onto his back. I hoped he felt okay. I hoped this wasn't all just hurting him.

After a few minutes of morning chit chat, the conversation took a turn. This is where what I call a secret-mission Tic Tac–sized comment embedded itself in my brain. I didn't even really notice it at the time, but I'm pointing it out now because we'll be referring back to it in, oh, say...twenty-four hours?

"So...am I supposed to tell you if I'm dating anyone?" he asked.

Um, well...considering you're lying in my bed with your arms wrapped around me...probably?

I wouldn't call the feeling that happened the surge necessarily. It was more like abruptly walking into a sliding glass door and trying to play it off like you didn't just face-plant into a wall of glass at a decent speed.

"Uh, I mean, I don't really think you should be sleeping in my bed if you are," I responded, completely thrown off guard.

"It's just someone I've been talking to, nothing has happened. We're just kind of getting to know each other. We're supposed to go on a date tomorrow night."

"Nope. Don't wanna know." I responded more quickly than I had time to actually think about it. *What the fuck, Gabrielle?* Not more than twelve hours ago you said, "I hope he's dating. He deserves to find someone incredible who loves him as much as he loves them." So why, when what you just said you hoped for appears to be happening, do you feel the need to book it like the roadrunner in the other direction? Please hold, Tyler, I need a Thought Onion for breakfast. And maybe a mimosa. Superficial thought?

- I love this person and want him to be happy.

Yes. That is 100% accurate. On my brain's conscious level. Authentic thought?

- What if he finds someone and I don't?

That's interesting. I've never had a problem finding someone to have a relationship with. Besides, it's not a freaking race. But I had never felt ready to pack up and move on to someone new since Tyler and I had broken up. Javier was moving backwards and was just physical. Okay, subconscious thought?

- What if he leaves me?

Yes. There it was. My little six-year-old girl watching her father possibly leave. Obviously, Ty is not my father—I mean, ew. *But* he is older, with a similar energy and so many parallel qualities. I felt protected by him, safe with him, and closer to him than almost any other person in my life. Okay, you nasty fucking abandonment wound, I see you, and you will *not* have power over me. I *want* this human to be happy.

"Okay." He snapped me out of my thoughts.

"Just, if it becomes a thing, you need to tell me. Obviously, we can't be cuddling on the couch and sleeping in the same bed," I said.

"Of course. You know I would never do that."

"I know."

After a very long hug goodbye, I got ready to go about my day. As I threw clothes on, the secret-mission comment was slowly embedding itself deep into my brain. For whatever reason, I could not stop wondering who he was taking on a date the next night—or why it even mattered to me. There is a downside of having a closer-than-close relationship like Tyler and I did. When normally you would just overthink and deal or discuss it over a bottle of wine with your girlfriends, I had no problem picking up the phone and calling him to just flat out ask. So, I did.

"The person you've been talking to...do I know her?' I asked as I climbed into my car.

"Um. You don't know her. I think you know *of* her," he answered warily, knowing where this was going.

"Oh, so she's famous," I concluded.

"I mean, she's well known."

My heart then took an elevator ride down to my stomach—because I knew exactly who it was. "It's Nicole Conrad, isn't it?"

A very long, very affirmative pause. "Yes." His voice sounded almost pained when he said it—because no matter what we had gone through, or the fact that I had been the one who left him, he knew this was going to hurt me. And that was the last thing he ever wanted to do. Now it was time for the surge.

"I have to go," I said, quickly hanging up. Nicole Conrad was an actress you most definitely know if you weren't living under a rock in the 90s. She was Ty's age now, still beautiful, and you know, Nicole fucking Conrad. My anxiety immediately shot through the roof. As I drove and my phone rang repeatedly, I, fucking, bawled.

Was I having this reaction because he was talking to *someone*? Or because of *who* that someone was? I felt physically sick as my phone racked up another two missed calls from Tyler. I finally answered.

"I just need some time to process everything."

"Okay, I'm sorry, I don't want you to be upset. Nothing has even happened."

That wasn't the issue. I'd left *him*. Twice. He had every right to go be with whomever he wanted. I mean, hello, I had been sleeping with *THE* ex of all exes. He shouldn't be apologizing. I was the one who had gotten us here.

"Can you call me when you get home?" he pleaded.

"Okay." I cried, like my little six-year-old self, into the phone.

"Okay, I love you," he said.

Seriously, system overload. First Javier, now Tyler. I was at my breaking point in the panic/abandonment department. As I tried to breath and calm myself, a text from Ty came in.

Tyler: It's brutally important that you hear this: When I told you yesterday that I have yet to hook up with or even kiss ANYONE since you…that was the absolute truth. Nothing happened on set. She and I are very slowly figuring things out. Please call me when you're done.

When I finally got home, I sat on my couch and cried. So much overwhelm was pouring out of me. The last two weeks that the book had been out, I had been in a constant state of not knowing whether to jump up and down with barely containable excitement or burst into tears of *what the fuck am I doing*. I needed my person. I needed Ty. So I picked up the phone and called.

"Peanut," he said, as if he had been waiting for the phone to ring.

"I'm so freaking sad," I cried into the phone.

"Me too."

"I just need to be in your arms," I pushed out through the tears.

"I'm on my way." He never missed a beat. He really was my knight in shining armor.

Twenty minutes later, I opened the door, fell into his arms, and sobbed.

"Why do you think you're feeling like this?" he asked.

"I don't know," I said, wishing I had a better answer. "I just feel like you're going to go on this date, fall for each other, and be together. Like truly, in my gut, that's how I feel."

"Come on, Gabs, it's just a date."

"I just feel it. I know you. I feel physically sick. I don't know what's wrong with me."

I'd known Javier had been with other people since we'd broken up. I knew he had dated. But I had never felt *this* way. I had never felt like my heart was literally breaking inside my chest. I had, truthfully, never felt this feeling in my life.

Tyler and I sat and talked about everything. I don't think I've ever felt more at ease with someone. I knew I could say anything without judgment and without fear of being met with anger.

"I was just saying yesterday that I want you to be dating and I want you to be happy. I don't know why I'm having this reaction." I flopped down on the floor and took a deep breath. He came down beside me and held me. A few moments later, he looked into my eyes, and it was as if we were physically pulled into each other. It was the first time we had kissed since February—and the first time I had suddenly felt the desire to tear his clothes off. After a few passionate moments of kissing, he sat up.

"What am I gonna do with you, Peanut?" He sighed.

"I'm sorry. I don't know," I answered.

"What's going on, what are you feeling?"

"I know that, since February, I haven't wanted to sleep with you but for some reason right now, I really do." Honest, yet probably going to backfire into further complications.

"So why is that bad?" he asked.

"You know why."

"I'm not going to assume it means anything. I just want to be with you." He leaned down to kiss me again.

"Okay." I gave in. He lifted me up from the floor and carried me to my bed.

I didn't even need a Thought Onion. It was very clear to me what had just taken place. My fear of abandonment had kicked in, *big time*. And, like in the past, I turned to sex to protect myself—to not feel abandoned. But something unexpected happened instead. My heart broke wide open, totally gave in, and we ended up making love the way you hear about in romance novels and watch in *The Notebook*—looking deep into each other's eyes, breathing heavily, whispering what we had said that first night we were ever together: *I don't want you to be with anyone else.* Tears began to swell in my eyes. I wasn't sure what they meant. Overcome with emotion? Terrified of losing this human? Letting him go?

When we collapsed on the bed, I began to cry. He didn't ask if I was okay. He didn't even seem taken aback. He just pulled me into his chest, wrapped me in his arms, and held me. I felt his chest vibrate as he held tears in too.

The next morning, I again woke up in his arms. I didn't feel any type of regret—but the anxiety in the pit of my stomach flared up anytime I thought about him taking Nicole on a date later that day.

I made us something to eat, and we sat in the living room to talk.

"Are you okay?" he asked.

"Yeah," I answered, although I had no idea if it was true or not.

"You realize that what you're feeling seems like your fear of abandonment kicking in, right?"

"Yes. I know."

"Gabs. I am *not* abandoning you. I will *never* abandon you. I'm here for life. No woman, or person, will ever change that. You're my family."

"It's really easy to say that now, but things change." I knew this all too well from my own experience with Javier.

"Things may change and be different, but I will never not be in your life or not be here for you," he assured me.

"Okay," I said. Luckily, the tear well had dried up after the day before.

We hugged and I watched him head to his car. I shut the door and sat on my couch, trying to control my anxiety. Then, as if on a timer, the secret-mission comment exploded like a fucking atomic bomb. *Panic.*

Do a Thought Onion. And for the love of God breathe so you don't pass out. Superficial thought?

• What the fuck are you doing, you stupid woman? You're making the biggest mistake of your goddamn life.

That was pretty much where my panicked brain was at. Authentic thought?

- Don't let your fear of abandonment dictate what your next move is.

Yes. This was really important. I could not put this amazing human whom I love so much through this—again. Taking that into account, what is the subconscious thought of it all?

- What if what was missing with this person was the fact that I hadn't had closure with—or closed the door to—Javier.

Well, fuck. That notion made me panic even more. I had finally seen that Javier was never going to be the guy who showed up for me. This human who had infiltrated my being and haunted my thoughts. I had finally opened my own door and walked through. What if I was letting my soulmate slip away when it could be different now? If we both started on level ground, instead of me starting at the bottom of the hill? This connection we had, this love I felt for him, didn't that deserve one last shot now that the toxic element had been removed?

I called my mother in hopes she would talk me off the ledge. Either back into a calm zone we call the single life or off the edge into Tyler's arms. I couldn't handle wobbling on the ledge any longer.

"I'm freaking out," I said into the phone. "I don't know if I'm making the biggest mistake of my life or if this is my abandonment fears kicking in hard."

"Well, baby, you haven't ever really been able to let him go. Maybe there's a reason for that," she said.

I hung up, got in my car, and drove to his house.

He opened the door, surprised to see me—especially in the state I was in.

"I'm sorry, I messed up, I don't want to not be with you. I don't want you to date other people, I want to be with you." He probably understood a third of it through my heavy tears and hiccupped breathing. *Jesus, Gabrielle, pull it together.* I dug my face into his chest and grabbed on for dear life.

"It's okay, it's okay, come inside." He guided me to the couch. I tried to calm down a bit and control my breathing—and emotions.

"I don't want to not be with you. I love you so much, you're my person. I want you, I want Blue, I want all of it. I'm just scared. I'm sorry, you probably think I'm crazy," I said.

He paused. "This is just a lot to hear because it's all I've wanted to hear for the last year." He held my hand tightly.

"I know. I don't know what happened—just with everything last night something changed." I continued to pour my emotional messy heart out.

"I know. I've never experienced anything like that. You know I want to be with you. I want nothing more than that. But I just cannot do this again. I've barely been hanging on, Peanut. I can't go through this again—I won't make it," he confessed. That worried me. You're going to take this man's heart in your hands and *hope* it will work a third time around?

"I know," I said—and I did know. That was the last thing I wanted.

"And I can't keep letting Blue get her hopes up—she loves you so much."

"I know," I repeated. More pressure, more panic. We sat there holding each other's hands. He kissed me and wiped away a mess of tears.

"If you need to take her on the date tonight, I understand. I just needed you to know how I feel and that I want to be with you." It was so interesting. The younger me would have been doing this as a manipulation tactic, not wanting him to go on a date with this person. This was *so* the opposite. I wanted him to do what was best for him and made *him* happy. I felt guilty about the epically awful timing of it all. I wished I would have had this poorly timed epiphany sooner.

"I'm not even thinking about that right now. I'm just scared," he admitted.

"I understand."

There was a long pause. My heart began to pound in my chest with nervousness. I knew that if I was going to commit to moving forward with this man, it would have to be with a clean slate. And that meant being fully honest. There was no way I would be able to do that without telling him about Javier. *Fuck.*

"I do have to tell you something," I said, trying to control my nerves and mild need to projectile vomit. I did *not* want to have this conversation. "But I need you to, please, be my best friend and unicorn right now and be here for me without judgment."

"Okay. I already know what you're going to say." His whole demeanor instantly changed.

"Just let me explain and tell you, okay?" I asked. He sat quietly, waiting. "When we were apart, Javier and I slept together. I don't regret it. I needed to get some kind of closure with all of it and it helped me do that. It was necessary for me." Somehow, none of this was sounding as convincing out loud.

"How many times?" he asked. What a strange first question.

"What?" I stalled.

"How many times?" he repeated.

"Two," I lied—and instantly felt awful. So much for starting with an honest clean slate, Gabrielle. He stood up with the cup of tea he was holding and *hurled* it against the kitchen wall. It smashed into a hundred pieces, the way his heart had moments before. I stood up, mouth open, shocked. He walked into the kitchen and punched the washing machine—*hard*. I had never seen him like this.

"Tyler, it helped me heal. I needed to close that chapter," I said, still mildly shocked at what I had just witnessed.

"Not twice," he answered, fuming.

"Why does it matter how many times?"

"We're done." His words cut into me like a sharp knife. *Panic.*

"Stop, please. I'm trying to be honest with you. We weren't together," I pleaded.

"It doesn't matter. After all he put you through, what he did to you, how he treated you...you went back to him."

"I had zero closure, Ty, I had—"

"YOU WROTE A FUCKING BOOK ABOUT THE GUY!" he yelled. "YOU DIDN'T GO BACK ONCE, YOU WENT BACK TWICE!" he said, as my guilt spewed into my throat, attempting to choke me.

"Look, I'm here, telling you I want to be with you."

"It doesn't matter. We're done." It cut just as badly the second time. He pulled away from me.

"Really, just like that?" I cried.

"I can't even look at you right now." He balled his fists tightly. I sat there, completely defeated, but not willing to accept all this and just...leave. After a few moments, he said, "You have to tell your mom."

"What?" I said, mildly shocked.

"You have to tell your mom, or I will. You've been lying to both of us."

"I haven't been lying. It's no one's business!" I defended. He stared daggers into my eyes. A long pause. "Okay. Okay, I'll tell her," I agreed. I think in that moment, he was so hurt, so blindsided, he needed someone else who hated Javier just as much to understand and share his pain. "Do you just want me to go?" I asked, hoping he wouldn't say yes. A long, painful pause. Then he spoke more softly.

"I am not abandoning you," he said, unable to look at me.

My heart nearly exploded. I had unintentionally put this man through hell and back, and he loved me so goddamn much that, even when I said the most hurtful thing to him, he *still* made sure he didn't trigger my wounds. Tyler taught me something so valuable in that moment—when you love someone and you know their wounds, you do not pick and prod at them. You do not walk away to let them bleed and ache. You stay and tend to them with care, compassion, and comfort—especially when those wounds mirror your own. I was so incredibly thankful that in his deepest hurt, he still chose to take care of mine.

"I need you to know that I am not abandoning you. I just need to process this and calm down." He slightly loosened his clenched fists.

"Okay. I understand," I said. "I love you." I stood and hugged his head to my chest. "I'm so sorry."

"I love you too," he said softly.

I walked out the front door and got into my car. As I drove home in tears, all I could hear in my head were his words. *We're done.* Jesus Christ, Gabrielle. *What the fuck did you just do?*

191

The Ridiculous Misadventures
of...
THE ROMANCE MOVIE

After calling my mother and begrudgingly telling her that I had slept with Javier—to which she replied she already knew and, although she wasn't thrilled, she was glad I'd gotten the closure I needed—I called Tyler's aunt, Louise, who had been a maternal figure to him since he had lost his mother.

"Well shit, honey, I'm not surprised. I read the book. You needed some freaking closure," she replied matter-of-factly. Louise was a licensed therapist, and I was thankful *someone* finally saw it the same way I did. "He's just in reaction and needs to process it all. Give him some time to calm down. He'll get over it."

Uh, I don't know if you heard about the mug throwing or the washing machine punch but the whole "get over it" thing is not looking like a strong bet.

"I just feel like he's going to go on this date and fall for her. I feel it in my gut. And I'm a little worried about his safety," I said. I know it sounds dramatic, but Tyler's genetic makeup consists of grand affairs, intense emotions, and shit out of romance movies. Plus, we all know how Jedi mind freak my intuition can be.

"Don't be silly, it's only a date. He loves you more than I've ever seen him love anybody. There's no doubt in my mind it will be fine," she assured me. I felt like I was going to puke. Then a text from Tyler came in. Just a single broken heart emoji.

Me: I'm here.

Tyler: I just spoke with my aunt. I want you to know that I'm okay. I'm just trying to find my way back to this planet.

Me: I understand. I'm here when you're ready. I'm done around six tonight if you need me or want to talk, or I can come to you. Unless you're going on your date in which case I hope you have a really good time, and I'm sorry for the bad timing and stress this has all caused.

Please say you're not going. Please say you're not going.

Tyler: I will be going tonight. Although rather begrudgingly. I'm just utterly confused and frankly a little sick to my stomach right now. I really don't know what to do.

Me: I hope you have a really good time and get some clarity. Sorry again for the awful timing. Last night was just a lot.

Not only did I feel like an asshole for hurting this amazing person that I loved, I also genuinely felt sick thinking about him going on a date with the chick from the 90s movie I watched a dozen times when I was twelve. That was *not* an age jab—I was actually twelve when it came out. I went to the gym to try and run off some anxiety. It failed. So I went home, unable to eat (which we all know means I was *seriously* not okay), and turned on some trashy reality TV to try and get my mind on *anything* else. *Ding*. My phone went off.

Tyler: You NEED to know this. I've never in my life had a night like last night. EVER. Everything in my soul leads me and pushes me toward you. But at this point, after last night and followed by today...I'm just in a state of shock. And when the shock subsides, the door of fear awaits.

Me: I get it. I'm kind of in the same boat too in a different way. And I'm sick to my stomach about all of it. I just keep telling myself that I know everything, and I mean everything, happens for a reason. So today was all I could do.

Tyler: I'm proud of you. I really am. And I'm extraordinarily happy for your closure and clarity. I know this all weighed on you so heavily.

Even in the thick of it, he continually supported and loved me. And yet here I was, letting this one-of-a-kind man go on a date with someone else. Jesus. Every time I thought about them at dinner, him being his handsome, charming self, I felt like I would never have an appetite again. A mere seventy-two hours earlier I'd been preaching that I wanted him to date and find someone who'd make him the happiest ever because he deserves that. And now here I was in a full-blown state of panic because he was doing just that. God, Gabrielle, this is why women get called crazy.

All I could do was wait, feeling like the minutes were moving in slow motion. One TV show ended. Then another. *What were they talking about? Was he already asking her on a second date? Oh God, was he fucking kissing her goodnight? Did it go that well? Clearly, they're still there. What if he—*

Knock, knock, knock. My front door thankfully interrupted my downward tailspin just in time. Who the hell was at my door at 10 p.m. on a Monday?

I opened it to see Tyler standing outside. My heart didn't know whether to jump for joy or drop straight out my ass and run.

"Hi," I finally said as we stared at each other.

"I sat across from her the whole time and could only think about you," he said with a mixture of love and sadness. He stepped inside, and I threw my arms around him as he picked me up in his huge, safe, grasp. My unicorn had come back and chosen me. It felt like a scene out of an epic romance film. And we lived happily ever after...

Oh, how I *wish* this story ended here.

*****

I was on cloud nine. I was back with the man that made me feel like I was the center of his world, getting my hair and makeup done for the official release party of *Eat, Pray, #FML*, and then jetting off to

Hawaii with Tyler for ten days in Maui. The second half of July and all of August was like a dream—and I felt as if I had finally found my solace.

The night of the book launch, Tyler showed up in a navy-blue suit looking like he had stepped off the pages of *GQ* magazine. I will forever remember that night. So many of my friends, past work acquaintances, and faces I hadn't seen in much too long gathered to celebrate this new accomplishment in my life. Rhonda from Barcelona came, and we laughed and reminisced about how ridiculous it was that we'd met across the world and were now standing on a red carpet as a product of it. Manny was there, and he met Tyler with all the respect and grace I would expect from each of them. My mother beamed at what the worst and lowest time in her daughter's life had now become. I got a text from my ex-brother- and sister-in-law that they had both finished and loved the book, and how proud they were of me. Tess, Elizabeth, and Jess were there—all of the women who had helped get me through some of the darkest times in my life. We all celebrated, laughed, and toasted to the new career path I was about to embark on: *author*.

The following week, Tyler and I escaped reality and headed back to where we had fallen more in love the year before. On the plane we snuggled like we were a newlywed couple and talked the entire five hours. Everything was finally falling into place.

"You're so beautiful." He smiled at me.

"I look like death right now." I laughed, makeup-free, with a messy bun.

"With makeup, with no makeup, with shit all over your face, you are the most beautiful goddamn woman I have ever seen."

I smiled, as my heart melted into this man.

"Should we do the road to Hana?" he asked.

"We should totally do the road to Hana," I responded with a smile.

The road to Hana was where Daniel had proposed to me—and it just so happened that we were in Hawaii on the same week he had gotten down on one knee six years earlier.

We not only did the road to Hana, we went to the same waterfall, stood on the same rock, and reveled in the fact that I did not—and could not—regret one goddamn decision I had made. Because saying yes to that proposal, getting stuck in a narcissistic and loveless marriage, and everything that had ensued after the day I'd handed him the papers, had led me to exactly where I was. Standing on the same rock, holding up a copy of what had bloomed from it all. Tyler snapped a photo of me flipping off the camera—because as much as I was grateful to him...*fuck you, Daniel.*

Tyler even surprised me and took me to the Hyatt Regency for a few nights. There were so many memories at the hotel that was my mother's favorite place on earth. Yes, I had gotten engaged while we were staying at that hotel. But I had also said goodbye to my father there. As we watched his ashes be taken out to sea, I had said farewell as a seven-year-old little girl, not knowing what a monumental amount of grief I would carry with me because of it. And in those few days, Tyler and I redefined all the negative memories of Daniel, embraced the beautiful memories of my father, and created our own wonderful new ones.

I'd received hundreds and hundreds of messages, mostly from readers, people I had never met, that felt like they were now my best friends. People who had healed, gained strength, overcome fears, and learned to love themselves from my journey. I'd also received messages from girls (who were now in college) that Daniel used to coach. Messages about the way they felt emotionally abused, leaving them with crippling anxiety and a jaded memory of the sport they once loved—and how reading my story in the book helped them see that none of it was *their fault.* So, as I stood in the place we had celebrated our engagement, I let out a sigh of relief. Because I had shown them that he was no longer the big scary monster in the closet—he was just a sad, angry, damaged human.

We flew home and spent a blissful month and a half together. And then it came: September 4th, 2019. The day that had once been my wedding anniversary. The day that then became when I left on my infamous FML trip. It was now a day I celebrated my fearless independence. The day I'd taken my life back and decided to heal.

And just then, like internal clockwork, a little and familiar voice whispered to me from the very pit of my stomach—*Gabrielle, your journey can't end here.*

The Ridiculous Misadventures

of...

THE FRIEND ZONE

t happened after a night that wasn't terribly significant—unless you really knew what to look for. It was early October, which is always subconsciously a tough month for me. The month my dad died. Tyler and I were sitting in bed, watching reruns of *Grey's Anatomy*, when Izzy Stevens walks in to find the love of her life, Denny Duquette, dead from heart failure. As I lay there, wrapped in Tyler's arms, watching her heart-wrenching breakdown, I began to cry. Not the single tear that rolls down your cheek when you watch an emotional scene. No, the type of cry where you begin to hyperventilate from the deep-rooted pain it's bringing to the surface—full-on ugly cry. Why, you may ask? Because in that moment, watching the blonde cry tears of grief over the actor who could be Tyler's brother—I saw myself. It was my greatest fear—losing someone I love—and I was quite literally watching it play out in front of my eyes.

"What's wrong? What's going on?" Tyler asked as he held me.

"I don't want you to die. I don't want to be left like my mom was. I'm fifteen years younger than you. What am I going to do when you die?" I sobbed and hiccupped in between panicked breaths.

"I'm not going anywhere. I'm not going to die." He stroked my head.

It was in that moment that I first realized—maybe there wasn't something *missing*. Maybe it was one of my biggest fears being shoved directly into my face. Here was this amazing man, who even my mother saw qualities of my father in, who was a decade and a half older than me. And here I was, subconsciously terrified that our story would be the same as the one I witnessed as a little girl. And that fear was simply too much to fight my way through.

The next few days I pulled back—and Tyler could feel that. I tried to walk through the discomfort, the fear, the deeply ingrained subconscious terror. Until one day, he flat-out asked me if I could, without any doubt, say that I didn't have any questions or feel there was anything missing—and I just couldn't. As we sat there, looking at each other with tears in our eyes, unable to figure out what piece of the puzzle was missing, I knew deep down that I had something else to learn before whatever piece I found would actually fucking fit—and whatever it was, it was going to be big.

We both knew that it just wasn't fair to him—and I was *so* fucking sad. Not only did I want to be able to throw my arms up, blow the whistle, and say, "I'm done and set for the rest of my life with this man," but I genuinely missed my best friend. I felt all the grief on my end, but also all the guilt—because without ever intending to, I had become this amazing man's personal Javier—*and that fucking killed me.*

Tyler and I always fought to remain friends when we broke up. As painful as it was, the thought of not being in each other's lives was even *more* painful. Unicorns first—that was always our promise from the very beginning.

> Tyler: Just so you know…and I stand by this: You have deserved every single ounce of love that I showed to you. There is no single person on this planet that I think is more ambitious, talented, compassionate, loving, sexy, and beautiful than you. Stop at nothing until you find someone that feels exactly the same way as I do. Because that's what you deserve.

It was texts like these that made me want to punch myself for walking away from this man. But I had *tried.* I had tried three times and until I could figure out what it was that was missing, or how to walk through this paralyzing fear, it just seemed as if it wasn't in the cards.

While I had been riding the wave of adding author to my resume and posting about all the amazing things that were happening,

I felt a responsibility to all of the people following my journey to continue to be real. I had created a reputation for being authentic and raw on my social media and I was proud of that. But that meant sharing the lows with the highs—and I had been seriously struggling the past few weeks. I hadn't outright said that I was dealing with a breakup, but I was open about the fact that I was dealing with some personal things and that I was, for lack of better words, really fucking sad—and Javier saw that.

"Hey, Gabs," he said when I answered the phone call.

"Hey," I replied somberly.

"I know you're having a tough time, but I'm a better human because of you. You're super special. I'm always here for you if you need me. Even though I'm sure your mom and Tyler have it covered." I let out a big sigh. Hearing from my ex how well taken care of I was by the man I had just chosen to walk away from stabbed me like a freaking knife in the face.

"Yeah. Thank you," I answered.

"What's going on, why are you upset?"

"I'll be fine. I always am."

"Is it your dad?

"I think October is always hard subconsciously. But Ty and I broke up and it's been really difficult." I felt myself wanting to cry.

"I'm sorry, Gabs. I know your connection with him is really strong and it must make it that much harder."

"He's definitely one of my soul people. It's so frustrating to wish someone could be your person and deep down you just know something is off, but you don't know what it is or how to fix it. It's heartbreaking. I've never been loved like that or treated like that. And it's terrifying to walk away from." I let out a small chuckle. "I'm aware I'm literally preaching to the choir right now."

He laughed. "YEP! I'm sure it will make sense over time. But I know how badly it sucks."

"Fuck these soul people coming in and upheaving my world."

But like, actually, I get it, universe. You're sending these men to teach me some massive lessons so I could write a book to help others heal and to put me on the path I'm supposed to be on—but for the love of God, could you give me a moment to catch my breath?

"I get back in a few days. Let's get dinner Monday?" he asked.

"Sure," I agreed.

I realized something. This was the first time I had made plans with Javier and not felt this crazy surge of excitement or anticipation. In fact, it felt like the comfort of getting to see an old friend you hadn't seen in a while. We had done the romance, the heartbreak, the no communication, the casual fuck-buddy dynamic, and it finally felt like we were able to be what he had claimed he wanted back in Europe: *friends.* So, when Monday rolled around, I was looking forward to dinner and a movie with someone who I didn't have to put on a happy show for, I knew would make me laugh, and who really knew me.

After my day, I headed out to meet Javier at his house. The house I'd been to so many times for casual hot-and-heavy sex. The house where I had slept in his arms, eaten many meals, and somehow, through it all, managed to maintain a friendship with my ex.

He opened the door, scooped me up in his arms, and gave me a huge hug. I held back some residual tears of missing being held in Tyler's giant grasp. I never realized how...small Javier was compared to Tyler.

We sat at the kitchen table, and he brought a maté cup and some hot water over. After catching me up on his recent travels, he dove into the subject I wasn't particularly excited to talk about.

"What happened with you and Tyler?" he asked.

"I don't know. I just felt like there was something missing. I can't explain it." My eyes immediately watered.

"Yeah, I know that feeling."

"I just feel like a fucking awful human. Since we came back from Europe, I have said I don't ever want to make anyone feel the way you made me feel. And that's exactly what I've done."

"Ouch," he said with a chuckle.

"Sorry." I laughed in return. "He's just the best person. I wanted it to work really badly. And I just really miss him." Some tears finally fell. I had nothing to hide from the person sitting across from me.

"Yeah, I understand. But if you were feeling that way, you did the right thing," he assured me.

"Yeah. I know."

We changed the subject as we continued to pass the maté cup back and forth.

"How is everything going with the book? It seems like it's doing really well and people are loving it," he said.

"It's been a whirlwind. But super fulfilling getting all the messages how it's helping people." I smiled.

"I bet. I'm so proud of you, Gabs. You're a freaking author!"

"Thank you. So, did you finish it?"

"I did."

Let's just pause for a second to acknowledge the weight of this particular conversation. So many times, when I had been pouring my soul into writing *Eat, Pray, #FML*, I would stop and think, *What the hell is he going to think when he reads all of this?* Countless hours during the edit process wondering, *How is he going to feel, reliving it all?* It had been two years of these thoughts circling my brain, and I was finally about to get the answer.

"It was really difficult for me to read," he finally said.

"Why?" I asked.

"As bad as I felt for the way I hurt you and how I handled everything, it's not every day you have to then read about the other person's emotions and feelings of how *you* broke their heart," he admitted.

"Yeah, I bet."

"It made me hate myself all over again for it. There were many times I had to stop and put it down. It took me a week just to get past the chapters before the trip. It was really hard reliving it all."

"Imagine how it's been being in it for the past two years." I laughed.

"I don't know how you did it. Honestly. I would get to a part where I knew it was like sex and fun and it was still terrible to read—I still felt awful about it all. The more I read, the more I wanted to punch Javier in the face and tell him to be more aware of what you were dealing with."

I sat there listening to this and had a giant realization—I had come *so, freaking, far*. There I was, sitting with the man who'd fractured my heart into a million little pieces, who I had cried count-less tears over, never thinking I would ever be able to fully breathe from again—*and I felt nothing.* No surge, no longing for what could have been, just…nothing. It felt like I was finally back in the driver's seat—I felt *free.*

"I really learned a lot reading it though." He snapped me out of my thoughts.

"How so?"

"Patience, for one. I don't know if I would've been so under-standing like you were, but it definitely taught me to be more patient with people. And to never assume what someone is feeling or that they're okay, and to be there and support them even if you think that's not what they want. I promise I will never hurt you like that again, Gabs."

"Good." I smiled. "Was there anything you read that you felt wasn't accurate or that you didn't remember happening that way?" I asked, knowing how often our brains contort situations when we remember them.

"Not one thing. I would read conversations and say to myself that's literally word for word what I said to her. It was wild to read it all," he answered. "I'm so freaking proud of you, Gabs. It's so well written, and it's going to help so many people."

"I've gotten a handful of DMs from people saying that reading about your grieving experience with your brother has helped them understand things about their own grief," I told him. His face lit up.

"That's incredible. Wow, thank you for telling me that." He smiled.

As he got up to refill the hot water and bring a snack to the ta-ble, I asked him about his time in Bali. After everything had finally fallen apart with Tyler, I was having the urge to go on my second solo trip—only this time, it wasn't to run away from things. It was to face things head-on and figure out *why* I needed to run from things.

After twenty minutes of travel talk, Javier made a hard freaking left in the conversation.

"So…how often do you think about our sexscapades?"

I almost spit out the tea I was sipping.

"...What?" was all that I could get out.

"How often do you think about our sex?" he asked again.

"Did you just say sexscapades?" I laughed, still trying to regain my balance from being so drastically caught off guard.

"Yes. I'm serious. Cause I think about it all the time," he said matter-of-factly.

I looked around, waiting for Ashton Kutcher to jump out and tell me I was being Punk'd. He couldn't possibly be serious...right?

"Uh...I...I mean, I think about it sometimes. Why?" I finally said.

"Just wondering. You hungry?"

What, we're going to just blow past this one like you *didn't* just bring this up?

"Um...yes?" I laughed.

"Great, let's go eat." He stood up to clear the table.

We headed out the door and began to walk to the nearby plaza for dinner. As we walked, we passed by a guy walking in the opposite direction who very overtly looked me up and down.

"Take a picture, man," Javier snapped at him.

"Javier!" I shrieked, surprised, as I hit his arm.

"What? He was undressing you with his eyes," he said in defense.

Uh, yes, and you are not my boyfriend who gets to say a damn thing about it, my inner sassiness scoffed.

After we got to the restaurant and sat down to eat, the conversation went from a hard left to an off-roading area with no freaking seatbelt.

"Okay, I'm still totally thrown off by what you said. Why do you think about our sex all the time?" I asked, taking a bite of my food.

"Because it's amazing. Our sex is unlike anything I have ever experienced. I have an addiction to you, Stone. You're like a drug," he told me, still not losing his suave demeanor.

I stopped chewing. I was so not used to this very raw, very forward Javier.

"I'm just saying that, whenever you're single, I would be happy to be the one to assist you with whatever needs you might have. Whenever you want it," he continued.

I felt like I had left his house and walked onto the set of a lame yet sexy soap opera. "Oh, is that so?" I laughed.

"Yes."

"I mean, I'm not denying the fact that our sex was amazing," I admitted. He took a bite of his food.

"Beyond." He swallowed.

"Haven't you been with other people the last few months?" I asked.

"Yeah, but no one I've really been serious about. Just casual stuff. And I've thought about you every time."

I coughed on the bite of food I was chewing.

"Javier! That's terrible." I laughed, but it was more than slightly satisfying to hear.

"What? It's not like I told them that, they had no idea. And besides, it made it ten times better."

"I cannot even process this information right now." I put my hand to my head, hiding my smirk.

"I think about you when I'm by myself too."

"What do you..." I looked at him confused. "Oh my God, Javier!" I dropped my fork down dramatically as I realized what he was telling me.

"I told you. Like a drug." He smiled.

There were so many different random thoughts flying around my head at that moment. For starters, the idiocy of a man leaving a woman he apparently can't stop thinking about only to go and think about her while being intimate with other women. Secondly, the fact that the type of sex he was referring to doesn't happen with just anyone—it happens with someone you're deeply emotionally invested in. Some might even say love. But who am I to tell him what an idiot he was for walking away from that? And lastly, what the fuck was I supposed to do with this information from the person I thought had finally made it into my mental friend zone? It yet again felt like his internal alarm clock had gone off and, just as I was back on my feet and walking safely away from the Javier tornado, he would do something shocking that would make me stop and look over my shoulder.

We got to the movie and sat down in the dim lighting, our usual witty banter continuing with an extra dash of flirtation. As the previews began, Javier grabbed my hand in his and leaned into me, putting his head on my shoulder. This, my friends, is where Javier made his first mistake...well, in this half of the book, anyway. During the times we'd been casually hooking up, he had never *once* held my hand. In fact, every time I had gone to his house for sex, it had been just that—sex. There was no romance, no flirtation, nothing beyond the bedroom. We would leave his bed and become friends that made fun of each other, talked about my troubles with Tyler, and called each other *dude*. There was never anything that felt like he wanted me in more than a sexual way—until the two hours of hand-holding and cuddling during the movie that night.

We walked home hand in hand, having a stimulating conversation about the cinematic masterpiece we had just seen. When we got back to his house, he turned to face me.

"Why don't you just stay here tonight?" he asked.

"You're just horny." I laughed.

"I mean, yes, I am, but I want you to stay with me." He pulled me a little closer to him.

"I can't." It wasn't that I didn't *want* to—my vagina was literally screaming at me to walk inside. It was my heart that told me to get in the goddamn car.

"Why? You have something to do tomorrow?"

"No. Because I just broke up with my boyfriend two weeks ago."

"Right. Of course." He pulled me in and hugged me tightly.

"I mean, I can't, right?" I said out loud, although I intended it to be an internal thought.

"You can. I want you to. But I understand."

"I can't," I decided.

"Let's go dancing with everyone Friday," he said into my neck.

"Okay." I laughed. Mostly at how insane this all seemed to be.

"Text me when you get home?" he asked, lifting his head up to look at me.

"Of course. Thank you for dinner," I said, looking up at him.

He kissed my cheek, and I headed to my car. Driving home, I tried to unpack all of the unexpected items that had been presented to me over the night. I was definitely not looking for another casual sexual relationship—but something about this night felt...different. I knew this man, and this was *not* typical behavior for him, even when he wanted to sleep with me. Did I dare even begin to venture down the road that had proven to be cataclysmically devastating to my heart? Did I even think after all this time and everything that had happened there was any chance that we somehow were going to find our way back to each other? Had he finally woken up out of the scared fuckboy mentality I had come to know all too well? I was standing at the beginning of a path that had warning signs, flashing red lights, and caution tape all around the entrance. Well, Gabrielle, are you going to heed the warning this time or walk down the path to an unknown beginning? Rest assured, the path would definitely lead to a beginning. The beginning of the end.

The Ridiculous Misadventures
of...
THE BEGINNING OF THE END

The next morning, I woke up wondering if I had dreamed the weird events of the night before. No, I definitely did *not* imagine hearing all of the shocking sex secrets Javier was apparently harboring, nor did I know what the hell I was supposed to do with this information. I really thought we had closed that bedroom door after rolling around in his bed for what was supposed to be twenty-four hours and turned into a month.

I did something that day—something big. I had finally decided it was time. Time to go on my second solo adventure. Time to stop putting it off, take the leap, and go. Part of me was terrified. For one, solo trips can be a weird mix of total excitement and utter panic— but mostly because I knew that whatever I was going to learn on this trip was going to be life altering. My intuition had been internally screaming at me for weeks now, and it was finally time to stop bitching and pull the trigger—well, book the ticket at least. It was set: I was turning thirty-one in Southeast Asia.

That night I snuggled onto my couch in the cozy little apartment I had grown to absolutely love being alone in. Half of me felt like a total badass for booking the trip and the other half of me wanted to throw up. I poured myself a glass of wine, turned on a recorded episode of *The Bachelorette*, and felt completely content on Monday night—and then my phone rang.

Well, technically, my FaceTime rang. I freaking hate when people just FaceTime you out of the blue—like, hello, what if I'm naked? Or taking a shit? Or trying to freaking decompress after a long-ass day and have my goddamn wine and watch my trashy reality TV? *Rude.*

"What do you want?" I answered, taking a sip of my wine.

"Oh, did I interrupt something?" Javier laughed.

"Don't you always?" I smiled back.

"My mistake. I just wanted to see if you had thought about my proposal," he said confidently, as if he had offered me some incredible voucher for an all-inclusive vacation.

"Oh my God, you are freaking relentless."

"I can't help it. I told you, it's a drug."

Now if you're wondering why this chapter is entitled "The Beginning of the End," it is really due to three seemingly minor occurrences that took place over the following week and a half. *Strikes,* if you will—and about an hour in, the first strike came.

"That photo you posted of you and your mom the other night, what was that from?" he asked casually. It was a photo of us on the red carpet. I had worn a silver rocker top, black pants, and a bold rep lip.

"Rob's new movie she was in. Such a wild ride," I told him.

"Oh, nice!"

"Yeah, she played such a fun character."

"I don't like when you wear bold-colored lipstick," he said, looking at my bare, makeup-free face through the phone.

A beat—I scoffed.

"What? I've worn lipstick around you since I've known you." I laughed at the ridiculous statement I'd just heard.

"I know. You just look so much better without it. The angles of your face, it just doesn't work," he said, somehow in a way that didn't make it sound totally inappropriate and rude.

"Luckily, I'm not wearing it for you," I said with another laugh, brushing it off.

"No, of course, I know. You looked beautiful that night." He smiled. "What are your plans the rest of the week?" He aimed to redirect the conversation.

After spending another hour on the phone, I realized it was now 11 p.m., and I still had an entire episode of *The Bachelorette* to watch. We said goodbye, and I returned to my couch to finish my wine and zone out. As Hannah Brown had sex in a windmill (four times, apparently), I started to replay parts of my conversation with Javier. He really was insistent on this whole sexual servant proposal—and I knew that I needed to make some type of decision before the upcoming night out on Friday because, let's be real, if I didn't go in with a hard plan, I was no match for Rico fucking Suave on the dance floor. *You can't go down this road again, Gabrielle. You know exactly where it leads,* I said to my own brain. *Besides, Friday you're going to be in a group so you can totally get away with holding off a bit longer.*

I turned off the TV, stood up, and was taking the last gulp of my wine when the striking comment Javier said suddenly popped back into my head. I rolled my eyes.

"And I look fucking great in lipstick."

Strike, one.

*****

By hump day that week, two things were beginning to happen. The first was a continued mix of emotions about my impending second solo adventure. The second? Serious sexual frustration. Javier wasn't helping the situation by sending me messages and constant reminders that he was waiting to complete a list of endless tasks for me in his bedroom.

I was out at a friend's show when a message came in on my phone. A photo of a can of whipped cream.

Me: You're. Literally. The. Worst.

The thing about Javier and this entire situation that made it so utterly messy and confusing is that we had a perfect balance of dirty sex talk and meaningful heartfelt talk. The following day was a perfect example of that.

"I just had a conversation with someone and gave them a ton of advice about what I learned from our relationship," he said to me over FaceTime.

Javier giving relationship advice to someone felt like the Cheshire Cat trying to explain to Alice how to get the fuck out of Wonderland.

"And what advice was that?" I asked, genuinely amused and curious.

"That you always have a responsibility to respect the other person's process. To understand and communicate what the other person is going through, even if you're on a different journey."

Huh. Apparently, reading a book about wrecking your ex-girlfriend's heart can shed some light on your world after all.

"It was nice to be able to help someone not make the same shitty mistakes I've made," he concluded.

"That's great. How did they respond?"

"Really grateful. Although they did think it was weird I sold them your book for double the price after." We both laughed.

"So...I booked my ticket."

"Holy shit. That's amazing, Gabs."

"Yeah, so why do I feel so nervous? I go back and forth between excited and like shitting my pants."

"It's normal. You're going to have the time of your life the second you arrive."

"I'm sure. I just want to be in a hut by myself writing."

"Knowing you, you'll meet people and have a huge adventure."

"It's a balance." I laughed. "I mean I did write a book on my last one."

"You're right. Oh, can't wait for the sequel."

I'm sure he was joking at that moment but will fully regret saying that by the time he reads this. We continued to talk, and the conversation of course ended up taking a slight right into our ongoing dilemma. Well, *my* ongoing dilemma.

"Look, I know it's easier on my end, so I'll stop pushing the sex offer so much while you figure it out."

"I'm glad it's so easy for you while I'm over here trying to weigh out all the pros and cons."

"Cons? Tell me what they are."

"Part of me feels like the universe is testing me. Like 'Hey, Gabrielle, look at that shiny thing. Do you want to stay on your path to everything you're creating in your life or get distracted by the shiny thing?' And part of me feels like I can't just keep repeating a pattern of going back to someone when I separate from someone else."

"Those are valid cons, I see what you're saying. But as far as repeating the pattern and going back to someone, I don't agree with that."

"Oh? How do you figure that?" I scoffed.

"You're different this time. The last time we were sleeping together, you were still in love with Tyler. This time it feels like you're really ready to just be with yourself. I'm just offering assistance in a particular department," he explained.

Interesting. I sure as hell didn't feel like I was more over Tyler this time around. In fact, I felt more freaking heartbroken. Even hearing his name leave Javier's lips felt like a tiny knife in my side. If I was really going to make a decision by tomorrow, I needed to be brutally honest and get all the answers to the questions flying around in my head.

"Javier...when we were at the movies the other night, you were so different. You never used to be all cuddly and romantic. What was up with all of that?"

"I hadn't seen you in a long time. And I was super horny for you," he said without missing a beat.

"So it was just because you wanted me to stay over and sleep with you?"

"I mean, yes, I did, but you know I care about you, Gabs," he said.

"No, you can't do that. I'm asking you if there was something different going on or if it was just you wanting to sleep with me,"

"You mean something different, as in wanting something more?"

"Yes."

"I mean, not at this moment. Right now, what I want is to have amazing sex with someone I care about and am really comfortable with and connected to."

Ladies and gentlemen, this is where *yours truly* made her not first and certainly not last mistake of this journey—and it's a mistake that women make all, the, time: *I did not believe him.* There I sat, listening to him tell me that he did in fact want a straight-up fuck-boy, have-his-cake-and-eat-it-too dynamic with me. Sure, the words came wrapped in some bullshit "care" paper topped with a bow of "comfortable connection." And although I heard this answer loud and clear, I chose to consciously and blatantly *not* take it at face fucking value.

"Okay," I said, after a few moments of contemplation. "I'll think about it."

After another long FaceTime conversation, I was out of time. The next day was Friday, and I knew I had to be sure of where I stood going into the night. I went to sleep that night thinking I would decide in the morning and not put too much pressure on the situation at hand—because at the end of the day, it's just sex, right? What could *possibly* go wrong?

The Ridiculous Misadventures of...

STRIKE TWO

I walked into the restaurant where I was meeting Manny, Javier, Yeseña, and Yeseña's new boyfriend. I was wearing a red crop top, tight high-waist jeans, black high-heel boots, and a minor fucking attitude. I wasn't sure at the beginning of the night what exactly it was that made me feel like Megan Fox from *Jennifer's Body*, but I was out for fucking blood. However, at the beginning of the night, it was sitting just at the top of my subconscious, where it had been festering all week—and it needed something to fully pull it out.

The hostess showed me to the table where everyone else had just sat down. I said hello and gave hugs to everyone one at a time, lastly to Javier.

"God, you look amazing," he said in my ear as he inhaled the perfume I knew he was obsessed with.

"Thank you." I smiled as we turned to sit down across from our three friends.

"And no lipstick." He smiled.

DING. It was pulled out of my subconscious like a kid bobbing for an apple on Halloween. Ah, yes, that was what had been festering all week—*strike one*.

We sat down and ordered, and I made a conscious decision to refrain from drinking. To be completely honest? I left my house that night looking hot as hell because I knew there was a 95% chance I would be going home with Javier. However, until I decided on that five percent, it's best not to allow alcohol in the decision-making process.

"Do you want my jacket, Gabs?" Javier offered.

"Sure," I said as he took his jacket off and put it over my shoulders.

As we all caught up, laughed, and chatted, I couldn't help but notice I was not my normal happy self that I usually am around Javier. I was a bit quieter, not as quick to banter back and forth, and kind of just...down. I looked at the group around the table as if I was paying attention when I was really lost in a rabbit hole of my own thoughts.

"Don't you agree, Gabrielle?" Manny asked as the rest of the group looked over, awaiting my response.

"With what?" I had no idea what the hell they'd been talking about.

"Do you think it's ever okay to tell a woman she looks fat in something?"

"No," I said.

"You should just lie to her then?" Javier said, looking back at Manny.

"I'm saying if a woman asks me if she looks fat in something, I'm not going to tell her yes, go change, I'm going to tell her she looks beautiful," Manny continued.

"But shouldn't you tell her the truth if she's asking for your opinion?" Javier continued to hold firm on his side.

"This is coming from someone who made constant jokes about my weight when we were in San Vito, even without me asking." I laughed, solely to hide the discomfort of the conversation.

"I was joking with you, you know that," he insisted.

"But that's not okay to even joke with her about it," Manny defended me.

"Oh, come on, she knew I was kidding! I wished I was eating the way she was on that trip. But she definitely wasn't holding back." Javier laughed. The conversation felt like it was now happening without me even being there—and I didn't say a damn word.

"Javier, let me make this very clear." Yeseña's Cuban accent came out in full force. "It is *never, ever* okay to comment on a woman's weight." Her boyfriend nodded as he took a bite of food.

"Okay, okay, I was just playing devil's advocate and seeing both sides," he conceded.

They continued to discuss the topic as I just sat there, uncomfortable in the memories of my insecurity at such a fragile time.

"I have to go to the bathroom." I stood up, putting Javier's jacket beside me. Yeseña immediately rose to accompany me.

I didn't have to pee, I just needed to get the hell away from the conversation. I looked at my face in the mirror. Makeup done to perfection, just a gloss on my lips, looking better than I had in a long time—and I felt freaking *broken*.

"What the hell was that?" Yeseña asked me, flushing the toilet in her stall.

"What do you mean?" I asked, knowing damn well what she meant.

"I've never seen you not stand up for yourself like that," she said, joining me at the mirror.

"I don't know. I was just so uncomfortable. And then I got angry."

"Uh, yeah, rightfully so. You'd never let Tyler talk to you like that. You'd shut that shit down instantly," she pointed out, touching up her lipstick.

"Tyler would never talk to me like that in the first place. Do you know Javier told me he doesn't like when I wear bold lipstick? That it 'doesn't work with the angles in my face.'"

"Are you freaking kidding me?" Her hip popped out as she turned toward me.

"It's like he doesn't even realize he's being a dick," I said.

To make it worse, I was reminded what I had traded in for lipstick shaming and hurtful comments when a text from Tyler came in.

Tyler: Wherever you are tonight, Peanut, I hope your spirit is happy.

Ugh. Like an actual stake in my heart. Reading his words on the screen made tears pound at the back of my eyes like a freaking gorilla trying to escape his cage at the zoo. I stuffed them down, reminding myself that Tyler and I had tried three times—and something had still been missing.

We returned to the table, and Javier smiled at me like nothing monumental had taken place. So many of you reading this are probably yelling at your book pages, saying, *"COME ON, GABRIELLE, HOW ARE YOU NOT SEEING THIS?"* Was it because I once had such a love for this man that I felt I truly knew his heart and didn't believe he could *possibly* be intentionally making me feel so bad? Or that I always gave him the benefit of the doubt, to a fault sometimes, making things easier to brush off? Whatever it was, my fuse was now dangerously short, and I didn't even want to go dancing—which for me is like not wanting to breathe. *Strike two.*

After we all split the bill, we met Cesar at the club—and I headed *straight* for the bar. What's the expression? *She saw red.* Well, I saw tequila. It's never a good idea to use alcohol as a chaser for your anger, and tequila is arguably the worst. As I waited for my double shot at the bar, Manny came up beside me.

"Are you okay?" he asked.

"Yeah, why?" I smiled.

"That was rough even for me," he said. "I don't know why he's like that around you. It only happens when you're around."

"What do you mean?" I asked, curious.

"I don't know. It's like he becomes a different person when you're around and has to impress you."

"Funny fucking way of doing that." I scoffed.

"I know. That was not okay at dinner. I'm sorry." He motioned for the bartender to make it two shots.

"It's not your fault. But thank you." We clinked glasses and threw back a massive double shot of tequila.

I decided to somehow compartmentalize my feelings because I knew they were not going to be successfully sorted through that night. Instead, my friend tequila assisted me in stepping into my alter ego—who is bold, doesn't give a fuck, and is feisty as hell. I've never named her before, but to fully convey the night properly, let's call her...Lolita.

I danced with Manny and Cesar for the first half hour we were there. I could feel Javier's eyes on me anytime a random guy came to dance with me—and to be honest, I didn't freaking care. Three shots later, I had committed to a night of not giving a shit about anything—and that included Javier.

"How many shots have you had?" he asked as I picked up the cup of tequila the bartender had resorted to giving me.

"I'm not counting." I laughed as I raised it to my lips.

"Okay, maybe slow down then, Gabs." He laughed.

"Let her live, man!" Manny said as he grabbed my hand to head back to the dance floor. I looked back over my shoulder at Javier and gave him a smile that said, *See, even your friends love me. Loosen the fuck up.*

"I'm drunk," I shouted to Yeseña, dancing next to me.

"Same!" she shouted back. "He hasn't stopped staring at you," she added.

"I don't know if I want to rip his clothes off or punch him in the face. It's a dilemma," I shouted as I looked over and locked eyes with him.

"Do both then. But make it the last time because this is bull-shit." She twirled away from me on the dance floor just as the music changed.

I walked back to our table where Javier was and took the re-mainder of my shot and a swig of my water. He grabbed me to dance. This was always where Javier and I found ourselves in trouble when trying to stay away from each other—dancing—and he knew that. Add however many shots of tequila were in my system by this point and game over. Lolita has zero inhibitions when it comes to danc-ing, even when in a club full of people. Javier had his hands tightly on my hips and was breathing heavily into my hair as I pressed up against him.

"Jesus, Gabrielle, you're making me hard," he whispered in my ear.

I turned around to dance face-to-face with him, and that's when he did something even my alter ego was not expecting. There, in the middle of the club, in front of his two friends, he grabbed my face and kissed me. No one knew that we had secretly slept together for over a month. No one knew that we'd been in this weird messed-up web of sex and friendship. No one knew that we had crossed that line—way more than once. Quite frankly, I was shocked that Javier, who was so private and secretive, couldn't contain himself any longer and had just full-on publicly displayed what had been happening for months now. We stood there, passionately kissing while our bodies were still moving to the music, and I realized I was exactly where I was when this whole Javier fiasco started—making out in a club.

When I finally pulled away from him and came out of my toxic ex-boyfriend make-out bubble, my hand instinctually covered my mouth, like we had just been caught by paparazzi.

"What?" a still very sober Javier asked with a laugh.

"We're like...in public. And your friends are here," a very not-sober me replied.

"I don't care." He pulled me back in and kissed me again.

The next two hours consisted of a lot of dancing, a lot of making out, and a lot more tequila. Manny, Cesar, and I were having way too much fun joking around and taking turns buying rounds at the bar. Javier (who is usually the sober one anyway) was driving that night. I can't even imagine what we must have looked like from a sober person's perspective. At one point, I grabbed my tequila and Javier reached for it.

"Slow down!" He laughed as he pulled my glass out of my hand.

"I'm fine!" I argued.

Manny snatched my glass from him and handed it back to me, laughing.

"She's fine! We're having fun, relax!" he teased his sober friend.

"Sí, she's great!" Cesar added.

To be fair, Javier was right. I was setting myself up for a not terribly fun morning and some potentially bad decisions. But after the display at dinner, I (and apparently his friends too) would be dammed if he was going to tell me what I could and couldn't drink.

Yeseña and her boyfriend said their goodbyes to the group, and she pulled me aside.

"What are you going to do?" she asked.

I responded in true Lolita fashion. "I'm going to have wild sex with him and make him regret his entire life."

"Fine. Then be done," her equally drunk self said to me.

"Fine." I laughed.

I turned back around to where Javier was standing, walked over to him, and kissed his neck.

"Come home with me," Lolita said to Javier. He let out a deep groan.

"Why didn't you tell me this before? I drove Manny!" he said in frustration.

"Because I didn't know if I wanted to fuck your brains out at the beginning of the night." Oh, I didn't mention? Lolita is also a porn star.

"Fuck it, just come home with me. I'll bring you home tomorrow," Javier decided.

"You're going to drive me all the way back to Hollywood tomorrow?" I laughed, enjoying how badly he wanted me in his bed.

"Yes."

"What are you going to tell Manny?"

"I don't know, I'll figure it out."

I think this is a good time to let you all in on a well-known fact about me. Since college, I've been told that even when I'm blacked out drunk, I never really *seem* all that drunk. I'm never the girl falling, puking, or acting a freaking fool—in fact, it's quite the opposite. I'm just a heightened, fun, outrageous version of myself. You would never in a million years look at me and be like, *Shit, Gabrielle, you are never going to remember this tomorrow*. This talent has gotten me into a few bad situations and out of others. It's a gift.

Mid car ride, over the music, I heard drunken Manny in the front seat.

"So...what exactly is going on?"

"She's coming over to have sex," he said in true, ridiculous, yet matter-of-fact Javier fashion.

"That is a terrible idea," Manny stated, drunk and yet the voice of reason in this particular situation.

"No, no, we've talked about it a lot. We both decided it's just sex," he assured his rightfully skeptical friend.

"It's never going to be just sex with you two," Manny said, accurate as fuck, I might add.

We pulled into Javier's garage, and I hugged Manny goodbye. He gave me a look that said, *This is a terrible idea and I do not approve.*

I walked into Javier's place, stopped to pee on the first floor, then hiked up the two flights to his bedroom.

Javier came out of the shower, butt-ass naked, tore my clothes off, and for the first time, had sex with Lolita. From the commotion the neighbors apparently heard at 3 a.m., it was a damn good time. The nail and bite marks on him the next morning confirmed that story. Lolita was there for the sex with the hot, passionate Latin man that she wanted to have her way with. Gabrielle, on the other hand, would wake up with a massive hangover, a lot of questions, and one giant freaking recollection: *strike two.*

The Ridiculous Misadventures of...

THREE STRIKES, YOU'RE OUT

I squinted at the rude sunlight coming through the window and rolled over. I slightly opened one eye wider to try and make out the tiny numbers on my cell phone. Whatever the time was, it was too fucking early to be conscious after the night I'd had. *Shit, I have to pee.* I looked over at Javier, who was still sleeping, and slipped out of the bed, completely naked. After quietly shutting the door, I sat down to pee, still mildly drunk. The toilet always seems to be the place for deep reflecting—and in some cases, regretting—drunken debacles from the night before. *Jesus, Gabrielle, you're making me hard.* I laughed. *I wasn't sure if I wanted to fuck your brains out at the beginning of the night.* I covered my face with my hands. *Flashes of loud, wild sex.* I rolled my eyes, groaned, and wiped.

I walked back into the bedroom and picked up my phone, still completely naked because, at this point, where the hell could my clothes possibly be?

"Morning."

"Jesus!" I jumped. "You scared the shit out of me."

"How you feeling?" He laughed at my disheveled state.

"Ugh," I groaned in response.

"Yeah, I tried to help you last night..." he started, too early I might add.

"Shut up."

"Come on, I'll make you breakfast." He got up to get dressed.

"OH MY GOD." My mouth dropped open as I laid eyes on his upper body. He looked as if he had gotten in some type of primal fight with an angered cheetah on crack.

"Yeah. I know." He glared at me with a slight smile.

"Where are my clothes?"

He ducked under the bed, came up, and walked over to me with my jeans and one of his shirts. He kissed my neck as he handed me the clothes to put on.

"Comida. Vamanos," he said as he headed downstairs.

Another groan as I mustered up the energy to get dressed.

Javier cooked a delicious breakfast, and we sat out on his patio, where I attempted to stuff my stomach before it turned on me. *Please don't be hungover, Gabrielle. Please don't puke your brains out at Javier's house, Gabrielle.*

"You were intense last night." He laughed.

"I'm so sorry about your body," I said, although I wasn't really. "I'm uncontrollable when I'm drunk."

"You weren't that drunk."

"Javier, I had like eight shots of tequila."

"I'm pretty sure we woke all my neighbors up."

"Oh God." I laughed as I put my head back in my hands.

"So...you said something to me last night," he said. *No, no I didn't, Lolita said something to you. I cannot be held accountable for any ridiculous statements that were said in the last twelve hours.*

"Okay..." I waited, praying it was something I could easily get out of. "What?"

"I asked you to tell me what you wanted, and you said, 'You can't give me what I want.' What did that mean?"

It means you have never, except for the first five days of our whirlwind romance, been able to give me what the fuck I actually want. It means that you are not capable of being the guy who ever shows up for me or gives me what I actually want from you.

"I wanted it without a condom," I lied—because was I actually going to say what my inner dialogue had just screamed at him? That would be a big *no.* He paused, questioning me with a look.

"So you didn't mean anything more by that?"

"No, dude, calm down, I was just drunk. I'm well aware of what this is." I laughed and took a bite of my food.

"Promise?" He was totally not believing me. I gave him a look.

"I cannot believe Manny drove home with us." I changed the subject.

"I told him what was going on," he said casually. Suddenly, my eyes widened.

"Oh my God, and we, like, made out in the club...in front of people!" I remembered.

"That we did." He laughed.

"Oh God!" Head back in the hands.

"Didn't know you were so embarrassed of me," Javier teased.

"No, but I mean...it's *you*. Like, it's *you and I*," my hungover brain explained.

We finished breakfast, and Javier set me up on the couch while he went to go play his soccer game before taking me home. To be honest, I was counting down the seconds for him to leave so I could violently puke in his bathroom before cuddling up in the fetal position with his dog. God, I hate tequila.

Once I was finally home in the comfort of my own bed, I slept. I threw up. I slept some more. The way my hangovers are, you might wonder why I ever drink—it's just not fucking worth it. Finally, around 5 p.m. I felt like I could see the light at the end of the tunnel. I shakily went to the kitchen to attempt to find something that didn't invoke the urge to vomit. My phone rang.

"What do you want?" I said dramatically into the phone.

"Just wanted to see how you were feeling, princess!" Javier laughed on the other end.

"Like death. But I think I'm out of the depths of hell."

"I tried to stop you from drinking so much. I knew you were gonna be hurting," he reiterated.

"I know, and watching Manny tell you to leave me alone was hilarious," I responded. "I've become like his little sister."

Javier scoffed. "Manny doesn't give a shit about you. He just wanted to see you get drunk." He laughed. I paused. I must not have heard that right...*right?* "Anyway, I had so much fun with you. What are you doing the rest of the week?"

My hungover brain could not properly register statements as quickly as they were coming—I would have to analyze that last comment at a later time.

"Recovering." I laughed.

"Well, I want to see you," he said. "Sunday."

"Okay. Going back to bed now. Thanks for bringing me home."

"Of course. Feel better. Besos."

I hung up the phone, plopped back down on my bed, and stared up at my ceiling. My brain replayed the unsettling statement in my head. *Manny doesn't give a shit about you. He just wanted to see you get drunk*—and then it happened. I went through all the stages within a matter of ten seconds.

That was fucking rude.

I cannot believe he just said that.

Who the HELL says that to someone they claim to care about?

Who the hell says that to ANYONE AT ALL?

That was so not okay.

What a dick.

Strike.

Three.

It was then that it finally fucking dawned on me. Let's pause so you all can look at the book in your hands and say, "*JESUS CHRIST, IT'S ABOUT FUCKING TIME, GABRIELLE!*" Okay...get it out of your system? Good. If it helps, I'm aware how heavily my sexual blinders must have been on to have it take this goddamn long to come to the realization: *I should never be treated like this.* No one— friend, boyfriend, fuck buddy—should *ever* treat me like this. WHY ON EARTH AM I ALLOWING SOMEONE TO TREAT ME LIKE THIS? I knew in that moment that there must be an Origin Experience here—but it was one that came much later in life.

He's not doing anything *that* bad—not like *Daniel*—so it's *okay.*

My marriage had done one thing: it had given me a front row seat to how deep a narcissist can sink their claws into you without you even knowing you've been punctured. I'd been so mistreated for so long without even really knowing it. Looking back on it now, all the double standards, all the rules, all the times he made me feel like I was the one doing something wrong. When he told me that if I gave up my career and became a housewife, he would take care of all our bills—but if I chose to keep working, I had to pay my half. Every time he would call me when I was on set, crying and yelling because I had to kiss someone on screen. All while he was the one stepping outside of our marriage. The lies. The manipulation. The disrespect.

Now you see, compared to that, these comments from Javier didn't seem all that bad. It was then, in this moment, lying on my bed, that I realized my marriage had created a massive subconscious belief: *men will not treat you the way you deserve.* How ironic that I had walked away from the one who was doing just the opposite.

What was so confusing about the situation, and why I think it took me so freaking long to get it, is that 90% of the time, Javier was great to me. He made me feel desired, he made me laugh, he would have conversations with me that showed he cared about me as a person. But hello, Gabrielle, there is another 10%. A 10% made up of backhanded lipstick compliments, uncomfortable weight conversations, and remarks that were flat-out fucking inexcusable. How had I allowed this to be okay? How had I not spoken up for myself? Why was I still making excuses for this godforsaken man in my life? It was no longer okay. It was no longer acceptable—and I no longer had my blinders on. In fact, I was seeing more clearly than I had in a long-ass time, and the next few days would only give these new feelings time to fester and manifest a new fire inside of me. I had finally burned to the ground and become a pile of ashes. But magnificent things rise from ashes—and I planned to emerge on my own fucking terms.

It was time. Time for me to let go of the bullshit origin story my ex-husband had instilled deep in my subconscious. Time for me to finally let this man go. This man who had erupted into my life, invaded my heart, and continued to keep the door open with one foot in while the rest of him was running for the hills. I was going to end this two-year roller-coaster ride on my own terms. I was going to honor the fact that part of me desperately loved this broken fucking human. I was going to allow myself to have one final day with this man that had dismantled my world for the past two years—and then, I was going to do what had needed to be done for a very long time. *I was going to let go.*

The Ridiculous Misadventures of...

LETTING GO

pulled up to his house and parked. Deep breath. Not because I was nervous—I knew exactly how this day was going to go. But because I had *so* many different emotions swirling around inside.

- Anger. I was definitely angry at him.
- Hurt. Which was somehow even worse than the anger.
- Excited. Yes, I'm human, and I knew the sex I was about to have.
- Sadness. Because I knew deep down that this really was the last time.

What an interesting set of emotions. To be honest, I didn't know if I was going to be able to successfully compartmentalize it all. Only one way to find out.

I opened the door and was greeted with a wagging tail and wet kisses from his adorable dog.

"Hola, Gabs. ¿Cómo estás?" he shouted from the kitchen.

"Good," I responded while I loved on my four-legged friend.

"Feeling better?" he asked, joining me in the living room and giving me a hug and a kiss on the cheek.

No, but I'm about to fuck my feelings right out on you.

"Yeah." I smiled, keeping that inner dialogue to myself. We sat on the couch and talked about my trip to Asia for a bit. Javier had been to Bali years earlier.

"You're gonna absolutely love it, Gabs. I'm so excited for you."

"Yeah, I feel like it's happening at the perfect time. I need it."

"It'll be amazing."

After about ten minutes of small talk, I was ready to be naked.

"So, upstairs?" I said.

"Oh, damn, already?" He sounded surprised as he immediately stood up.

"I mean..." I grabbed my bag as we headed up to his bedroom.

The sex was, as it always was, passionate, intense, rough, yet intimate—although this time it included a blindfold and some other fun accessories I had brought with me for my final hoorah. I don't think I'd ever witnessed him climax as intensely as he did that day. So much so that when he fell on top of me, he proceeded to yell and ramble in Spanish for a full minute, which eventually made me begin to laugh.

"That was so intense, don't laugh," he said through a chuckle.

After a few minutes of regaining feeling in our bodies, he rolled over and kissed me.

"That was unbelievable. I'm exhausted." Yeah. He would never be forgetting what had just taken place.

After showering, we headed downstairs to recuperate and not move on the couch for a bit. I plopped down next to Javier as he scrolled through Netflix options. The irony was not lost on me—this is what they mean by "Netflix and chill."

"God, no one would ever understand the type of sex we have." He looked over at me.

"What do you mean?" I asked, though I had to admit, what had just taken place was next level.

"Even if I tried to talk to Manny or the guys about it, no one would understand how intense and incredible it is because of our connection," he explained. I smiled as he pressed play on a comedy special. I draped my legs over him and lay back on the couch. Yes... the intense connection. The insane sex. Why on earth would you want to keep something amazing like that once you've found it?

After the show, we picked up lunch and continued to be exactly how we normally were—great. Talking, laughing, and having an exceptional day together. As good of a time as it was, it was still very present in the back of my mind that I was eventually going to have to have *that* conversation with him. However, it was safe to say that I successfully compartmentalized.

Once our food had settled, it was time for round two. The bed. The balcony. Back to the bed. This time he blindfolded me. There's something about having one of your main senses taken away—you really have to trust the person you're with in order to let yourself go and surrender to the vulnerability of it all. Yet, I didn't really trust Javier completely—not anymore. How poetic that, while I was being blindfolded by this man in bed, the blindfold I had been wearing for over two years was finally coming off.

"I literally can't feel my feet," he said after we had finished, both sprawled out on his giant bed, once again. "I have nothing left in me." He laughed. As amazing as it was that day, something was missing. After everything that had happened the past week and how it had made me feel... It wasn't that the sex wasn't perfect. It's that *he* was no longer perfect.

We went downstairs and, while Javier made some coffee, I checked my phone for the first time that day. I had a text from Tyler.

Tyler: How's your date going?

The surge. Sheer and utter panic ran through my entire body. *What. The. Fuck.*

Me: Excuse me? Was this meant for someone else?

Tyler: No, it was meant for you.

Oh my God. He followed me here, he's outside, and he is going to murder Javier.

Me: What are you talking about?

Tyler: I just had an interesting feeling. I'm kinda playing.

I mean, COME ON. If you weren't convinced that this human and I were cosmically connected before, are you *now*? Unreal. I felt so guilty. Even if we were broken up and Tyler and I were talking less, I still felt so freaking guilty. Because this was the man who would ride into battle for me, no questions asked, and here I was, giving myself to the man who doesn't like me with bold lipstick. Stellar job, Gabrielle.

We went to dinner and a movie before returning to his house and yet again rolling around in his bed. That's the dangerous thing about spending time with Javier—when we were together it was nothing but laughter, intellectually stimulating conversation, great sex, and a really comfortable bond. But this last week had opened my eyes and closed my heart more than any other time in the last two and a half years.

"I'll make us some tea," he finally said after we'd been lying in bed for half an hour. "Oh, and here..." He went into the other room as I started to get dressed. He returned with his copy of my book. "Sign it for me?" He smiled. I smiled back as I took my newly published diary from his hands. Oh, the irony. This book was not only my story, it was our story. None of it would have taken place without him. We had been through a life-changing experience together, and it was now printed, forever, out in the world. What the hell was I supposed to write in his copy?

I had written all my deep thoughts in the postcard I had given him the day it released, which was stuck inside the book when I opened it. I settled on *"Thanks for the inspiration, Javier,"* signed my name, and with *bright red lipstick*, stuck a kiss right next to it.

I headed into the bathroom to pee. I looked at myself in the mirror and, out loud, gave myself a full-blown pep talk.

"You are doing this, Gabrielle. You are going downstairs and having this conversation. It is time—and you deserve *so* much better than this."

Once downstairs, I tossed the book on the table and cozied up on the couch.

"Ha! I love it. It's perfect. Thank you," he said, reading the personalized inscription.

I waited for Javier and the tea. It was around 11:30 p.m.—and it was time. *Deep breath, Gabrielle. You can do this.* He handed me my cup of tea and sat down beside me.

"So, I need to talk to you," I started with the cliché phrase that every man dreads hearing.

"Oh God." He immediately froze.

"Yeah." I wasn't trying to hide the type of conversation this was about to be.

"Okay...what's going on?"

"I haven't been honest with you about how I've been feeling."

"Alright." He waited.

"I didn't know if I was even going to talk to you about it or not—because I knew it would go one of two ways. Either you'd feel bad, which I never want to intentionally do, or worse, you'd try and defend yourself," I explained. He saw how serious I was and just sat there, for once not saying a thing. "You said some things that haven't sat well with me and actually really hurt and upset me. So I want to explain them to you. Just let me get through this before you jump in," I requested.

"Yeah, of course, go ahead." His demeanor reflected my emotions.

"It started when we were FaceTiming last week and you told me 'I don't like when you wear bold-colored lipstick. The angles of your face, it just doesn't work.' First of all, you are not my boyfriend, nor did I ask for your opinion, which doesn't matter to me in the slightest. Honestly, all I could think about was sitting across from Tyler and him saying, 'With makeup, with no makeup, with shit all over your face, you are the most beautiful goddamn woman I have ever seen.' And *that* is how I deserve to be treated. By a boyfriend, a friend, a fuck buddy—because that's how *I* treat people." I watched as he sat there, taking all this in.

"Then we went to dinner before the club, and you guys were all debating about being honest with women and if it's okay to tell a female she's gained weight. You may have been trying to make a stupid point or have a conversation, but it was *so* uncomfortable for me to sit there and listen to it. You may have told me *months* later that you loved my body like that but in Sicily, all I experienced was comments about my eating and my weight. Joking or not, I was heartbroken and feeling *so* insecure because of it all. So to sit there and listen to you defend it was just...not okay. I didn't even want to go to the club or be around you after that—hence the amount of tequila I chose to drink," I explained. He continued to sit, nod in understanding, and just listen. "Manny even pulled me aside when we got to the club and asked if I was okay—and said you never act like that unless I'm around, and he doesn't get it." His face fell. Still, he was quiet.

"When you called me Sunday and told me about Manny giving you shit for taking my drink away—and I said it's because he thinks of me like a little sister—you proceeded to say, 'Manny doesn't give a shit about you. He just wanted to see you get drunk.' You have *no* idea the type of relationship Manny and I have. He would smack you if he heard you say that. Even if we weren't friends, you don't say something like that to someone you care about." I was somewhat surprised I had gotten through this entire speech without any tears coming to the surface. To be honest, I felt powerful. I knew that I was finally standing up for what I deserved—standing up for myself—and finally speaking my truth.

"The last few days, it really started to fester and made me really angry. None of those things are things you do when you care about someone—and you tell me you love me and I'm so important to you? I finally just stopped and thought 'Jesus, has everyone been right this whole fucking time?'" His face fell and I could see he was holding back tears. "I've always defended you from day one, Javier. But with all these things, you've made it *impossible* for me to defend you anymore. You don't even treat me the way a friend deserves to be treated, much less someone you're sleeping with," I finished. I was shocked he hadn't said a single word the entire time. A long moment passed as I waited for his response.

"There is absolutely no excuse for this. God. I am so sorry, Gabs," he said finally. He looked like a little boy that had just been scolded by his mother. "I promised. I promised you I would never hurt you again. What is wrong with me, why do I do this?" he asked himself. A long pause. "It's like a defense mechanism."

"What do you mean?" I asked.

"Everyone knows what I did to you. Manny, Cesar, Yeseña, Jess, your mom, Tyler. They all try and protect you from me. Even *my* friends try and protect you from me. I'm toxic for you." I watched as this thirty-seven-year-old man had this huge, obvious, yet devastating realization in front of me.

"But what do you mean it's a defense mechanism?"

"It's like they all know I'm the bad guy. They all know the story or read the book—I just feel so bad for what I did to you and how I handled it all—I hate that I'm the bad guy," he said, full of hurt.

"Javier. You're not a bad guy. Everything we went through changed my life and happened for a reason."

"I know, but it's like I try to joke about it to make it less awful. God, why do I do this?" he repeated.

"Well, that makes sense for the conversation at dinner—not really for the lipstick comment," I said.

"I was trying to tell you you're beautiful and don't need all that makeup!" he interjected.

"Then that's what you should have said."

"You're right. There's no excuse for any of it. I feel so much guilt. I told you I'd never hurt you again." He looked so sad—so defeated.

"Javier. I've been hurting for two years now. Every time you flirted with me, or we'd sleep together, or you'd leave the door just a tiny bit open. I've been hurting this whole time—and for whatever reason, I haven't been able to, or didn't want to, let you go. But it's time." Those words had needed to be given life for so long now. He nodded solemnly. We sat there for a long while. I had never seen him at such a loss for words. It was like he was analyzing and processing all his thoughts before speaking.

"This feels like a cold bucket of water getting dumped on me after the day we just had," he said.

"Hey. What happened today was amazing. That will always be something we have—separate from this conversation."

"Right. Why didn't you tell me all of this before?"

"Well, first of all, I needed to process it all, and it didn't really feel like a phone conversation," I began. "And honestly, I wanted to be with you one more time," I said truthfully. He nodded, knowing he would have wanted it that way too. Another long moment as he thought.

"This is gonna be a hard transition," he finally said. "I've always felt like I've had you here in some way. This feels different." He fought harder to hold in tears. "I have abandonment issues too, you know."

Of course, I knew. Isn't that what made us so instantly close in the first place? Isn't that the wound he ripped open in me before Europe? But if I'd learned anything from Tyler, it was this: When you love someone and you know their wounds, you do not pick and prod at them. You do not walk away to let them bleed and ache. You *stay* and tend to them with love, compassion, and comfort. Especially when their wounds mirror your own. I moved closer to him on the couch, grabbed his hand, and looked him directly in the eyes.

"I am not abandoning you. I will always be here for you. It just won't be in the same way," I said. He looked at me, broken. "Did you hear me? *I'm not abandoning you.*"

"I just don't feel like I deserve to have you in my life." His voice cracked and the tears that he had kept at bay began to fall freely down his face.

"Javier. Please. Let go of the guilt. It must be exhausting. No one wants you to carry it. Your family doesn't, your brother doesn't, I don't." I put my arms around him, and he hung his head into me and cried. "I don't want you to be sad," I said. And I didn't. As hurt as I had been the past week—hell, the past two and a half years—I loved this person. And I didn't want him to hurt.

"Don't worry about me. You deserve so much more than this," he said.

"I've always worried about you. I've taken care of you from the moment you walked into my life. Why do you think that would suddenly change now?" I chuckled under my breath.

"It's really hard to know your mom and Tyler and all your friends think I'm horrible and want you to stay away from me," he said solemnly.

"Yeah. Imagine how hard it is for me." There was no further explanation needed for that sentiment. We sat for a moment, quiet.

"Do you need space?" he finally asked. I thought about it for a minute. I knew the answer.

"I know I don't want to talk to you or Tyler on my trip," I started. "You both have become crutches to me—and I need to know I can walk forward on my own."

"You don't need either of us," he said. "It's going to be so good for you."

"I know," I replied. Although I wasn't sure *I* fully believed that yet.

"I'm proud of you, Gabs. You're going to have an amazing time."

"Yeah," I said. Another long pause.

"I have to figure out why I do this. I don't want to hurt you, ever. I tell everyone when I talk about you how you changed my life and how amazing you are. I have to figure this out..." His voice trailed off. I could tell this had really hit him. Hard.

It was almost 1 a.m. I was physically, emotionally, and all-around exhausted.

"I should get home," I said.

"I'll walk you out."

I grabbed my bag and said goodbye to the dog. I swear breaking up with a dude you're with (or ending a fuck-buddy relationship with—whatever) is ten times harder when you love their dog.

We got to my car, and I tossed my stuff inside, then turned to face him.

"Please drive safe and text me when you get home," he said. I put my arms around him and stood there for a moment.

"I love you," I said, my face half buried in his neck.

"I love you too." He squeezed me a little tighter. When he let me go, I put my hands on his face and kissed him. Not a passionate, sexual kiss—the kind of kiss you just let linger without even opening your mouth. The kind that means goodbye.

I got in my car, plugged in my phone, and put on Selena Gomez's *Lose You to Love Me*. As the lyrics of my two-and-a-half-year saga played loudly, I waited for the tears that I assumed were inevitable, the tears that I had been conditioned to associate with this man since he erupted into my world—but they didn't come. Instead, I felt a weird sense of freedom—and even more so: *pride*.

After two years of looking for closure, saying it was the "last time" more than a few times and trying to find a way to get over this man, I realized something life-changing. The sex hadn't brought closure. The long confusing conversations hadn't brought closure. The not showing up, the not being treated the way I deserved—and most of all, the disrespect—*that...was the fucking closure.*

It takes a lot of mistakes, missteps, and healing to finally let go of the toxic wounds abandonment leaves. To finally stop attracting and accepting the men who don't show up for you. To finally know that you're worthy of healthy love. Worthy of safe love. Believe me, looking back on my journey, *I* wanted to shake me—so I can only imagine how you all felt reading. But those of you who have had the claws of toxic love embedded deep within your heart get it. So while it may have taken a long time—and more bad decisions than I care to admit—I finally made room for real love. And that? Makes it all fucking worth it.

I knew I had done the right thing. I was proud I had kept my promise to myself—even if it had taken a literal pep talk in the bathroom. Because finally, after two and a half years of heartache, confusion, mixed signals, casual sex, over-analyzation, and never-ending questions—I had *finally* chosen me. Chosen to let go. It was about fucking time, Gabrielle. And it felt damn good.

The Ridiculous Misadventures

of...

ART IMITATES LIFE

'm sure it was not by chance that after ending things with Tyler and *finally* closing—and deadbolting—the door with Javier, I was set to record the audiobook for *Eat, Pray, #FML*. And I was so excited to bring it to life with my own voice, the way I intended it to be heard.

Two days after I'd left Javier's house for the last time, my phone rang. After the generic "Hey, how are you after our porn star sexscapades and poorly timed fuck-buddy breakup convo," he began to tell me why he was calling.

"So, listen, I've been thinking about our talk and processing a lot. I think in order to be the type of friend you need and for me to deserve to have you in my life, I have to take a step back and do the work. I have to really figure out why I do this," he explained.

"Okay." I waited, knowing there was more.

"So if you go out with Manny or Cesar and I'm not there, just know that's why. I just really need to do the work so I can have a healthy friendship with you."

"Okay. I think that's great. I'm proud of you."

"But I love you, and I hope you have an amazing time on your trip. You deserve it."

"Thank you." I paused. "Promise me something?"

"What?"

"That we'll never let distance, time, assumptions, or other people affect how we know each other. On a soul level."

"That will never change, Gabrielle. Ever."

"Okay."

"Okay. Love you, Gabs."

"Love you too." Click. And just like that, our complicated, messy, dramatic, intense, relationship was redirected onto a new path. Where that road led? I had no fucking idea.

I wouldn't say I panicked. In fact, I was surprisingly calm, considering this was poking right at *my* abandonment issues. Funny how that works. Instead, I felt...grief. Because up until now, even when the door was "closed" it was never fully shut and locked—and this time it was.

That Sunday, Tyler and I had plans to get dinner and make sure everything between us was as fine as it could be. It had been roughly a month and a half of minimal talking, not seeing each other, and trying our best to not have a confusing and cloudy breakup. Not talking to Tyler was like instantly losing your absolute best friend and not knowing who to call when you wanted to tell someone about the random person who cut you off on the freeway. One second, we were fine, the next he hated me. Oh, the lovely waves of heartbroken grief. On Saturday afternoon, a text from him came in.

Tyler: God. My fucking life.

Jesus. *What now?* I thought. He was probably mad at me for something new he'd heard or seen. Oh no. That would be *much* too simple. After all, it's *my* life we're talking about, remember? My phone rang.

"What's up?" I said cautiously, bracing for impact.

"You're not going to believe this," he began.

"Okay...what?" For the love of God, spit it out and lower the chances of my impending heart attack.

"I was at a callback for a commercial just now," Oh, deep breath, not even about me. "And Javier walked in." Pause...are everyone's mouths hanging open? Good. Mine too. Let's continue.

"You're kidding," I said...or hoped.

"Nope. There were only five guys called back," he answered.

Now, let me paint this picture for my non-actor folks. I've been in the business for ten years now. Only *once* have I ever run into someone I knew at an audition. The odds of you being up for the same project, for the same role, *and* to be auditioning in the same exact time slot are seriously fucking slim. And that *one time* was a girl who is totally the same type as me. So does someone want to explain to me why the *fuck* a 5'10" *Latino* and a 6'3" bear of a *Persian white dude* are up for the same damn role? Why? Well, because they are the two men in *my* life, of course. And the universe chuckled and said, "Well, she finally closed the doors with both of them. Might as well have some fun!" The universe then decided it would be hilarious to puppeteer them right into the same fucking building. I swear, you can't write this shit.

"What did you do?" I managed to eventually get out of my stunned mouth.

"We locked eyes, knew exactly who each other were, and he headed directly into the bathroom," he told me. *Oh, well, thank God it was just that,* I thought. HA. "I went in and did my callback, then came out and waited," he said. Uh, I'm sorry, *what?* Oh my God, should I turn on the news? Is my ex-lover floating in a river somewhere?

"Okay..." I wished he would spit it out faster.

"When he came out, I walked straight up to him, shook his hand, and said, 'Hey, man, I'm Ty. Just wanted to introduce myself.'" I didn't know if the image in my head made me want to laugh, cry, or pass out. "He gave me a big hug and then, with his hands on my arms still, he looked at me and said, 'How's your heart? How's your spirit?'" he explained. Leave it to Javier to say something that Tyler would totally connect with and say to someone himself. "I said, 'I'm fine, I'm good.'" Which unfortunately was a total lie. "Then he asked how my daughter was."

There was a long pause. Fuck. To be fair, I could see it from both sides. Javier was really saying, "Hey, man, I know how hard this has been on Gabrielle, so I can imagine you and your daughter aren't great, but I hope you are." It was coming from a genuine place. From Tyler's perspective, I'm sure he heard something more along the lines of this: "So I know I've haunted you for the past two years but whenever the girl you love is with me after we sleep together, she talks about you and your child to me." Yeah. No bueno.

He continued to tell me how for the next five minutes they talked and joked that Javier was the only non-white guy there and the current state of the industry.

"Then I said goodbye and left," Tyler finished.

"I am fucking blown away," I responded. "But I am so proud of you."

"Yeah. It felt really good to face him after the past two years."

"I bet."

"And you know what, Gabs? I kind of get it."

"What do you mean?"

"I see it. Why you were so hung up on him. He's good-looking, he's charming, compassionate. I get his energy," he explained. Oh, if he only knew what the charming and compassionate man had made me feel that past week.

"I'm, like, in shock. What are the chances of that happening?" I said.

"Only in your life," he joked, still in shock himself.

You got that right. *Only in my fucking life.*

The following evening, I walked into the restaurant where we were meeting and saw him sitting at a table looking just as annoyingly handsome as the last time I'd seen him—if not more. My heart immediately did a backflip inside of my chest. I had missed him so freaking much—and I so badly wanted him not to be sad anymore.

"Hi," I said as I walked over, and he stood up to greet me.

"Hey." He smiled and put his arms around me. I took a deep breath, inhaling the scent of the man I had truly been longing for.

We sat and caught up on what our lives had brought each of us the past month. He had definitely been hitting the gym, and hearing he'd been spending a lot of great quality time with Blue made me happy. Strides had even been made in repairing the broken friendship between him and his ex-wife, Christine, and they were officially back to joint custody. It seemed, at least to those who didn't really know him, that he was doing really well. But I knew his heart was still very much broken—and that killed me.

"How is Blue doing?" I asked, feeling so guilty that I had vanished from her life in the way I never intended to.

"She's good. Really good. She misses you though," he said, sticking a knife in my side.

"How do you know that?"

"The other night we were driving, and I asked her how she felt about me maybe starting to date again. She looked at me and said, 'But I want you to be with Peanut.'" Knife, twisted.

"Oh my God." My bottom lip stuck out with nothing else to say—and hearing him say the word *dating* gave me a mini surge that I promptly buried.

"She'll be fine. She just loves you." He smiled.

"Well, hopefully, we can all eventually hang out if it's not too confusing."

We laughed, like we always did, as we ate and smiled at each other. God, I had really missed him.

When we were finished, we walked a few doors down to get coffee. We found two corner chairs and cozied in as we sipped our hot drinks.

"So..." I started.

"Oh God," he said, assuming the worst.

"What?"

"It's just never good when you say that." He chuckled. "But I guess you can't be breaking up with me." We both laughed.

"I booked a solo trip to Asia for my birthday," I told him.

"Really? That's great. When do you leave?" he asked, trying his best to sound excited for me.

"November 18th. I get there the day before my birthday. For a month."

"Wow. That's going to be awesome. Where are you going to go?" He sipped his coffee.

"Vietnam and Bali. I just really feel like I have to reset. I feel this constant anxiety in my chest. I need a soul trip," I explained.

"Like another FML trip?" he jabbed, referencing the men I had racked up abroad.

"No, idiot, like a me trip. I'm going to heal some shit. I can feel it. It's going to be big."

"I'm excited for you. I know you've wanted to do that since you came back from Europe." He smiled.

"Yeah." My smile faded.

"What?" he asked.

"I think I need to go and not talk to you or Javier or anyone for the month. You both, in different ways, have become like a crutch to me. Especially you—like my safety net. And I need to walk on my own again."

"I think that's great. I mean, I don't know how we'll be able to not talk for that long and it will absolutely suck, but I think it's going to be really powerful for you." He again reassured me with a smile that I so deeply appreciated.

"Thank you. I know, the thought of not talking to you all the time is...I don't even know." I chuckled over my sadness. "I start recording the audiobook tomorrow." I changed the subject.

"That's incredible. Are you excited?"

"Yes. And nervous."

"I get that. It's a lot to relive out loud. But you're going to be great. You always are."

We continued to bounce around different topics until we found ourselves laughing about the ridiculous encounter Tyler had with Javier.

"It was really like being in a movie. Only in your life. I'm sure he called you right away too," he said. A pause.

"Actually, we're not really talking right now," I finally said.

"Oh. Why is that?"

"There were some things that kind of upset me," I admitted. Tyler instantly looked like he was about to murder someone.

"What did he do now?" he asked intently.

"It's nothing. There were just things that didn't sit right with me."

"Like what things?" he persisted. Shit. How was I going to get out of explaining all of these details?

"Just things!" I laughed. "It's really nothing, calm down, Wolverine."

"It must be bad if you don't even want to talk about it." He knew me too well.

"Just stupid stuff that upset me. Anyways, how are Blue's acting classes going?"

He thankfully dropped it, and we continued to have a really good night, happy to just once again be in each other's presence. When the coffee shop was closing, Tyler walked me back to my car. We stood outside, lingering for a few minutes.

"Tell me what he did to upset you," he said out of nowhere.

"Tyler, really, it's nothing." I tried to hide the still rather fresh hurt on my face.

"God, he really hurt you, didn't he?" Clearly, I was failing.

"It was just stuff he said that hurt my feelings. Like that he didn't like me with lipstick on." I offered the least detailed of the many things that had led to Javier and I parting ways. He took a deep, controlled breath. I waited to see how this piece of information about someone I knew he was deeply triggered by was going to manifest. He put his hands firmly on my shoulders and leaned down close to my face.

"With makeup, with no makeup, with shit all over your face, you are the most beautiful goddamn woman I have ever seen." He held my gaze to make sure I took in what he'd said.

"Thank you." I looked down. He lifted my head back up to look at him.

"Don't you ever fucking forget that, Gabrielle. And fuck anyone who ever says different."

He pulled me forward and wrapped his arms around me. We stood there, for many moments, just breathing and holding on tightly.

Who the hell in their right mind would walk away from a man that so blatantly loved her? A man who thought the world of her? A man that wanted nothing more than to protect her from all the bad the world had thrown into her orbit the past two years. Apparently, that someone is me. *What the fuck, Gabrielle.*

*****

The next day was day one of five I would be recording the audiobook. It was my dream job really—drive a mile and a half to a studio, in my pajamas, to sit and act while I sipped on an endless supply of tea. Sign me up for life.

However, I have to admit, even with all the excitement I was feeling about this next step in my journey, I was a little bit nervous. I mean, I had never narrated anything before. I didn't know if there were certain rules or expectations of this profession, and I didn't really have anyone guiding me. I was on my own. As I scarfed down breakfast, a text from Tyler came in.

Tyler: This book was written for many reasons. It was a period in your life that has paved a way to growth, responsibility, self-love, and perseverance. Although it is in the past and you take each step of progress new and deliberate, it will always be a part of you. It will remind you of where you were and how far you've come. It will remind you of the kind of person you deserve in your life as a partner, and it will remind you of the beautiful soul you as an individual truly are. This week will prove as a final movement toward that progress. It will act as the closure to that chapter of your life in unspeakable ways. Clear your mind of any and all other aspects in your life during this week. That includes me. Make this week count. Relive that summer. Relive the book this week. Relive your feelings. Your sadness. Your joy. Your triumph. Immerse yourself in your emotions that were with you on that trip. Don't act it. Relive it. Put everything you have into this week so you can walk away with a fresh start and a sense of purpose to write your next one and to move on with your beautiful life. I'm so profoundly proud of you for everything that you do. For the person you were during your trip. For the person you've become thereafter. I'm proud of you for the air that you breathe and for the lipstick that you wear (wink). I love you like no other and am sending you all the strength through this week to conquer this mountain once and for all. To stick your flag at the top of that mountain and claim, "This mountain is mine." I love you.

And just like that, I wasn't so scared anymore.

When I arrived, I signed in and met Dave. Dave was going to be my engineer along for this wild ride—and I'm sure he had no idea what he was in for. He was short, somewhat reserved, and looked like he played Dungeons and Dragons with a fully outfitted headset on. Aesthetically, we looked like a pretty unlikely pair. But this was totally new territory for me, so Dave instantly needed to become my support system buddy.

As he began to tinker around on the computer in the dark windowless room, I walked through the door and into the room I'd be recording in.

"So what's your book about? I love the title," he said, keeping his eyes on the screen.

"Uh...it's a memoir, I guess? About the shit show my life turned into in 2017." I chuckled.

"Cool. I just finished recording a really boring sci-fi novel that was like five hundred pages. This will be a nice change of pace." *Oh, dude, you have no idea.*

I sat down in the chair that was set up in front of the podium where there was an iPad with my book downloaded onto it. A little table with a lamp was the only real light source in the small room where a paperback copy of my book sat. This was going to be my home for the next five days. My dark little sanctuary for therapy. With my new buddy Dave.

As we dove straight into day one, I was forced to quickly get over my long-standing discomfort with reading aloud. I also quickly realized that recounting this wild time in my life out loud was a totally different experience than reading any of the edits I had done.

I would often catch Dave chuckling as he stared into the computer screen on the other side of the glass, which made me feel a bit more at ease. As I read the words I had written more than a year before, I made a conscious decision. I would not read as if I was simply relaying my story, nor as a narrator telling a tale of someone's life— and not even as an actress attempting to evoke some sort of emotion out of whoever ended up listening. I decided that I would take this entire journey, all over again, so that whatever emotions I had felt during the actual experience would come through as I read—and *that* meant ripping open some old fucking wounds.

I felt the anger I'd experienced as I voiced a scene with my then husband. I allowed my voice to crack reading the open letter to the girl that had slept with him. I even experienced the same relief as I recounted driving away from the prison that had become my marriage.

I allowed myself to fall in love all over again—the blinding, all-encompassing love I felt toward Javier. The realness of those five days where we found ourselves falling for each other—and the fucking dagger that went through my chest as I found out he was going to be breaking my heart.

I felt the fear and panic of getting ready to board the plane with not a single clue where I was going or who I would meet. The exhilarating excitement of my first solo day in London. The adventure of not knowing where I was off to next.

Each day when my session ended, Dave would ask me what was coming next—where certain people were now, if I was still in touch with them. We quickly became the most unlikely of friends, and I knew that I was safe to rip open my heart in this space.

By day three, I had laughed more than I had in a long time. Yes, there were moments of sadness and pain, because when you so vividly speak every detail of your broken heart's biggest wounds, it is only natural to feel every emotion that helped stitch it back up. But overall, I think I had more fun that week than I'd had all year.

I felt the cold rain in Amsterdam, and Dave and I laughed our way through my ridiculous one-night stand. I relived the highs and lows that Paris brought me and reminded myself how epically awful my hangovers are. I partied through Barcelona and got to re-meet all of the amazing people that I still had in my life. I smiled as I read about everyone's favorite character, Chris—because I knew I had done him (and what he did for me) justice.

I yawned as I arrived in Mykonos, unsure of how the hell I was functioning on the amount of sleep I had been getting. I laughed as I watched Dave's reserved face react to me hopping into bed with Marcus—and got hungry reading about Jimmy's mouthwatering gyros.

I recalled the sadness and heaviness I experienced in Rome when it was again time to just be with myself. The bitterness I felt walking through the streets of the city where I was supposed to start my trip—and the utter anger toward Javier for how he'd handled it all.

On the final day of recording, I greeted Dave, who now knew me entirely too well, and took a seat with my tea. I knew today was going to be heavy—because today we were in San Vito.

As I acted out the conversation between Javier and me that I will never fully forget, my voice cracked as I said, "You broke my fucking heart," because he so carelessly had. And then, my own words hit me like a fucking freight train.

"You're telling me you want me in your life forever, and you want me to be your best friend, but you don't even treat me how a friend deserves to be treated." I stopped.

It was then, a full two years after this conversation had taken place, that I had the cold and abrupt realization: I was quite literally in the *same exact* place with this man that I'd been in sitting in the small apartment in Sicily. Only a few days earlier, I had sat at his house saying the *same exact* sentence to him. He had, for two years, continually showed me that he could not (or just would not) treat me how a friend *deserved* to be treated. And here I was, not only being a friend to him, but giving him my body, my time, my energy... giving him *me*. The fact that I had not only missed this but *allowed it* made me angry. If any of my girlfriends had been stuck in a dynamic like this, I would have been preaching to them as I deleted his number from their phone. Yet somehow, in the midst of the connection, the open endings, the fun and laughter, the sex, and the time we spent together, I completely missed the fact that this man, this goddamn Achilles' heel of a man, *didn't actually love me enough to respect me as a friend.* There has to be a juicy-ass Thought Onion somewhere in here...Superficial?

• FUCK YOU AND THE HORSE YOU ROAD IN ON, JAVIER.

Okay, Gabrielle. Do you feel better now that you got that out? Yes. Let's proceed. Authentic?

• I allowed and accepted disrespect from someone I thought really did love me.

That's part of what was making me so angry. Yes, of course, I was upset that he had in fact been doing this for the two years I had been entangled with him. But what was worse was that *I'd allowed it*. I'd come to the conclusion during our conversation in Sicily, yet it had taken me all of this back and forth, mental energy, and wasted time to figure out the same freaking revelation. *Why?* Why. Subconscious thought...

- I don't believe I deserve love.

Wait, what? I don't feel that way. That doesn't make any sense at all. I sat and really thought about it. Sure, I'd always believed that I deserved love—then my husband cheated on me. Still, I knew I deserved love—then the man I gave my heart to completely abandoned me. It all made sense. The things that had happened in 2017 reprogrammed me to subconsciously believe that I did not deserve love because, after all, that is what was being shown to me. And somewhere along the way, *I decided to believe it.* So, while I had finally walked away from my wounds of Javier, I now had a much bigger task at hand. *Heal my damn self.*

As I read the final words of my journey aloud, I turned to the acknowledgement page. A page I had published when Tyler and I weren't even together—yet I still felt it just as strongly.

"And Ty, for being my unicorn," I spoke into the microphone.

I drove home that night, knowing what a therapeutic, healing, and fun week it had been—but I couldn't stop thinking about that subconscious thought. *I don't believe I deserve love.* How could I possibly accept love if I didn't feel I deserved it? What if that was why I continually pushed Tyler away? The realization of that subconscious piece of the puzzle made me feel like my gut was leading me astray. What a predicament, Gabrielle.

When I flopped down on my bed, I reflected on how much of myself I had poured into the last five days. I had relived it. I had immersed myself in it. I had put everything into it. I smiled—because I knew that I had finally completed *Eat, Pray, #FML.* I had conquered the mountain once and for all. I had stuck my flag on top of that mountain and claimed, *"This mountain is mine."*

The Ridiculous Misadventures
of...
SOLO BY CHOICE

The morning of the day my flight left for Asia, I caved. As I sat in my apartment, realizing that I was about to get on a plane and fly across the world, I had a total and complete panic moment. Not about the fact that I hadn't spoken to Javier in about a month, or that I would be traveling farther and more alone than I had ever been. I panicked because I realized I wouldn't have Tyler. With all the ups and down, break-ups and reconciliations, and twisted time-lines, one thing had held true and strong: *that man was my person.* He had in fact, without me truly realizing it yet, become the only man in my life to never abandon me. Of course, my father hadn't *really* abandoned me. He didn't *choose* to die when I was a little girl. Yet the belief had manifested all the same. Daniel had abandoned our marriage—and me—in the most heinous and conniving way possible. Javier had abandoned my heart—more than once—in one of the most shocking ways I had ever experienced. But despite all that I had put Tyler through, what he had endured on my behalf—he *still* did not abandon me. He had been so patient with me and my journey. He knew my trigger and protected it fiercely—to a fault some might say—and to not have that? *Was fucking terrifying.*

I called him, holding back tears, and he didn't even ask—he just simply got in the car and drove to my house.

"It's going to be amazing." His comforting blue eyes and smile looked at me on my couch.

"I know. I can feel it's going to be a totally different trip—something big is coming." I tried to relish in the comfort his company gave me.

"It's only a month. We can do it." He smiled encouragingly at me.

"I haven't gone more than a day without talking to you in some way in two years."

"Yeah, I know, Peanut." He took a sip of the tea I'd made us. "Have you talked to Javier?"

"No," I said intently.

"Oh..." He looked at me.

"What?"

"He just must have really hurt you. I've never seen you like... this, about him."

Tyler was right. Something had massively shifted in me regarding Javier. But I didn't want to divulge everything that had gone down between us quite yet. There was still some processing to be done—and some fear that he would hate me for going back...again.

"Yeah, well. I need to go on this trip and not have either of you as a crutch. It's easier with him, I've done it before, and I'll do it again. You're a different story."

"I'm proud of you. You're going to have an incredible experience. I can feel it." He smiled, reached for a bag he'd brought in with him, and handed it to me.

"What's this?" I asked.

"Just a little something."

I opened it, and a small heart-shaped rock fell into my hand. I looked up at him.

"It's for anxiety. You can hold it in your hand and rub it if you're ever feeling anxious or alone. And a little something else in there for your birthday." I threw my arms around him and squeezed him tightly. My breath skipped a few beats as I tried to hold back tears. I didn't want him to let go.

"Thank you," I said, standing in his protective arms.

"You're gonna do great. I can't wait to see you when you get home."

When I finally stopped hugging him, I walked him to the door and watched the biggest form of comfort I had known the past two years leave. He waved and smiled as he drove away from my house, and I went in to open the gift he had given me. Inside was a letter and a silver bracelet with the engraved words *Forever my Unicorn* on the inside. I opened the letter and began to read it.

Peanut,

I see you. I have always seen you. From the very first time I laid eyes on you; I've seen you. I believe in you the same way that I see you. I believe in everything you do to the fullest. And always will. You're the one that can do no wrong in my book—regardless of your choices. Although sometimes causing me pain, I still believe in you, and I secretly know that you'll be alright. As we step into the vortex of our future as individuals, the plethora of emotions that come along with not being partners hits me like a ton of bricks. Fear and sadness. The sadness will go away with time. It will naturally turn into "what could've been," as opposed to "what should've been." The fear on the other hand is something to behold and work through. Not something to ignore. To me, fear is something that can always be overcome. It's just a matter of how and when we overcome it. Sometimes it consumes us and takes longer than expected. Sometimes it is never overcome. But there are other times, regardless of how long it takes, that one can turn that fear into something beautiful. Something extraordinarily powerful. And in those instances, fear can just be a doorway to power. Never forget that, if looked through the right lens, you'll see, "Where there is fear, there is power." As long as I've known you, as much as we've been through, as deep as I've loved you—I have never known someone else in my whole existence that has the power to turn their fears into something beautiful. I've never known someone who has the ambition to do exactly what she wants to and actually succeeds in doing so. You somehow walk through this life with an air of excellence about you without having a conceited bone in your body. You are extremely rare and extremely gifted for these very reasons. Your compassion, your patience, your ability to listen and understand. Your talent in everything you do and your strength of character. Your dedication and willpower. Your beauty. You quite literally take my breath away every time I look at you. The list goes on and on and will continue to grow each passing day. It is paramount that you see these qualities in yourself. That you believe in yourself to the fullest, like I believe in you, like your mom believes in you, and like your dad believed in you. Know that your life, sometimes rooted in fear, has turned out to be that of what dreams are made of, for your strength and perseverance molded that very fear into the power that defines you. To say that I'm proud of you is meager to how I really feel. To say that I honor you would be an understatement. To say that I appreciate you would be futile. To say that I respect you would be unworthy. To say that I love you will never be enough. You have changed my life, my outlook on this world, the very way I love, my relationship with my daughter, my relationship with myself, my health, my future, in such dramatic ways that I will forever feel an undying amount of gratitude for you...an undying amount of love, respect, appreciation, and honor. My feelings for you are limitless and profound all the while being so pure and true. Regardless of any pain that has taken place in the past or present or any pain that comes in the future...regardless of how and when we actually become the friends we will strive so hard to be...regardless of *absolutely anything*, one thing will never change: I will always have your back and I will always hold your heart as close to my very own as humanly possible. I will always be an ear to listen and a hug waiting. I will always pet your head and wipe your tears. I will always cook you dinner and make you laugh. I will always hold you and watch trashy TV. I will forever be your unicorn until the day I die because there has always been one terrific constant from the day I first met you in Michigan. One great wave that overcame me. That one bit of knowledge that has forever kept me smiling. Just one thought. One sentence. One way.

My heart has always been yours.

I love you,

Jacky

As I crumbled into a puddle of tears reading this man's deepest feelings about me, I asked myself (as I'm sure all of you are, too), *What the hell is wrong with me?* Why is this *not* my person? Why is he *not* my forever? What on earth could *possibly* be missing. I slowed my breathing as I clutched one of the most beautiful things anyone had ever written me. I could *feel* it. This trip, this journey—whatever it was going to bring—*was going to change the course of my life.*

*****

"You ready to go?" my mom asked as I double-checked my passport and license. I had a serious mixture of nerves, dread, and total excitement. I had been wanting to take my second solo trip since I'd stepped off the plane from Europe, and it was finally here—this time, by choice.

"Yeah. Let's do it." I grabbed my bag, which was much lighter than on my rookie trip. I knew how many clothes I wanted to buy in Asia, so I'd only packed a few outfits, two pairs of shoes, and essential toiletries. A tinted moisturizer and travel size mascara would be the only makeup needed for this trip. Who the hell was I trying to look pretty for? My soul was what needed work. What did add a slight bit of weight was two copies of *Eat, Pray, #FML* and the new journal I had bought to write in. I planned on giving a copy of the book to someone I connected with on my travels that could benefit from it. After all, it was only because of solo travel that I'm here with you all now...

"Okay, let's get a photo before we head out." My mom grabbed my phone from me. I sat on the front step of her home—my home—where I had spent the first eighteen years of my life and continued to come home to. I had sat on that step at every age of my life. Thirty years. I had been an innocent, carefree kid on that step. A grieving confused seven-year-old little girl on that step. A defiant, rebellious teenager on that step. An engaged, married, and divorced woman on that step. I had walked off that step to get on a plane to Europe after having my heart crushed. And now, I would walk off that step on yet another adventure, to hopefully find another piece of myself, and come back different than that step had ever seen me before. I sat with the same giant maroon backpack, a new travel-sized daypack, and my new journal. I posted the photo with the caption:

My first solo trip with this backpack was to Europe in 2017. While it was absolutely life changing and divinely right...it was most definitely not a solo trip by choice. Now, two and a half years later, it's time to do another one—by choice. There is something about solo travel. Liberating. Exciting. Terrifying. Empowering. Uncomfortable. Unknown. But there is growth in the uncomfortable—and change in the unknown. Many of you will ask, "Are you writing the sequel?" My answer to that is this: I'm not putting pressure on myself to do anything on this journey except nourish my soul and get in touch with *myself.* That being said—we all know what happened the last time I left the country with an empty journal. Peace out, USA—I'll see you on the other side.

"Why do I feel like crying?" I asked as we stood at the LAX drop off. My voice cracked with the tears that had been bubbling up since early that morning.

"Because you're finally doing it. And it's going to be big," my mom responded. She never failed to serve up the spiritual nail and hit it right on the fucking head. She reached over and grabbed my hand. I squeezed it tightly. *Breathe, Gabrielle. It's going to be amazing. Just breathe.*

I grabbed my backpack and slung it on my back, then put my arms through my smaller one so it sat on my front. I was ready. Well, I was technically ready, with my bags, ticket, and location.

Was I *actually* ready? Emotionally, mentally, spiritually? Well, we were about to find out.

I hugged my mom, squeezed her tight, and let out a few cries buried in her shoulder.

"I'm so proud of you. You're going to do great. I love you," she said as she held me.

"I love you too." I wiped my tears, smiled at the woman who has never failed me, and headed into the airport.

I checked my large bag and headed through security. The international terminal at LAX is like being in a high-end shopping mall that's in outer space. It feels almost otherworldly. As I walked around with my daypack on my back, I continued to feel really anxious. It was 10:30 p.m., and I had an hour before my flight was supposed to board. Why could I not stop tears from filling my eyes? It was like my internal cup was overflowing, and they just needed to get out. Ugh, okay. What else is there to do anyway. Superficial thought?

- What the HELL were you thinking choosing to go across the entire world by your FREAKING SELF?

Well, it's something you've wanted to do for two years now. So why is it freaking you out now that it's finally here?

- What if I'm not capable of doing all of this on my own? No Emma to welcome me off the plane, no Javier...no Tyler.

Those people didn't make you capable. Just because they were there doesn't mean they were what made you capable. So...what's the subconscious thought?

- What if you don't find what you're looking for?

Ah. Well, that makes sense. This whole month I'd been feeling like some huge change was coming. From closing things with Javier, to navigating the end of Tyler and I, to knowing that my soul is hav-

ing some type of awakening. Somehow, I allowed it to become pressure—pressure to find some type of answer on this journey. Pressure
to go find out why my soul has been uneasy, what I want in life, how
to truly be happy. None of that was going to happen under pressure.
So I decided right then that I was just going to allow myself to be. To
explore, to discover, to heal, and to *just, freaking, be.*

As I sat with my thoughts and building anxiety, I felt it in my
heart. Tyler. I was so scared that this month was somehow going to
ruin the bond I had with this human. Yes, I had chosen to leave. Yes,
we had just spent the day talking about the fact that he would never
abandon me. So why, in all this emotion, was he the only person that
was totally overwhelming my brain. Fuck it. The trip hadn't technically started yet.

Me: Why do I feel like I'm about to have a full-blown panic attack?

Tyler: Because you're about to go on a life-changing trip.

Me: Can you talk?

Tyler: Of course.

I popped my headphones in, and his soothing voice came
through the other end, immediately calming me.

"I've been so calm and ready the past few days. I don't know
why I suddenly feel so freaked out." I was now outright crying in my
little airport seating section.

"Hey. Just breathe. It's going to be amazing. Once you get there,
you're going to be so happy you decided to do this. Feeling like this
is totally normal."

"I'm just really scared, dude," I confessed.

"Of what? You've done this before, you're a pro."

"Of not talking to you for a whole month. Of not being connected to you. It's really terrifying for me." We were committed—both
blocked on social media, rules in place. There was a long pause as I

wiped my tears, hoping other travelers weren't wondering who the weirdo crying in the corner was.

"Yeah. Me too, Peanut. Me too." Another pause. "But you know what, it's only a month. I'm always in your corner. I'm always here. That's never going to change."

"I just miss you," I cried, knowing full well that what I was saying was confusing and not fair. Hell, it was confusing to me. I had made this decision—again—and chosen to be on my own. So why did I miss this person so much already?

"I miss you too. I always miss you. But you're going to do great. It will be an amazing trip. I'm proud of you," he said. Only this man would go through all this pain, heartache, ups and downs with me— many *caused* by me—and *still* be cheering me on.

"Thank you. I love you," I said. *Try and pull it together, Gabrielle.*

"I love you too."

"I'm about to board. Thank you for talking to me."

"I will always be here to talk to you. I hope you have an amazing trip." I could hear his tone shift, knowing I was about to get on a plane.

"I guess I'll talk to you in a month." I half laughed and half cried.

"Be safe. I love you," he said.

"I will. I love you too."

I hung up the phone, grabbed my bags, and got in line to board. Damn. This was actually happening.

As I neared the ticket counter, my phone rang. It was Tyler.

"Hey," I answered. I heard quiet tears on the other end.

"Please be safe. I love you, forever and ever. And I will always be here."

"I love you too. So much. Thank you," I said back in the middle of the line.

"Bye, Gabs."

"Bye, Jacky."

I handed my ticket to the lady at the counter and smiled. I headed down the jetway, found my seat, and got situated. As the cabin doors closed, I thanked my lucky stars that the two seats next to me were empty on this fourteen-hour flight.

It was time. Time to step away from my safety net. Time to repair what the men in my life had broken inside me—to remember that I deserve love. Time to figure out how to feel totally safe and secure all on my own. Without any assistance. Without Tyler.

The plane took off and we ascended into the sky. I took a deep breath and smiled. All the anxiety suddenly melted away—because once again, I knew how epically life-changing this was about to be. Yes, Gabrielle, you can *totally* do this. Here we go—*solo by choice.*

The Ridiculous Misadventures of...
VIETNAM

After a connection in Taipei and a thankfully shorter two-and-a-half-hour second flight, I was in Vietnam. I'd made the not-so-smart choice of watching *Crazy, Stupid, Love* on the plane which, by the way, I don't recommend watching if you're going through any type of love issues or missing someone. The weird signs that reminded me of Ty happened no more than a few hours into my trip while I was watching *Toy Story 3* and waiting for my sleeping pill to kick in. We use many GIFs regularly when we text but one of our favorites was a little stuffed unicorn dramatically rolling his eyes. I never knew this was anything more than a GIF until I saw this little unicorn pop up on the screen in front of me in the movie I just happened to choose. It may sound small, insignificant, or coincidental, but it made my eyes well up and my heart thump inside of my chest. It felt like a little sign that Tyler was with me.

Traveling from the airport to my hostel in Vietnam was nothing short of death-defying. It's as if the people driving think they're in a virtual game of bumper cars and no harm will come if they happen to collide. There were probably twelve times I legitimately thought I was going to die on the forty-minute ride.

When I finally arrived at Old Quarter View Hanoi Hostel (*alive*, surprisingly), I checked in to my wildly inexpensive $6.75 a night room. Thank you, Asia, I can totally get used to your room rates. I had booked an all-female dorm for my first stop, and it was on the sixth and top floor. Hiking up six flights of stairs with two backpacks after twenty plus hours of flying, and a time zone change, was much

261

harder than you might think—but the outdoor patio overlooking the entire city made it all worth it.

I showered, changed clothes, and headed back down to join the hostel walking tour that was about to start. I mean, why not just jump right into it, eh? It was 1 p.m. so, regardless of if I was tired or not, I had a full day ahead of me.

There were about fifteen people in the lobby ready to get out and see Hanoi. As we all strolled along, we tried to keep up with our guide, learn where everyone was from, and not get hit by frantic motorbikes whizzing by like we didn't exist. That was the first thing I learned in Vietnam—good freaking luck crossing the street. Pedestrians *don't* have the right of way, *no one* cares if you're trying to get across, and they *will* hit you. Your best shot is to find a local who can see the sheer and utter panic on your face, hold on for dear life, and run when they run.

I met three girls and started chatting as we adventured around the bustling streets of Hanoi. One was from Australia, one from the Netherlands, and one from the U.S. We got to know each other as we weaved in and out of different things for sale in Dong Xuan Market. Apart from fruits, spices, and to my horror, small animals for sale, there was an inside four-story swap meet filled with so many clothes and fabrics you wondered how anyone ever sold anything. It was magnificent, wild, and overwhelming, all at the same time.

That night, once the tour had ended, one of my new friends and I set out to find a place to eat. Kristy, the girl from the States, had been living in Ho Chi Minh, Vietnam, for about six months, teaching at a school, and was visiting Hanoi on a long weekend. Her story was pretty incredible. She had always been a travel junkie, but trips suddenly weren't enough for her—she wanted to live abroad. I found this especially inspiring because she had a boyfriend at home whom she loved but knew she needed to fill this void within her. They were doing long distance while she lived and taught across the world. What a badass.

We sat down at one of a few small tables with folding chairs outside on one of the busy streets.

"Banh mi is one of my favorites. The best are usually the random little street carts," she said as we took a seat at the table next to, of course, a random little street cart. A woman approached us and asked what we wanted. Kristy ordered two Banh mis and the woman went back to make them fresh for us. She returned with two delicious sandwiches that included savory meat and toppings on a full baguette. As we sat and I ate my first meal in Vietnam, she asked about the ins and outs of my life back home in the States. We clicked right off the bat, and she reminded me a lot of Mallory, whom I had met in Barcelona.

After we had finished our Banh mi, we walked around the streets that were now coming alive with lights, smells, and even more people.

"Are you still hungry?" she asked as we walked. *Is that ever even a question?*

"Yes. Take me to the next food station!" We laughed.

We ended up settling on one of the many restaurants on Pub Street with small plastic tables and chairs. This was the norm in Vietnam, seating set-ups that looked like you'd find them in a child's playroom—and it was awesome. Kristy ordered us a slew of dishes, two bowls of pho, and two beers to toast our new friendship. We ate like kings, stuffed our faces, and ended up with a bill that was roughly three dollars a piece in American.

With full and happy bellies, we headed off to get a foot massage. I quickly learned that taking advantage of the ridiculously cheap foot massages was not only a no-brainer but imperative after the amount of walking you do. We laughed as she told me about the different parts of Vietnam she had visited so far. Since I didn't have any set plans, I soaked it all in, thinking about where I might want to venture next. Then, the second little sign appeared. Well, rather, played. There, in a random massage parlor in Vietnam, "Linger," the song that had become a staple in my and Tyler's relationship, played through the small speakers. I smiled—because my heart felt a little safer knowing his energy was with me on my journey.

Somewhere in the middle of our foot massage, my internal alarm clock went off, and the jetlag gods (or...devils) charged into the room and smacked me in the face. It was time to go to bed. Walking back to our hostel, I even started to see spots. I had been up for over twenty-four hours and had switched time zones—it was time to take my ass to bed.

As I lay in my first hostel bunk of my trip on November 19th, I reflected on the fact that I would be waking up the next day on my thirty-first birthday. Not exactly where I thought I would be at thirty-one. In fact, the high school me would have told you I would be married by twenty-seven with kids by thirty. Yet here I was, single and childless after a failed marriage and divorce. I smiled because, in that moment—jet-lagged and snuggled into a bunk bed across the world—that was *exactly* where I wanted to be.

*****

I opened my eyes, praying that it was a somewhat acceptable time to get up for the day—because you know what? IT WAS MY FUCKING BIRTHDAY. 6:24 a.m. Good enough! I was officially not in my twenties, not the heroic thirty, but on the other side at thirty-one. Not only was I thirty-one, I was on the other end of the freaking world, by myself, divorced, single, and ready to figure out where the hell my life was about to take me. Okay, Vietnam, *let's fucking celebrate.*

I was solo. Yes, day one I had met some awesome girls at my hostel, but they were all off on excursions, and more importantly, I hadn't flown across the globe to be surrounded by new friends this time. I had come to be with *myself.* So I threw on some elephant pants and a light blue crop top and ventured out for my day of birth.

First stop? The Note Coffee. Let me take this well-worth-it paragraph to accurately describe to you what a treasure this place is. The Note Coffee is three stories. The coffee shop is right at the entrance with an assortment of Vietnamese coffees and delicious pastries. Once you give your order (and pay the *ridiculously* cheap tab you racked up), they show you to a seat on one of the next two stories. I was lucky enough to be taken to the top level, where you have a perfect view of the bustling street below and the lake just across the main road. But that's not what's special about The Note Coffee—it is 90% covered in different colored Post-It notes. At each table there is an assortment of little paper tabs that you can write whatever you feel on. You then pull it off and stick it wherever you feel called to do so. The table, the floor, the walls...you are literally in a structure that is entirely covered by Post-It note messages from people around the world.

I sat down at a quaint table by the window and thought about what the hell I wanted to write to leave a little piece of me behind. The sweet waitress brought my coffee and smiled at me.

"Where you from?" she asked in the English she knew.

"California," I replied.

"Ah, amazing! You like Vietnam?"

"Very much!" I responded.

"Enjoy," she told me with another warm smile.

Each coffee comes in a mug with a saying on it. Ready for what mine said? *Always remember that you are special, you are unique and absolutely important. Never doubt it for a moment, ok?* It also comes with a Post-It note that the staff writes a message on. Mine read: *Every day is a new, better day!*

How appropriate, I thought. I sipped my coffee and thought about what I should write on my little message to future travelers in Vietnam. I settled on the following four:

1. The light at the end of the tunnel is more beautiful than you can ever imagine. Keep going.

2. If you broke your heart or need to love yourself, read Eat, Pray, #FML.

A note to bring my family together once again. Mine, my father's and mother's names.

3. From: Here
To: Heaven
Chris, Dee, Gabrielle

And finally...

4. From: Peanut
To: Jacky
Thank you. I love you. You will always be my unicorn.

I hadn't been able to stop thinking about Tyler. It felt like a piece of my heart had been cut out and taken away from my body. Which, of course, was incredibly ironic considering the fact that when I was *with* Tyler, I had continually felt like something was missing. Such a contradiction. *Could you get it together, heart?* Thanks.

I took my time enjoying my coffee and chatted with a few other solo travelers who came and left. Then it was time. Time to begin what everyone had been asking for since *Eat, Pray, #FML* released five months earlier—book number two.

However, there was a slight problem. While it filled my heart with complete joy that so many people were resonating with and healing from my crazy 2017 journey, I didn't exactly know how book number two ended. So how was I supposed to follow up something that I was so unwaveringly proud of? Everyone was now expecting a certain standard. *Well,* I thought to myself as I opened my journal, *you didn't know how the fucking first one was going to end either. So just shut up and write.* Thank you, Gabrielle. You're always so eloquent when you yell at yourself.

After about an hour and a half of writing, I decided it was time to move on to the next birthday stop. Before I left, I wanted to post something special for my birthday. I snapped a photo of myself at my table in The Note Coffee (amazing what you can capture with a self-timed front camera) as well as one of the notes I had left. I wanted to show the people following my journey that it's okay to be vulnerable, it's okay to be scared, and it's never too late to change old beliefs. For me, this was *so much more* than another birthday. I posted it with the following caption:

> "Why do you think it is that you always have anxiety around your birthday, Gabrielle?"
> I sat there, thinking.
> "When was it your father passed?" she asked.
> It was only then—sitting in therapy, at the ripe age of thirty—that I put it all together. One month. Exactly one month before my seventh birthday. My mother had thrown me a party that year, and I vividly remember the feeling: Every-

one is having *fun, right?* We're all *okay, right?* And since then, I have *always* had a fear that I wouldn't be happy on my birthday. So, I surrounded myself with people, events, things, to make sure I was fulfilled.

This year, I decided to *break* that belief. So today, on my thirty-first birthday, I adventured around the streets of Vietnam. All the way across the world.

With *me, myself*, and *I*.

That day in therapy, I had discovered a massive Origin Experience. The sense memory of trying to still celebrate turning seven after my dad had left this earth, desperately trying to pretend we were okay. What belief did that Origin Experience create?

Even when you're hurting, pretend you're okay.

I had unconsciously picked up the innate need to mask what I was feeling and pretend that everything was *fine*. I had done it when my dad died. I had done it after my divorce. I had done it with Javier. In some capacity, I had been doing it all my life. So, across the world from all the comfort that always made me feel fine, I closed my eyes and spoke to my little girl. *You don't need to be okay, Gabrielle. You're safe even though you don't feel fine. You're allowed to not feel fine.*

My next stop was train street. Train street was a narrow yet stunning old street with a few small cafés, beautiful overgrown plants and ivy, and train tracks running straight down the middle. The kicker? Twice a day, a real full-speed train rode straight through it. Numerous people had told me I needed to check it out, so I set out on a twenty-five-minute walk to see this incredible site. As I strolled through the city, I popped in and out of a few shops, grabbing an awesome pair of green pants that I have yet to see anywhere else.

When I finally made it to train street, it was like walking into the pages of an old storybook. It truly didn't feel real. I strolled along the tracks, taking in the cascading greenery falling down the buildings that bordered this special little street. After walking its length, I settled on a spot with a small table and chair set up and ordered a fruit smoothie and egg rolls from a lady whose eyes were so thankful I had chosen her restaurant. I had found my next writing spot.

For whatever reason, I'd chosen to write the chapter about saying goodbye to Javier. Why I decided this would be a fun chapter to write on my birthday, I have no idea. Maybe because it was so fresh in my mind. Or because I knew I had finally let go—and what better way than to physically write it all out. If I learned anything from my Europe trip, it's that writing is *therapy*. And, oddly enough, writing about it didn't set off any surges in me. In fact, I felt rather disconnected from my overly drawn-out saga with Javier. I was expecting to miss him—to feel that ache I had become so familiar with. But that day, it was just a woman sitting at a little table in Vietnam, writing about a love affair that once was—and that felt *wonderful*.

About an hour into my writing session, all the restaurant workers came out and started ushering people to the sides of the narrow street. We all stood flush up against the walls, hearing the sounds of loud whistle blows approaching. Suddenly, a massive train came full speed down the street, whooshing by our faces only inches away. It sounds terrifying, doesn't it? *It was*—but exhilarating at the same time. Kind of how this trip felt. Shit, kind of how my life felt.

After a once-in-a-lifetime experience at train street, I took my time on what became a forty-five-minute walk back to where my hostel was. I changed into some comfy clothes and sat on my bunk to relax. I looked through my phone at all the birthday messages that had come through from friends across the world. It was so strange to be totally alone on a day I was normally surrounded by people. I opened the birthday card my mom had included in her stack of *open these if you need a little pick-me-up* parting gift. It was the only thing I really needed this year.

When dinnertime rolled around, I debated seeing if anyone from the hostel was around to grab a bite. My conditioned brain thought I should at least have some type of dinner with someone to celebrate with. Then I remembered why I was really there. Why I had taken this trip for my birthday in the first place. Happy birthday, Gabrielle, here's your gift—a Thought Onion. Superficial thought?

- It's fucking sad that I'm about to go have dinner alone on my birthday.

That is a valid thing that every past version of Gabrielle would think and feel—but I was no longer little Gaby, or teenage Gabrielle, or even thirty-year-old Gabrielle. This was the new thirty-one-year-old Gabrielle, who was breaking old beliefs and had learned to be not only okay by herself, but enjoy it, at that. Authentic thought?

- Am I going to be alone forever?

This might seem slightly dramatic, but I had literally just walked away from everyone's perfect dream man, who would have loved me until the day I died. So excuse me while I worry about a surplus number of cats in my future.

- What if I'm not enough?

That was the core of it. The core of everything really. What if I am not enough to create a life that I am fulfilled with—or enough to become a woman who is proud, fearless, and unwavering in who she is. *What if I am not enough with just...me.*

Isn't that what the majority of us feel, what society programs us to believe from the time we are little girls? Dream of the big white wedding, wait for prince charming, you're lucky if you can find someone who will treat you right. Don't have kids too late, keep your figure right, get an acceptable job. I'm sorry, where were all the messages that you can be alone and happy? That you don't need a man to ensure your safety or success in life? I, for one, had gotten the big white wedding and a man who looked like prince charming, and look where the fuck that left me. Maybe it's time the world starts teaching our youth that the only thing that *truly* matters is self-love and personal happiness—because *that* is when you're able to attract everything you want in life. Because in the end, *you have to be enough.*

And with that, I grabbed my bag, found a restaurant on the lively Pub Street, and took me, myself, and I to celebrate my birthday. Because goddammit—*I am enough.*

The Ridiculous Misadventures of...

THE BIGGEST

O
n my fourth day in Vietnam, after taking myself to a beautiful spa, getting the largest package they had, and spending a whopping one hundred dollars on a six-hour luxurious treat for my birthday, Liz arrived. Liz was a fellow traveler, about to turn thirty, who had caught my attention in an all-female Facebook group called Girls Love Travel. Two weeks before I boarded a plane to Asia, I had seen a post from her, vulnerably opening up about her failed marriage and divorce, the recent death of her father, and the fact that she was packing a bag, jetting off to Asia, and, you guessed it, writing a book about it. So naturally I thought—holy shit—*she's me.*

I messaged her, and we met at a coffee shop in Los Angeles where we clicked and found out our stories had too many parallels to be considered a coincidence—even the current on-and-off man that for me was Tyler. She had already been in Asia for about two and a half weeks and had taken a copy of my book with her to read. When she found out I was starting my trip in Vietnam, she decided to catch a short flight from Thailand to join me.

Liz walked into the hostel, and we threw our arms around each other like we had been best friends for much longer than a two-hour coffee date. As we hiked up the six stories to the top floor, I realized that she was exactly where I had been two years ago on my Europe trip.

We got settled in and met three new girls that had checked into our room that day—Emily, a spunky beauty from London, who was a teacher by day, polyamorous vixen by night; Kara, a seemingly quiet and reserved soul from Wyoming; and Coco, an adventurous spirit from Connecticut who was on her last hoorah after living in Italy for two years.

Sometimes, when you're lucky, you meet and instantly click with a group of women on your travels, and that night, the stars all perfectly aligned. We headed off to dinner on Pub Street, followed by the infamous Vietnamese egg coffee in a hidden famous spot. We all shared our troubles and insecurities and the current dilemmas we were trying to sort through with the medicine they call travel. As we scarfed down food, I looked around at the women sitting next to me.

"Oh my God." I smiled. "I'm so freaking happy in this moment."

"I'm so with you. It's perfect." Emily beamed back at me.

We finished the night clinking drinks while dancing to Britney Spears, Sir Mix-a-Lot, Ying Yang Twins, and every other *"Oh shit, this is my jam"* song you can think of. We sweat and smiled until our cheeks hurt, and topped the night off with a 2 a.m. crepe on a street corner that was still alive with people.

The following morning, I took the girls to The Note Coffee before Liz and I were hopping on a three-hour bus ride to our next stop—Ninh Binh.

However I describe Ninh Binh to you, I assure you it will not do its beauty justice. This is the location that a lot of *King Kong* was shot in, with massive stone formations standing tall into the clouds, moss and greenery growing high and low, and water surrounding you in many different directions. It looked as if you were entering an untouched world where dinosaurs once roamed, humans hadn't damaged the earth, and everything was existing in pure harmony. *It was heaven.*

After arriving at our hostel, which overlooked calm water and rock-like giants, we headed off to one of the main draws of Ninh Binh, the beautiful canals in Tam Coc.

The sweetest (and apparently strongest) Vietnamese woman welcomed us aboard a traditional sampan boat with one other solo traveler from Scotland. She had the same name as my grandmother, and when she introduced herself, I smiled—another little sign that I was being watched over.

All three of our mouths hung open as we stared up at the massive chunks of stone that were now up close and personal. Every way you turned felt like you'd stepped back in time. We ducked as she rowed us through caves that allowed us to pass through the thick stone to the other side, hopping off at different islands that had sacred temples, hundred-step stairways, and stunning lookouts.

"I don't know if I've ever been somewhere so beautiful," I said as I took in my breathtaking surroundings.

"It feels like we're on another planet," Liz agreed.

After thanking our guide, we rode our bikes back to the dirt road where our hostel was. Well, I rode, Liz crashed—more than once.

As we basked in the sun and waited for our food at the little restaurant we stopped at, Liz looked at me quizzically.

"You seem sad," she said, intuitively.

As fulfilled as I was with my stunning surroundings and newfound strength, there was definitely a little piece of me that just felt—empty.

"You miss him, don't you?" she asked.

"No, actually. This is the first time I feel free from him," I answered, knowing she had just finished reading my book.

"Not Javier, Gabrielle." She paused. "Tyler."

Even hearing his name from someone else's lips made my heart sting. I did. In fact, as much as I was trying to ignore it—*I missed him desperately.*

"Yeah." My voice cracked as I unexpectedly found myself holding back tears.

About ten minutes further into our conversation, my new friend and I both had tears running down our faces as we talked about the different experiences and relationships that had really impacted our lives—and our stories.

"What's crazy is that you'd assume my marriage, my ex-husband, the person I was with the longest would be the most impactful relationship of my life—but that's so far from true," I shared, wiping my tears. "Up until last year, I would have said it was Javier—but it has become so incredibly clear that it's not that relationship either. He was absolutely the biggest heartbreak and the thing that broke me—but it's the person who loved me while I was rebuilding it all that has changed me the most."

"I have so much fear that I will never find that," Liz said through her just as wet eyes.

"Yeah...and I left it," I said softly.

"There was a reason—whether you know what it is yet or not— there was a reason," she assured me.

"I don't feel like my heart has been settling the way I thought it would on this trip. I'm not sure how to explain it, but Vietnam hasn't wrapped me up the way I was expecting it to," I told my new friend.

"Yeah, it's been beautiful, but I know what you mean. I think Thailand was my favorite. That's where I felt the most at peace."

"What was your favorite place?" I asked.

"Pai." A warm smile came across her face and her entire energy shifted as she remembered the magical city.

"Interesting." I thought for a moment. I had been planning all along to do two weeks in Vietnam and then two weeks in Bali—but the beauty of solo travel is that you aren't on anyone else's schedule. There were no rules. Only a feeling I was chasing inside myself.

We bonded more during that hour-long lunch than I have with some people over the span of years. The type of bond where you don't have to talk or stay close but if one of you calls, there's no hesitation on jumping into the depths of the emotional deep end. The kind that will last for the simple fact that, in that moment, we saw each other.

That night in bed, I scrolled through photos on my phone. I stopped on a screenshot of a text Tyler had sent me after one of our many break-ups. I read the words over and over. Then I posted a photo from our day on the river. My Instagram had become my personal (yet ironically so public) diary. And since Tyler was safely blocked, I poured out and posted exactly what I was feeling.

"You have deserved *every* single ounce of love that I showed you. There is no *single* person on this planet that I think is more ambitious, talented, compassionate, loving, sexy, or beautiful than *you*. Stop at *nothing* until you find someone that feels *exactly* the same way as I do...because that is what you *deserve*."

Today, in the midst of all the beauty—*I missed this.*

As I sat at lunch telling my new friend about the relationships that have affected my life, changed my path, and left an imprint on me—this was *by far* the biggest.

The Ridiculous Misadventures of...

REGRET

A few different things happened during our three-night stay in Ninh Binh. For one, we both got a lot of writing done. Sitting out on the beautiful dock that overlooked the picturesque scenery while sipping fresh ginger tea, I poured my inner struggles onto the pages of yet another empty journal. Secondly, we adventured around some of the most breathtaking landscapes I had ever laid eyes on. We hiked to the tops of the Mua Caves, floated through the still waters of Ngo Dong river, and biked through the untouched roads of Ninh Binh. And third, we decided on our next adventure—Ha Long Bay. Ha Long Bay is a massive bay with the same magnificent giants made of limestone, glistening water for miles, and endless areas to explore. There are many different ways you can experience this newly dubbed wonder of the world but after doing a good amount of research, Liz and I decided that it was time to spice things up a bit.

While Liz had definitely been living her best life, attracting men in every different city she planted her feet in, and collecting stories that would rival my #FML trip, I was most definitely *not* on that type of trip. I'd had my hangover of regret in Amsterdam, broken hearts in Barcelona, mingled in Mykonos, and played with fucking fire in Sicily—and I was not looking to repeat *any* of those things.

However, I had to admit, a party cruise filled with fun and outgoing travelers, good drinks, and endless music to dance to didn't sound all that bad. Besides, I needed to climb out of this emotional sinkhole I had stumbled into.

Without knowing what we were getting into, we piled onto a bus that would be picking up the rest of the wild travelers ready to embark on a two-night, three-day otherworldly adventure—with unlimited alcohol.

As we all chatted and got to know each other on the bus, I noticed two younger guys sitting just across from me. One of them was tall and tan, with sandy brown hair and light eyes. Ugh, sound familiar? Oh...*just wait.*

"What's your name?" that ever-so-familiar type asked me.

"Gabrielle. From Los Angeles. You?"

Are you all braced and ready for this fucking response?

"Chris." He smiled at me. "This is my brother Jack."

My mouth hung open, which I'm sure was incredibly odd to witness from the brothers' point of view, but there wasn't a damn thing I could do about it. Yes, there, in Vietnam, on the bus next to me, looking freakishly similar to the boy who had captured my attention in Barcelona, was book two's official *Chris 2.0.*

We piled onto the giant ship we'd be calling home for the weekend. The first two levels were all the rooms. Liz and I had each sprung for our own, which included a king-size bed, stunning bathroom, a balcony, and windows that let you look out onto the endless bay.

The third level was a dining area, a mini club complete with a stage, huge bar, and two outdoor hot tubs. And finally, on the top level, endless space to enjoy the magnificent views.

After lunch, the ship pulled into a cove where we all hopped into canoes to paddle around the open waters enclosed only by the mountainous rocks topped with rainforest. Chris and Jack followed behind us in a separate boat. We laughed, sang Pocahontas's "Just Around the Riverbend," and joked as we maneuvered through the crisp clear water. It was peaceful, serene, and totally soul-nourishing—and then we got back on the boat.

Drinks in hand and music blaring, the "party" part of the party cruise had officially begun—and I had *no* freaking idea what I was in for.

The crew made sure we were all having the complete party cruise experience, complete with dance competitions, games, and drunk yoga—yes, I did indeed just say *drunk yoga.*

Many drinks later, around 11 p.m., I remember Liz getting up from the corner a bunch of us were laughing our asses off in. She had been flirting up a storm with this wildly hot guy from Amsterdam (*why is it always Amsterdam?*), and they had officially made the call that they would be heading back to her room to continue the party in her bed. She hugged me goodbye and squealed as she headed off with her hot choice from this leg of her trip.

A few more of our group peeled off as Chris and I sat and talked. He was a very genuinely sweet guy, and I could tell he had a good heart (*don't they always?*). After hitting a few different deeper topics, he finally asked.

"Do you wanna get in the jacuzzi?"

"Yeah, sure!" I replied, already knowing where this was headed but, per usual, convincing myself that it was totally fine to just get into a jacuzzi where "nothing has to happen."

After I changed into my suit, I met him in the hot tub on the deck as we floated on the water under the star-filled sky. We talked for a solid twenty minutes, none of which was apparently important enough for me to remember, and then he kissed me.

This next entire portion of the night makes me cringe for so many different reasons. First, because for this *one night* on my Asia soul-searching adventure, I totally and completely fell back into old patterns—feeling like I needed a man and something from him to not feel empty. Second, because, I kid you not, I remember lying in my bed that night thinking, *Fuck, I'm going to have to write about this.* And lastly, because I knew damn well from the moment I'd met Chris 2.0 that I had absolutely no interest in him romantically. So, as I sit here uncomfortably writing, I promise there's a lesson in here somewhere. Ugh. Here we go.

Ten minutes into making out in the hot tub like we were in high school, he used some suave line to insinuate we should take our jacuzzi party to my room. Or honestly, maybe I made that initial offer—between the long day, the sun, and the number of drinks had, I couldn't tell you exactly how we ended up in my shower.

As we rinsed the chlorine off and lost our bathing suits, the inner dialogue I know all too well had already begun.

Gabrielle. Don't do this. You know where this leads. You know how you will feel after. Just tell him you're tired and you need to go to sleep.

The sadness that had been enveloping me from the inside hushed my conscience and continued to kiss the man I had met ten hours earlier. He attempted to start having sex, right there, in the shower—without any sort of protection.

I mean seriously, dude, you don't know a freaking thing about me. For all you know, I could have slept with someone the night before, have all kinds of awful diseases I can't pronounce, or be inherently psycho and be looking to get pregnant by a random dude on a party cruise ship.

I will never understand the mentality men have around this particular subject. I pushed him off and laughed as I finished rinsing off, he smiled and immediately got the hint.

"Sorry, of course. Let me run back to my room really quick," he said as he dried off.

Actually, let's just call it a night—random dick is so not going to make me feel better about my life.

I flopped down onto my bed in my towel and waited. Waited to get this over with. Who the hell goes into having sex thinking that way? Like, why not just speak the fuck up and say, "Yo, dude, not really trying to have sex. Have a good night!" Well, might as well do a naked Thought Onion while I wait for my impending doom—uh—I mean, for Chris to return. Superficial thought?

• Why are you about to do something you so clearly do not want to be doing?

I had already discovered on my Europe trip in Mykonos that I used sex as some weird tool to keep men close to me so that I

wouldn't be abandoned. So deeply fucked up on so many levels—
and the realization of that belief had made me seriously look at my
sexual history. But that wasn't what was going on here. I didn't want
this man to stay, take care of me, or fix me. So, what the hell was the
authentic layer?

- I have to stay in control—and it's easier to just do it rather than
  retreat.

It had definitely been a pattern in my life. I could remember a
number of times that I hadn't physically wanted to have sex yet ended up doing it anyway because, why not? In some way, deep down,
it had become a defense mechanism, to protect myself. Because, like
so many women, there has been more than a few times where I felt
pressured, convinced, and guilted into being intimate. So, what's
deep at the subconscious level?

- If I minimize the importance of this act, I won't be taken advantage of.

Wow. It made *so, much, fucking, sense.* Ever since my first sexual experience, society, my parents, the media, and every health
class I had ever taken had instilled one thing in me: *don't let a man
take advantage of you.* In fact, over the years of failed relationships
and getting my heart bruised and beaten, I had developed my own
method to protect myself. If I take away the one *thing* that everyone
always warns you people want to take advantage of, if I make it *not*
sacred, *not* important, *not* a big deal—if it's *just sex*—I *can't* be tak-
en advantage of. And if I can't be taken advantage of? *Then I can't
fucking be hurt.*

I would love to report that I smacked myself across the face,
put on my big girl pants (and, you know, my actual pants), and told
Chris that I would not be sleeping with him that night. Unfortunately, then there would be no massive pool of regret to swim in the next
morning—and in turn, no massive lesson to be learned.

On the outside, all Chris saw was a wildly fun and sexually free
woman that knew what the hell she was doing in the bedroom. It

was in no way his fault that he wasn't psychic, didn't know how broken I was, and couldn't see the tiniest of tears escape the corner of my eye when we finished and fell down on the bed.

I made it clear that I wanted to get some sleep and was *so* thankful that he took the hint and headed back to his room. Relieved that I wasn't punished with someone who wanted to cuddle the entire night, I washed my face, crawled into bed, and *just, freaking, bawled.*

The worst part about all of it? All I could think about was Tyler. Not just that I wished it was him I had been with that night, or wanting to be with him, in his arms, safe from my failed choices and bad decisions—but that I knew how epically disappointed he would be in me. To tell you the truth, I was even more epically disappointed in myself.

It isn't that I don't think women should go out, have a good time, take home any freaking man they want, and roll around their sheets feeling like empowered sex goddesses once in a while. I mean, hello, look whose book you're reading. It was that for me, personally, that was all a big fucking front. Sure, I used that as my exterior shell to justify my bad decisions, which stemmed from a deep sadness and a long-running protection plan—but it wasn't real. What was real was that this pattern, this unhealthy relationship with sex that had covertly developed inside of me over the last fifteen years had to fucking stop. I had learned the lesson one too many times and just been too damn afraid to peel back the layers to learn where it was truly coming from. And there, on a massive ship, in the middle of an Asian bay, it all finally clicked. I am important. Intimacy is important. *And I will never break in order to falsely protect myself, ever again.*

In that rock-bottom moment, I made the decision—*fuck this, I'm going to Thailand.*

The Ridiculous Misadventures of...

PAI

I awoke in a new country, ready to find what my soul had been so desperately searching for since I'd left home—peace. I checked out of my hostel and headed to a random café with a street view of Chiang Mai for breakfast. I was already feeling lighter in some way now that I was in Thailand. Perhaps it was because I just needed a change of energy—or maybe it was because subconsciously I knew what Pai had in store for me.

I scarfed down my fresh fruit and granola, grabbed my pack, and headed to where the shuttle would be taking me to my next destination.

The streets of Chiang Mai were much less hectic than the death-defying streets of Vietnam. It was easier to glance around in wonderment as I made my way through the city.

Once I made it to the pick-up location, we were informed that we would be split up into groups and that we should use the restroom prior to the three-hour ride. I had heard two things about the ride up to Pai—it was indeed long, and it was by far the most winding road in the world.

Let me tell you—winding road does not even *begin* to describe it. It made Lombard Street in San Francisco seem like you could drive it with your eyes closed. Thankfully, I don't get car sick. Looking out the window, it felt like we were leaving a city and suddenly driving into FernGulley or Jurassic Park. Lush greenery and massive trees passed us by as we looked out the windows in awe. You could feel it—whatever was at the end of this twisty beautiful road was going to be magical. *And it was.*

Sometimes when you've heard amazing things about a place from *so* many different people, it sets your expectations way too high and you end up slightly disappointed with what you get. *Every* person I'd met on my trip who had traveled to Thailand had one thing in common: *they all said there was no place like Pai.* I didn't really know what I was expecting—but I knew damn well what I needed. To feel better. To get clarity. To heal.

My feet hit the dirt as I stepped off the bus. We were smack in the middle of the main market street—vibrant colors, hanging handmade clothes, delicious smells, and excitement permeating from the people who felt so at home there. Every way I turned it was like seeing a slice out of a mythical world. It was sensory overload in the best possible way.

I'd made friends with a German photographer and a sweet girl from the Netherlands, and we shared a cab to the hostel we were all staying at. Pai is pretty walkable for the main areas, but our hostel was on the outskirts of town, and we all had packs that made the twenty-minute walk not too desirable. I'd done some research on Hostelworld to figure out where I wanted to stay. Some were fancier and had beautiful infinity pools, others were super close to the main attractions in town, but the one I chose was where every review raved about the specialness and the people they had encountered there—and that was Deejai Pai.

I had looked at the photos. I had seen the vastly stunning view from the main common area. I saw the very plain and modest rooms and bunks. Nothing...I mean none of it, *did it any justice.*

As my eyes adjusted to the view I would be calling home for at least a few days, my entire body suddenly relaxed. It felt like I had stepped into *The Lion King* and our hostel was Pride Rock. It was freaking *magical.* People sat around talking, laughing on the swing-style seats, and napping in the hammocks. It was pretty damn close to heaven on earth.

"Checking in?" An Israeli accent snapped me out of my magical trance.

"Yes!" I smiled back at the small vibrant red-haired girl behind the counter.

"Cool, let me get you set up," she said. There was a distinctive *this is my place, I don't give a shit about anything* badass vibe to her.

As she explained when the kitchen was open and told me about the morning yoga class and how best to get into town, I took in everything around me. I could hardly believe this place was real. Whenever you arrive at a new hostel, there is a mixture of excitement, nervousness, and uncertainty—it's inevitable. But this one time, at Deejai Pai, all of those emotions were noticeably absent. I simply felt...home.

"I'm Red. If you need anything else, let me know." She smiled and headed out of the room she'd shown me to.

I dropped my stuff on my bunk in the very adequate room I'd be staying in. It was what you would imagine summer camp to look like—basic metal bunk beds, cement floors, and a bathroom that was shared by the twelve people the room could hold. I had booked three nights at this hostel. My plan was to spend a few days here and another two nights at another hostel, and then head down to one of the islands in southern Thailand before heading over to Bali.

It was about an hour until sunset, and Germany, Netherlands, and I decided to hike up to the famous white Buddha. We got to know each other as we strolled down our hostel road to the hill that took you up to the entrance. Germany had his massive fancy camera and snapped photos as we hiked up the steps to the top.

As I stood on the expansive platform, I looked up at the beautiful white Buddha, which had Pai's glowing sunset reflecting off it. It reminded me of being in Paris and looking up at the Eiffel Tower—but this time, instead of instinctually feeling incredibly small, I allowed myself to open my heart and sink into the beauty that this massive statue offered. You could really feel a spiritual presence emanating from it.

I sat and watched the sunset in Pai on my first night from the most magnificent and scenic spot to witness the sun hide from the world. As I allowed my eyes to admire what my brain couldn't comprehend was real, I recognized one feeling that had come with me from Vietnam to Chiang Mai to Pai—I really missed Ty.

I snapped a photo of myself with the beautiful Buddha behind me. Once we returned to the hostel, I sat in one of the hammocks in the common area, lost in my thoughts. I wrote out a conversation I'd had with Arna during one of our sessions that had really stuck with me. It would be the first photo I posted in Pai.

"Do you believe in soulmates?" she asked.
"No," I replied. "I believe in soul people."
"Yes." She smiled. "I think you've definitely met two of the four kinds so far…"

Healing Soulmate:
One who arrives with an intention to provide you with life lessons that heal your memories by mirroring you. They appear by divine timing—at the time we most need to learn from them. They teach us how to move forward in life. A healing friendship exists only as long as you need it until your purposes are aligned. When your relationship escalates fast, then you'll know you've found a healing soulmate. Sometimes painful, it might not last forever.

"Yes. That was him," I agreed.
"But it was conditional," she said.
"Yes."

Past Life Soulmate:
You'll feel like you've known them forever. The connection is instant. You may feel like you will be mates for a lifetime—no matter how much time has passed or how far apart you are—and you're probably right. This relationship will likely last forever because you will never feel the need to run or hide from this soulmate. They teach you to trust and believe in yourself. You're both accepted for who you are. The friend who'll help you grow into the person

you are meant to be. They can propel you toward your fate without pain or suffering. They'll always have your best interest at heart. This type of friendship can last a lifetime. You just need to stay connected. They're crucial in shaping you into the best version of yourself.

"That is without a doubt him."
"Yes. But unconditional," she added.
"Yes."

It's crazy how life works—the first I met six years before our story ever began. The second I met nine years before a single page was ever written—although we both somehow knew even back then. And today I sit here—alone—knowing how beautiful the story of love, loss, and life really is.

How freakishly accurate both of those descriptions were. The first described Javier and I in every way. After all, without him and the life lesson he'd brought me, I wouldn't be who I am now. And yeah, it escalated ridiculously quickly, and it was *fucking painful.*

The second described Tyler in better words than I could ever come up with myself. I identified with every single bit of it—and maybe that was why I felt like a piece of me was now gone.

I could feel it. I could feel that this was going to be the place that was going to unearth some deep-rooted things in my soul. I could feel that whatever this trip was going to end up bringing, it was going to begin here, in this place—because you see...*there is no place like Pai.*

The Ridiculous Misadventures of...

YOU CAN'T RUSH YOUR HEALING

The next morning, I woke up early for the yoga class our hostel offered. In the common area there was a big open space covered by the tented ceiling that overlooked the breathtaking view. Admittedly, I'm not much of a yoga person. When I work out, I need to be dying and drenched by the end of it or else it feels like a waste of time. But you know, when in Rome—well, Thailand.

I grabbed a mat and took a seat with roughly ten other travelers. In what other place would you be taking a yoga class with people from all over the world? I took a deep breath in as I sat still in the chilly morning air.

"Whatever you've been feeling in your chest, whatever heaviness, or pain, or fear, I want you to breathe into it and let it all go," our teacher spoke softly to us.

There was definitely a heaviness—in fact, I felt every single thing she had mentioned. It had lessened since I'd arrived in Pai, but there was no doubt that something inside of me just felt...off. As I stretched and breathed on cue, I focused on the one thing I was really longing for—*clarity*. I so desperately wanted to get clear on why I felt so confident in breaking up with Tyler, time and time again, only to come across the world and feel like there was a giant gaping hole in my heart. It made no sense to me, but one thing I was sure of—I could not go back to him without an answer. I couldn't do that to him again—I *wouldn't*.

As the class ended and we bowed our heads with a namaste, I saw a different perspective of yoga. While some do it as a workout, that was totally not what it was about for me. It was about getting centered, connecting with myself and the earth, and allowing myself to shut off my never-ending brain—and that made it an hour well spent.

I decided to explore that day with my new friend from the Netherlands, another girl from the UK, and a French Canadian who had been in Pai for a few weeks. In Pai, the best way to get around is on a scooter. I'd heard absolute horror stories of tourists eating shit, having near death experiences, and gaining more than a few scars as souvenirs, so I was more than happy when the French Canadian offered me the back of his bike. The four of us hopped onto the scooters and headed off to our first stop: breakfast at Fat Cat.

It's an odd name, but it is one of the coolest restaurants I've ever been to. It's completely exposed with bamboo roofing slats and mismatched colorful cushions on the ground around low-level tables—*and it's in a fucking tree.* Yes, this café is high above the ground, with strong branches and brightly colored leaves all around you. If you've ever imagined what it would be like to eat in a fairytale world, this is the place that can fulfill that curiosity. And to be honest, it was pretty magical.

"We're going to head to the lookout point. It's a must see," the French Canadian, who had been in Pai much longer than the rest of us, stated.

As I admired the scenery around the road we drove down, thankful I could get lost in the beauty and not need to focus on not killing myself via motor bike, I let out a big sigh.

"Ah, I know that sigh. That is the sigh of a broken heart," the French Canadian shouted over the wind speeding past us as we zoomed down the road. Turns out he was on an eight-month backpacking trip after having his own heart broken back in Canada.

"It's complicated. I don't really know what it is." I laughed.

"Is that what you were writing about last night? I saw you journaling."

"Kind of. I'm a writer. I'm working on my second book right now," I shouted back.

"Really? That's so cool. I've always wanted to write a book. I feel like I could write one about me and my ex. What is it about?"

"Well, funny you should say that. It's about my massive heart-break and the solo trip I took after it."

"Oh, I'll have to read it. I feel like I'm just now starting to heal from mine."

That thought was exhausting to me. Since *Eat, Pray, #FML* had come out, I had received countless messages from heartbroken women around the world asking me, "When does it lessen?" or "When does it get easier?" The answer to that question can be terrifying, uncertain, and defeating—*it just takes time.* I for one have never been a patient person. In fact, it is probably my biggest weakness. If there is an issue, I want it fixed immediately. If I'm hurting, I want the pain to go away. To be fair, it's one of the reasons I get shit done and can accomplish things in my life, because on one side of the coin is drive. But the other side of that coin is impatience—and there is no hell like frustrated impatience in your healing.

"Lookout point" doesn't even begin to describe it. This spot overlooked the entire valley of Pai. It was as if you were standing at the very top of a snow globe, inside the glass. You could see the infamous white Buddha far in the distance, the vast landscape stretching as far as the eye could see in every different direction, and the colorful rooftops below. A little structure at the top sold tea in authentic glass teapots and cups. I ordered one and took a seat on the bench that overlooked the world below. *How on earth did I get here?* I thought to myself. So many things had changed in my life over the course of two years. I was no longer married—*thank God.* I had gotten my heart broken for the first time—*which fucking sucked.* I had shifted into a new career path when I wrote a book about it all—*totally life changing.* And most recently, I had decided to run away from the one person I had felt truly safe with...ever. *Why, Gabrielle? What was missing for you?* As I looked out over the incredible scenery before me, I smiled, because it was not a bad freaking place for a Thought Onion. Superficial thought?

• There was something missing in my relationship with Tyler.

Yes, thank you, superficial brain for stating the fucking obvious. Hopefully, the authentic thought can be a little more helpful than that.

- I didn't feel that intoxicating passion I felt with Javier.

Interesting choice of words there, Gabrielle. Yes, my fast and furious relationship with Javier had been a constant intense honeymoon—*because he fucking broke up with you before it could go anywhere else*. With Tyler, I had felt passion. I had felt love. I had felt deeply connected. I had felt all of those things. So what's underneath all this?

- My definition of love is *fucking toxic*.

What? No. I grew up witnessing healthy, amazing, soulmate love. My parents were the epitome of that. *Well, yes, and then he died*, my heart reminded me. And so, the belief was created: *when I love someone, they die*. Okay...then I had what I would consider a pretty happy and healthy relationship with my college sweetheart. *Sure, until you got bored because he became like your best friend.* My brain rolled its imaginary eyes at me. That cemented the false belief: *love is boring without drama*. Oh, what I wouldn't give to have *never* picked up *that* terrible belief. Years later, I entered into a relationship that turned into a marriage with more toxic and narcissistic traits than I care to list. My relationship with Daniel was the definition of toxic—and it was my first real-life experience of marriage. This is where I welcomed a new belief: *I can't trust someone who says they love me*. That was then thrust back into my face tenfold when Javier decided to leave me sitting on my bed, wallowing in my tears, after he had made me feel like I was his forever.

Well, shit...I guess my definition of love *is* fucking toxic. Tyler hadn't died. He wasn't boring. He hadn't vowed to love me and then abandoned me. He wasn't toxic—and apparently a part of me had been conditioned into thinking that feeling was a requirement for "love." How incredibly fucked up is that?

Later that evening, everyone was getting ready to head to the night market, which is really the best place to be in Pai on any given night. Red led the way, with her hippie backpack and oversized elephant pants. We strolled through the warm air and gentle breeze as we conversed and laughed our way into town.

How do I even begin to describe the magic that is the night market? It is one long street lined with all different kinds of shops—beautiful Thai clothing hanging from storefronts, jewelry out on tables, handmade crafts of all kinds, stunning restaurants with live music and twinkling lights. But what really made it the best place to be was *the food*—cart after cart of fresh tasty creations being cooked and prepared right in front of you: the best pad thai you've ever tasted, the most colorful salad with dressings from scratch, delectable desserts like crepes and mango sticky rice, dumplings of every kind, and the infamous chicken lady who served the best fried chicken with her secret sauce. Is anyone else drooling reading this? But the best part of this magical street of endless food and shopping was that you could stuff yourself silly for roughly five dollars.

We all walked along the bustling street, branching off from the group to get something yummy that caught our eye. The smells alone made you never want to eat anywhere else. I knew that this street is where I would be getting my bracelet from—and realistically more than a few more articles of the clothing I had fallen in love with.

When our bellies were too stuffed to do another lap, a few of us decided to call it an early night and head back to the hostel.

I took my shoes off and hopped into the hammock that hung in the common area, away from the few people hanging out and listening to music. My heart definitely felt more at ease in Pai than it had in Vietnam—but I still had this overwhelming sadness in my chest. It almost felt like my soul was crying inside to alert me that some major shift was about to take place—and that this was the breakdown phase. It was overwhelming. I noticed tears coming up, wanting to escape from behind my eyes, but I held them in. If I let them out, I was unsure when they would ever stop.

All of a sudden, the music that was playing changed and a serene and calming voice came through the speakers. As I looked out at the dark land and the sky filled with stars above, I began to hear the lyrics entering my ears.

So, you can't rush your healing
Darkness has its teachings
Love is never leaving
You can't rush your healing
Your healing
Maw-maw, well, she told me time is such a wonderful gift
You're not running out
You're really running in
Confusion clouds the heart but it also points the way
Quiet down the mind
The more the song will play
So, you can't rush your healing
Darkness has its teachings
Love is never leaving
You can't rush your healing
Your healing

The tears were no longer hidden. They were freely and quietly running down my cheeks. I had never heard words in a song that spoke so directly to the depths of my soul the way Trevor Hall's did in that moment. It was as if the universe had turned on the exact song that my entire being needed to hear at that precise moment. It was then, crying in a hammock in Pai, that I felt myself breaking wide open to begin to heal. *How incredibly lucky I was to be doing it here.*

The Ridiculous Misadventures of...

SIGNS

The next morning, I awoke early for yoga, still teetering on the edge of a cliff of sadness—one that I knew I did not want to fall off of.

As I made a cup of hot tea in the crisp Thailand air, I looked out at the view that stretched for miles beyond the hostel. It was the most beautiful place to feel sad.

I breathed deeply as our yoga instructor guided us through an hour of stretching and connecting with ourselves.

"Whatever you may be feeling, validate it. Allow it. Accept it," she said as we changed into a different pose that hid our faces.

Allow it. Accept it, I repeated in my head. I took a deep breath and let the tears that were left over from the night before fall onto the mat.

"Tell the universe you're open. You're open to all signs it may bring you today. That you're ready to see them."

When the class concluded, everyone lingered and broke off into the different spaces the common area offered. I went to sit on the edge of the platform to watch the view continue to wake up with the sun. *Okay, universe*, I thought, *I'm open to whatever signs you want to bring me today. Hopefully to help me not feel so fucking—*

"Hey." A cute petite brunette with a bandaged knee interrupted my conversation with the universe.

"Hey! I'm Gabrielle," I introduced myself.

"Nina." She smiled as she awkwardly plopped down next to me.

"What happened to your knee?" I asked.

"Motor bike crash. I was supposed to leave five days ago, but the universe said stay put." She smiled.

"See, and people think I'm crazy for hitching rides everywhere." I laughed. She had a warm, open energy about her.

"So...how does it feel to be somewhere where no one knows who you are?" she asked. I was a bit thrown off.

"What...what do you mean?"

"You're that author...from LA, right?" I was completely shocked.

"I...uh...yes?" I answered, assuming she probably thought I was someone I wasn't. She smiled.

"I heard you on the *Whine Down* podcast recently. I've been wanting to read your book."

"Oh my God. That's amazing. And so sweet you think people in LA know me." I laughed.

"I connected with a lot of your story. One of my exes is a lot like your Javier—only over a longer time span." She chuckled.

"You have no idea how often I hear that." I smiled at her. "So how long do you think you're here for?"

"Depends. I can't really do anything until my knee heals a bit more. I already pushed my flight back a week, so hopefully I'll be good to go by then."

"I mean, if you have to get stuck somewhere..." I motioned to the view in front of us.

"Right? Just trying to let go of some control. This is forcing me to." She laughed.

"Can you actually wait here for a sec? I'm gonna grab something from my room." I hopped up.

"Sure!"

I knew without a doubt this was the first person I was supposed to give a copy of the book to. How wild that I was across the entire world, at a random hostel, in a country I was never originally supposed to be in, meeting someone who knew who I was. And as fate would have it, she was supposed to have left before I ever even arrived. This was the first time I had ever been recognized—and it happened across the freaking globe. What may seem like a superficial coincidence was enough to turn my entire morning around.

Because I knew it wasn't simply a coincidence—it was a sign. *Well... thank you, universe, that was quick.*

I returned with a copy of the book and handed it to my new friend, Nina, who was overjoyed to receive something that could relieve her boredom from not being able to move.

"Oh my God, I'm so excited!" she squealed.

"I only brought two copies. To give to special people I met along the way." I smiled.

"This is awesome. Seriously, thank you."

"No, girl, thank you. You totally just turned my whole morning around."

"What are your plans today?" she asked.

"I think I'm going to head to a café and just write for the day."

"Are you writing the sequel?"

"Slowly but surely." I chuckled. "You're welcome to come with me if you don't have any plans?" I offered.

"Oh my God, I'd love to. I'm so sick of sitting around the hostel. But..." She trailed off.

"What?" I asked.

"Is it weird if I bring your book to read?" We both laughed.

"No! That's amazing. We just have to find someone to drive us!" It felt like we'd been friends for much longer than a brief morning, and I knew she was someone I wanted to spend time with while I was in Pai.

We had a couple of the guys drop us at what would become one of my many sanctuaries in this town. The House Café was only a half mile from our hostel. Normally, I would have walked but since I was now accompanied by an immobile Nina, a chauffeured motorbike ride was necessary.

The House Café was at the end of a dirt road, tucked away in rice fields far from town or any other restaurants. The entrance was covered with greenery, an archway that welcomed you into the calm space where the sound of water trickled into the ponds that led you to the entrance. Ducks greeted you as they floated in the water, and the path brought you to the massive stairway entrance. The house itself was made mostly of stone and had huge windows and open-air spaces—it was the perfect blend of Thai soul and modern décor. If I ever built a dream house, it would look a lot like The House Café. And if you're ever in Pai the same time I am, there's a good chance you will find me there.

Nina and I found an area to sit and ordered some breakfast from the rather stern woman who owned the place. We would smile warmly at her, and she would look at us like she was contemplating killing us...and was 95% sure.

"Kap khun ka," Nina said as she took her meal from the serious woman who just nodded in return.

"What does that mean?" I asked.

"Thank you. And sawadee ka is used for, like, any hello or good-bye," she explained.

"Look at you!" I exclaimed.

"I mean, I've been here long enough to start learning it!"

We both began feasting on the beautiful food that had come to the table.

"So, this ex of yours, what's the story?" I asked.

"We were together for a while. I loved his family and his family absolutely adored me. I swear sometimes breaking up with the family is worse." We both laughed. I knew that all too well.

"Girl, I so feel you."

"Anyways, he just started to panic and gave me all these cop-out reasons for why he couldn't commit and be with me. It turned into this whole back and forth thing that I allowed to happen because I loved him and had this intense pull toward him. Kind of like your Javier."

"You seriously have no idea." I laughed. "That damn pull that makes you so stupidly blind to things you should never allow or accept."

"Yes! Exactly!" she agreed. "He also had a kid, so it added this whole other complicated layer."

"Ah. Yeah, I totally get that. Tyler has a kid too, and it completely changes the entire dynamic of it all."

"Who's Tyler?" she asked.

"The guy I've been on and off with for the last two years. He's 100% my soulmate, but I've always felt like there's something missing. But honestly, since the moment I got on the plane, I have felt this actual aching in my heart for him. A feeling I've never felt before. I miss him so much. I think about him constantly."

"What's he like?"

"The best fucking human you've ever met." I laughed. "We have so much fun together, he's so supportive and just loves me so unconditionally. I don't know what's wrong with me," I said.

"Well, maybe this trip is meant for you to find out." She smiled.

"Yeah. Whatever this trip is doing to me, it's big. I can feel it."

I opened my journal and began to write. She opened my book and began to read—we laughed. There were times she'd burst into laughter or gasp out loud, and I would stop writing and laugh as she told me what she was reading or how she related.

"Do you still talk to Javier?" she asked, after about an hour of reading.

"Isn't that the million-dollar question." I laughed out of the pure exhaustion that question—and that man—had brought to my existence.

"You don't have to answer."

"Oh, girl, it's a freaking saga. Actually, right before this trip, I decided not to talk to him or Tyler for the month," I explained.

As I divulged to my new friend what had gone down between Javier and me in the past few months, I realized how tired I was of telling this story. I was so tired of *him* being my story—and I was so tired of letting my feelings for him define me. I mean, it was really ridiculous. There I was, sitting across the world, writing a chapter about the final day I spent with this man—as my new friend read about our hot and heavy love affair two years earlier. It was then, sitting in my favorite café in Pai, Thailand, that I finally decided. Just like Daniel had so quickly become nothing more than a character in my story, it was time that Javier become the same. He was no longer the man who rocked my world, devastated my heart, changed my course, or kept me on the roller-coaster ride. He was Javier—the character from *Eat, Pray, #FML,* who so many readers around the world have experienced their own versions of. The character that made people want to scream, cry, and shake the living shit out of me. The character who allowed others to deeply identify with their own grief and therefore begin to address and heal it. And the character who, like it or not, was the catalyst to my biggest life's journey. But it was now time for the story to change its origin. Because what has bloomed from the ashes of the destruction of my heart is unequivocally due to the fact that it was *my heart* he broke—and *my* heart...*bloomed a fucking movement.*

We spent the entire day at The House Café. As I completed the chapter, I shut my journal and walked out onto the patio overlooking the rice field and smiled. I could feel it—I had truly let go. I looked back at Nina engrossed in the story that had started it all. *Full, fucking, circle.*

*****

The next three days were filled with delicious food, wonderous sites, and bonding with not only Nina, but Red, Paula (a sweet soul from Mexico with round cheeks and an infectious smile), and a few others that were staying at the hostel. Nina and I would usually start our day with breakfast at Earth Tone, which I completely blame for ruining all other smoothie bowls for me. Besides how colorful and artistic they looked arriving at your table, the fact that they are no more than $1.50 and completely shit on every $17.00 unimpressive smoothie bowl in Los Angeles makes it hard to ever justify buying one stateside again.

Every evening we would stroll through the whimsical night market, bumping into people we now knew as if we'd all lived in this little slice of heaven for much longer than a week. They call Pai "the piehole" because everyone who visits loves it so much, they end up choosing not to leave as planned. I had now become one of those people. Not only was I not changing hostels, I knew I wouldn't be leaving until I absolutely had to, and that was only because I had a retreat booked in Bali. Even Liz had found herself back in the piehole for a second time, and we laughed as we found ourselves in our second country together.

One day, Nina and I were strolling around town with two new guys from our hostel. Sawyer was a soft-spoken and mysterious type that almost every girl at the hostel was drooling over. Derek was traveling from Canada with an open mind and spiritual energy. Thankfully, Nina's knee was on the mend, and she was finally able to walk short distances. While we were getting money out of the ATM, I turned around and happened to look up. There, right in front of me, was a sign that read *Unicorn at Pai Resort*. I froze, looking up at the sign. Here, on a busy main street in Thailand, where hardly anything was in English, was the *one word* that connected Tyler and I most.

"What?" Nina snapped me out of my trance.

"That's what Tyler and I call each other," I told her.

"Shut up," she said.

"Seriously."

"It's a sign." She smiled.

"They seem to be everywhere on this trip. But this...I mean, come on."

Across the way, a tattoo shop caught my eye. I had asked my mother to write out the words *I love you* before I left because I was toying with the idea of getting a piece on my trip that included these words in her handwriting. I hadn't gotten one in over six years, so I was doubtful I'd actually go through with it, but Nina was wanting to get something small for her first one, so we all crossed the street to check it out.

Turns out Monkey Magic Tattoo is home to some world-known artists, and Red had gotten a huge back piece done by an artist there named Jeanne. I chatted with him about the idea I had in my head but wasn't totally 100% sure about. We agreed that he would draw up a few sketches for me and if I decided I didn't want it, I would just pay him for the artwork.

"Email me the images you want to use," he said as he headed to his computer. After handing him the writing my mom had done, which I kept in my journal, I sent him two things: a picture of the map art piece Tyler had made for me for my thirtieth birthday and the dedication words in *Eat, Pray, #FML*. Nina and I both made an appointment for the day after next, thanked Jeanne, and headed to grab a coffee.

Art in Chai was a whimsical indoor café that felt as if you had stepped into the pages of Aladdin. Cushions sat around the low and colorfully eclectic tables. Lights, teapots, and trinkets hung from the ceiling, and there were books stacked around, encouraging travelers to never leave. We ordered at the counter and took a seat in the corner on a low couch padded with boldly colored cushions.

As we sipped on the most satisfying chai my lips had ever tasted out of random mismatched mugs, the four of us talked about what our trips had brought us thus far and what we were hoping the remainders would bring.

"I really just want to figure out what direction I'm heading in. I feel like I don't really know what I want to do or where I want to be in life," Sawyer said. You could tell he took a bit to warm up to people. It was almost like he had a thin protective layer that was keeping him from truly connecting.

"I just want to travel, see the world and other cultures," Derek said as he went on to tell us about the month he'd just spent in the Philippines. He'd been traveling for months on a journey that had no real end date—which I was so incredibly jealous of. "I was only supposed to be in Pai for a few nights, but I just booked another week at the hostel." We all laughed because that was precisely what had happened to each of us.

"Anyone thinking of taking shrooms while we're here?" Sawyer asked. Magic mushrooms were about as common in Pai as oat milk lattes were in Los Angeles.

"I've only done them once and I thought I was legit going to die." I laughed. Seriously, my shroom experience felt like I was trapped in a horror movie and was never going to escape—not a fun time.

"I've never done them," Nina added.

"I haven't either, but I'm considering trying them. I mean, what better place than Pai, right?" Sawyer said.

"Maybe it will help you figure out what direction you're heading in." I smiled.

"What are you looking for on your trip, Gabrielle?" Derek asked.

I told the guys about Tyler and how I felt like I was on this big soul journey to really find what was missing. Not missing with him—

missing within myself. Just from the way I spoke about Tyler, they could see how much I cared for him and what a struggle it was being away from him and not speaking.

"Do you think you guys will get back together?" Derek asked. I sighed.

"I know that I can't even entertain going back to him in that way unless I am 100% sure. I can't do that to him all over again."

"Can I see what he looks like?" Nina asked. I grabbed my phone and pulled up a photo of him.

"He's Persian and Irish." I smiled, looking at his grinning handsome face.

"He's gorgeous," Nina added.

"That's crazy..." Derek said as he smiled at Sawyer.

"What is?" I asked.

"I'm Irish, and Derek is Persian," Sawyer pointed out. Everyone smiled as my mouth once again hung open.

"It's a sign!" Nina laughed.

See, here's the thing about signs. You can choose to ignore them and write them off as little random occurrences that are bound to happen now and again in your long lifetime—or you can choose to *fucking believe*. You can think that the one English word that means more to Tyler and me than any other hanging on a sign in Thailand is simply an arbitrary coincidence. Or that the two male friends sitting across from me just so happened to be the two things that make Tyler whole. You can even think that hearing The Cranberries' "Linger" in almost every location I had been in thus far was simply because Asia is apparently filled with nostalgic 90s fans. But isn't life so much more magical than that? Doesn't the universe get bored of letting us wander through life without throwing some unarguable messages in our paths? Because you see, my friends, it is only when we *believe* in the magic that our lives hold that we can truly decide to *create* that magic. And after all we've endured, survived, and overcome...I'd say that's all the proof we need.

As I sipped my chai and got lost in my thoughts, my ears focused on the soft background music that had been playing. *Want to take a guess what song it was?*

The Ridiculous Misadventures
of...
THE MAGIC CHAIR

The following morning, Nina and I headed into town with our day all mapped out, fulfilling the need to plan things that we were both genetically cursed with. Breakfast at the highly recommended OM Garden, coffee at Art in Chai, and some shopping in town.

We ordered and sat in the lush garden, with vines and flowers hanging all around us.

"I'm so glad you're staying an extra full day." I smiled at my new friend.

"I know. I'm so happy our paths crossed." She sipped on her green juice.

"Me too. Not to be weird, but you're definitely the person I've connected with the most on my trip." It was so nice to be saying that to a female, considering my solo Europe trip was definitely male heavy.

"Aw! I feel the same way." She smiled. *Ding.* Her phone got a message. "Sawyer said he's going to take shrooms today."

"I've been thinking about it since we talked about it yesterday." I laughed.

"I know, me too." She looked at me. A long pause as we both smiled.

"Oh God, are we doing shrooms today?" I asked.

"Yeah, I think we are." And just like that, our structured plans for the day went completely out the window...here goes nothing!

Derek was off on a day trip, so it ended up being me, Nina, and Sawyer. Paula took us over to one of the sun decks at the hostel, and we all sat in a circle surrounding the tray she had prepared: a bowl of the finely chopped mushrooms soaked in lemon juice, three small cups of honey with little spoons, and a box of cacao.

"Mushrooms are a medicine. In Mexico, we use them for getting in touch with the earth, to go on spiritual journeys, and accepting whatever the universe wants to bring you," Paula said in her thick Latin accent. "We feel that the medicine always knows how much you need and will bring you whatever your journey is supposed to be." She opened up the cacao. "The cacao is a heart opener. We eat this first to open your heart and put you in tune with love." She handed each of us one of the bitter chocolate balls. We ate them as we continued to take in every word she spoke.

Next, she handed us the honey cups.

"I would like to ask what each of your intentions are for this journey. We can start with you." She looked to Nina.

"Well, I mean firstly I just want to try it and open myself up to new experiences I might not try at home. But I guess to let go of expectations and fear. To trust in the unknown. That's what scares me. And not being able to control everything," she shared. Paula smiled.

"Beautiful. And you?" She looked at Sawyer.

"I didn't really have a set intention. I just wanted to experience something new," he said softly in his Irish accent. "Um...I guess to get out of my head a bit. I feel like I don't really have any direction in my life so maybe to accept the present and get some direction."

"Wonderful." She smiled warmly. "Gabriella?" I sighed and took a moment to let my heart tell me what my intention was.

"Clarity," I said after a few moments. I felt like every yoga class, meditation, and affirmation had all been searching for one thing—clarity.

"Clarity around what?" she questioned.

"Around a specific person and the path I'm on."

"Amazing." She nodded. Next, she instructed us to decide on a blessing to speak into our honey. We all closed our eyes and silently sent an intention, blessing, vibe, whatever you want to call it, into our honey. I sent the vibration of love and peace into my little cup of sticky goodness.

"Now pass your honey to each other so you all receive a different blessing for your journey." I handed mine to Nina, Nina passed hers to Sawyer, and I took his.

Paula handed us a deck of tarot cards and said if we were called to, we should pull one during our journey. She then said a prayer from her ancestors in Mexico City, and told us to eat the entire contents of the bowl. Spoon by spoon, we began to take sips of the mushroom lemon concoction with honey. It was honestly delicious. Shrooms are notoriously known for tasting like absolute ass, so the fact that we felt like we were eating some funky healthy dish at an organic café was phenomenal.

When the bowl was done, we thanked Paula for such a wonderful experience and headed over to the other side of the hostel to find a place to set up our little base camp. We found a great spot under a magnificent tree with three huge trunks that looked out onto the vast scenic view of rice fields, forest, mountains, and endless sky. Nina and Sawyer brought out their blankets and two pillows from their rooms, and we made our little spot under the tree.

"God. It's stunningly beautiful even without anything," I said. I wanted to appreciate the incredible beauty before any outside effects began.

"It really is," Nina said. "I don't feel anything, do you feel anything?"

"I feel tired," Sawyer said as he yawned, lying down. "What happens if I go to sleep?"

"I mean...I don't think you will—but if you mean is it safe, you won't like, die, no." I laughed.

I leaned back with my elbows supporting me to gaze out over this epic landscape that looked like a painting.

"This is what always makes me anxious, the not knowing when it's going to start part," Nina said. I gently put my hand on her arm.

"Okay, so anytime that thought comes up, just smile and breathe. It will physically calm you," I said to her.

"Oh, you feel something don't you?" she asked eagerly.

"I feel...good. Like, happy." That's the last fully sober moment I can recall. I'm not sure how it started but, somehow, we ended up in a hysterical fit of belly laughs. First me, then Nina, then finally, and rather begrudgingly, Sawyer. And when I say laughing, I mean tears rolling down our faces, barely able to breathe, *uncontrollable* laughing.

"You have such a shell protecting you, Sawyer," Nina managed to get out between massive amounts of giggles and not fully functioning motor skills. He really did. You could tell he was brought up in an environment where men were not meant to be emotional and expressive. Even at the ripe age of twenty-five, on psychedelic mushrooms, the wall Sawyer had built around his heart was holding strong.

"I don't even know why I'm laughing, nothing is funny!" Nina cried happy tears as we laughed and cried with her.

"Why don't we do this when we're not on drugs?" Sawyer said. "Like, just let ourselves laugh about nothing."

Minutes sometimes felt like hours. Long stretches of time felt like it didn't even happen. It was all so strange.

"I'm not sad, my eyes are just leaking!" Nina said, still in a total laughing fit.

"Me too!" I exclaimed.

We all finally took a breath and looked out at the scenic stretch before us. It was like someone had taken a stunning photo, then put the contrast, vibrancy, and saturation all the way up. The trees bled into more rows than existed and the wheat stalks swayed back and forth without any wind blowing. It was freaking *magical.* I wanted to lie down, but I felt like I would be missing so much beauty. When my body finally said, "Lie down, bitch, I can't keep you up anymore," I reclined and looked up at the massive tree branches that were hanging above us.

"You guys. This tree," I said, lost in the leaves. They lay down on each side of me to match my gaze. "The leaves look like when you fold a piece of paper, cut parts, and open it to make a pattern," I badly explained. Sober translation: a paper snowflake.

"It totally does!" Nina shrieked. We lay next to each other, watching the intricately designed leaves move around (without *actually* moving at all). "Did you guys ever see the show *Blue's Clues*?" she asked.

"Yeah, when I was like...eight." I laughed.

"You know when the guy used to go hunt for a clue and would have to jump into the painting?" she said through more hysterical laughs.

"Yeah..."

"It's like we're *in* that painting!" All three of us lost it. Because as funny as it was, it was totally freaking accurate in that moment.

Two other people who were staying at the hostel came over to check on us, and Nina and Sawyer sat up to chat with them. I stayed lying down. How were they having such a clear conversation right now? I was so *not* able to do that at the moment. I was lost in my thoughts. *Sit up, Gabrielle! You're missing the view!* my inner voice said. I sat up, still on the outside of the little circle my friends were sitting and talking in. I stared out into the field—it was so rich with color. I couldn't believe how breathtaking it was. Then I noticed a single chair off to my right.

I really want to go to that chair, my brain thought. *But it's really far*. In actuality, it was probably only about fifty feet from where we were sitting, right at the edge of the concrete foundation that had never been built on, looking out toward the view. I continued to look at the view in front of me as it moved, and I realized I was feeling as if we were on some type of swing. Like if a large rectangle area was hanging by four ropes and was just gently swaying back and forth. Yet I was completely aware that my ass was planted firmly on the non-moving earth below me. It seemed like I was wearing colored glasses, looking out at the nature before me. It was so intense that, for a moment, it almost made me panic. But then it hit me. It's *so* beautiful. Why would you not *want* to see the world in such beauty. No matter how intense or seemingly daunting it may be, why would you not choose to embrace it all? Isn't that what life is really all about? I knew I needed to write that revelation down.

"I feel like I'm high times thirty." Nina's voice pulled me out of the full-blown epiphany I was silently having. She and Sawyer were still having a totally deep conversation in a way I could not comprehend.

"I have to write it down," I announced as I forced my motor skills to function enough to dig through my bag to get my journal. Come on, hand, you can do it. Grab, the, pen...

Why would you not *want* to see it all through rose-colored glasses? It's a choice. Take the magnificent one.

I felt like it took a solid five minutes and way too much brain power to write those few sentences. *I wonder if I'll even be able to read it later*, I thought to myself. *God, I really want to go to that fucking chair.* I couldn't stop thinking about it. It felt like something was calling me, saying, "Yo, Gabrielle. All the answers are over here. What the hell are you waiting for?"

Nina and I began to chat, and our laughter suddenly turned into tears.

"I'm not sad but I need to cry," she said through tears.

"Same," I agreed.

"And you get it. We cry, we're emotional. That's why we're like the same person."

"I know. Honestly, I've needed this kind of cry for a while now. I don't know why I've been holding it in. I know it's good to cry, it's just...I don't know, it almost feels like whatever is inside of me won't get fixed by crying. It needs to be released another way," I explained.

"Yes! Me too. Mine is anger." She began to tell me some very heavy news about her family that she had been trying to deal with. I put my arms around her, and we both just held each other and cried.

I really want to go to that chair, my brain thought again as I looked over her shoulder at it. *But it's so damn far—and what if once I get there, I don't like it?* I thought.

"Guys," I announced to my two shrooming companions. "I've been thinking about going to that chair for what seems like five years."

"Then go!" Nina encouraged.

"I've actually had an entire conversation with myself about it." I laughed.

"What about?" Sawyer chimed in from the mental conversation he was having with the tarot card he had pulled.

"Well, it's like...really far. And if I make the journey to get all the way over there—what if I don't like it once I'm there? What if I get there and it doesn't measure up to my expectations? What if I don't like being alone?" I explained all the reasons I had come up with to keep myself from *not* going. "But I guess if I get there and I don't like it, I can always just...come back." I laughed as I discovered the simple notion.

"If you want to go to the chair, you should go to the chair," Nina declared.

"Yeah, you can always come back," Sawyer added.

I thought about it. Isn't that true of most things in life? We always let our conscious mind direct and dictate things—usually driven by *fear* that is *unfounded*. None of it is in our control. So why would we let the fear infiltrate our decisions, feelings, and beliefs? Maybe, just maybe, when we get to the chair, it will be *everything* we had ever hoped for—and *more*.

"I'm going to go to the chair," I announced. They cheered. We all laughed. I took a deep breath, grabbed my bag, and stood up.

"You're okay if I go?" I asked Nina, my promised buddy for this journey.

"Yes," she assured me.

Okay, Gabrielle. Let's go to the chair.

As I walked farther and farther away from my safety spot under my new friend, the tree, I questioned if I had made the right decision. *You can always go back*, I thought to myself. It was so interesting—any time I had *ever* done *any* form of drug, I had never wanted to be alone. It had always been (just like my former sober self) my biggest fear—being alone. Yet here I was, on a solo trip across the freaking world, *choosing* to walk away from my safety net and venture into the unknown. Well...fifty feet away at least.

It wasn't a straight walk—in fact, I had to climb down the edge of the grass-covered hill, walk across tons of little rocks, and make my way up the side of the cement platform just to get onto the stretch where my mystical chair sat. Mind you, this is all with bare feet, on psychedelic drugs. Ever play the game hot lava as a kid, where you pretend the ground is lava and you put pillows or whatever you could find on the floor and carefully jump from item to item, super wobbly, like a baby deer trying to walk for the first time? Yeah. That was me. It was a quest—and I was on it. When I *finally* emerged on the flat cement surface safe and sound, I felt like I had freaking conquered Mount Everest.

"You guys!" I turned back and waved to my friends who seemed like they were suddenly *really* far away. I put my arms up in a victory motion as they cheered and clapped.

"I feel like I'm in *The Neverending Story* where he has to go through the thingy!" I yelled over to them.

"What thingy?" Sawyer yelled back.

"You know, the thingy!" I said. There was no way I was going to find the words to explain that I meant the part where the boy crosses the giant sphinx statues in the desert, and he has to make it past before they shoot fire lasers out of their eyes. Huh. Writing this now makes me think that whoever wrote that film was on a way bigger shroom trip than I was currently on.

I continued across the cement clearing, now only a mere ten feet from the infamous chair. Just before reaching it, I turned back one more time. Okay, remember when Nina had joked about the landscape view looking like one of the paintings from the show *Blue's Clues*? Please pause your reading to google a clip of the actor saying, "Let's go!" giving a thumbs up, and jumping into the painting. Otherwise, you are totally depriving yourself of how freaking hilarious this next part is.

"Nina!" I exclaimed as I started to laugh hysterically.

"What?" she shouted back.

"I'm jumping into the painting!" I gave a wave, an overly dramatic thumbs up, and pretended to jump into the backdrop. We all died laughing. I can't even imagine what witnessing this as a sober person must have looked like.

I turned back around, took a few final steps, and made it to the chair. I felt like I had just won the fucking Olympics. I sat down, put Trevor Hall on shuffle, and looked out into the distance.

I don't really know how to explain what took place over the following...hour? Maybe? It honestly felt more like five. I don't know how it started but, as I looked out onto the heavenly landscape, it somehow turned into a tunnel. The space to the right and left of me was no longer flat and linear. It was as if I was in a sphere of the landscape. It was so intense. I felt like I was lost. I began to cry, thankful that I felt I could finally let it out all by myself. It felt good—it felt needed. Then my mind started to think—about Tyler. When I thought about him, my whole being felt such a profound feeling of pure love. Like, this feeling is what my mother must have felt when she held me for the first time. That was how it felt when I thought of Tyler. Pure, enveloping love. It was overwhelming. My mind started to go through different thoughts and scenarios, questioning my feelings and decisions and asking me to dig deeper. Then, as if my subconscious took form and yelled the answer at me, I heard it—clear as fucking day. So clear, I grabbed my journal and wrote it down.

When it comes down to it: I can change all my surroundings, all my exterior factors—but what is the constant? I love him. All roads, somehow, someway—lead back to him. Because he is home.

Wow. I mean *WOW*. The love I felt was so intense, so all encompassing. And it was true. Every road I had ventured down away from him—whether it was to be alone, with Javier, or apparently to Asia—they all somehow led my heart back to Tyler. Then a thought came in. *What if he's at home with someone else? With Nicole?* It literally made me feel sick. The warm tunnel went away, and my surroundings suddenly felt flat and cold. I forced my brain to go elsewhere.

You can't control that. Let it go, I said to myself. Woosh—I was back in my tunnel. My brain felt like it was swimming through thick pudding, searching for some big piece of important information. It was so close—I could feel it. *What am I missing?* It felt like I was one step away from grabbing a key that would unlock some giant well of answers. And then—I gasped inward. I had found it.

I've been asking for clarity this whole time. I'm clear. I know it's him. I'm just afraid of the epicness that it is.

It was powerful, profound, and clear. I just have to let go and fall. I know he'll catch me. I know he won't abandon me. Why on earth has my conscious self not let me get there? *But what if he's with someone else?*

Bam. Anxiety. Panic. *No, Gabrielle, you can't control it. Let it go.*

Woosh—back in the tunnel. I continued to let my thoughts, tears, and this feeling of overpowering love flow out of me as I got lost in the vibrant visuals of the beautiful picture-perfect environment in front of me.

After what seemed like forever, the last song on my playlist ended. As the music disappeared, the tunnel dissolved away, and the scenery was flat again. I knew my time in the chair had been completed, and I had gotten a huge piece of information from a deep part of my subconscious.

I slowly stood up and turned around to start the journey back to my safe little tree and trusted companions. As my gaze found our spot and focused, I realized no one was there. I was most definitely still tripping—hard. And I was, most definitely, all alone. Oh...*Fuck.*

The Ridiculous Misadventures

of...

COMING BACK TO EARTH

After what seemed like a journey across the Sahara Desert, I successfully made it back to the safety of the massive tree that our little blanket lay underneath. As I sat there, totally alone, I internally attempted to convince myself not to panic.

Just as my inner convincing was about to epically lose the battle, I heard a voice.

"Gabrielle!" the voice shouted.

Um...is that real or is the tree talking to me?

"Gabrielle, I'm coming!" the voice said. I looked up to see none other than Sawyer waving at me from the upper level of the hostel building.

Oh, thank God. It's not a tree, and I'm not alone to deal with the drug-induced workings of my messed-up brain.

"How was the chair?" Sawyer said as he plopped down beside me. "Was it everything you imagined?"

"It was pretty magical. I've never experienced anything like it, actually." I looked at what he was holding in his hands. "What's that?"

"An angel card from the deck Paula gave us. I can't stop staring at the picture. I've been lost in it for...actually, I don't know. How long were you gone?"

"It felt like five hours." I laughed.

"You should pick a card too!" He was suddenly so much more open and engaging.

"Where's Nina?" I asked, looking around.

"Here I am!" Her little frame popped out from around the corner.

As I breathed a sigh of relief, knowing our little group had found its way back to each other, the magic little mushrooms began to (thankfully) wear off. I can still, as spiritually amazing as this trip was, confirm that they are *not* the drug for me.

We decided to walk it off and head to the night market to get some food into our systems. Red joined us, a professional at all things mushrooms, eager to hear how our journeys had been. The four of us laughed, ate, and continued to dissect the different experiences we'd all had.

"I'm so jealous. I feel like you both had this crazy spiritual awakening and mine was just, fun," Nina whined.

"Maybe that's the lesson—to let go of control and just have fun." I smiled back at her. I had spent almost a week with Nina and if I had learned anything about her, it was that she, like yours truly, had a serious need to control things. It was time for both of us to let that shit go. Ironically, that's what I hate about mushrooms—you feel *completely* out of control.

"Look at this photo from today." I pulled up a photo I had taken of the view from our little tree spot that looked just as magnificent as it had on psychedelics. Three massive beams of light spurted out from the white cloud.

"Oh my God, what a freaking shot!" Nina beamed.

"That's incredible. It reminds me of my family," Sawyer said, still feeling the end of his trip.

"What do you mean?" I asked, slightly confused how the scenic photo reminded him of that.

"The three rays remind me of the three strong women in my family. My mother, my sister, and my grandma. We just lost my grandma earlier this year."

"Oh, I'm so sorry." Nina put her hand on his shoulder.

"I feel like this is all of them watching over me."

"I love that," I said.

"Me too." He smiled.

We walked the night market as I waited for the residual foreign feeling to fully leave my body. Back at the hostel, Sawyer again insisted Nina and I pull one of the angel cards he had been so entranced with. I did—and this is what it read.

This oracle comes to you with a special message. You are an inspiration. You are helping those around you and even many of whom you are unaware. You are doing this because this is your path, this is your way, this is your gift. You're also being gifted through this oracle with a sign: an issue too difficult for you to understand, no matter how hard you have been working on it, is about to be resolved. You have no need to hold on to it or become 'more worthy' of that resolution. It is going to happen. Your job is to allow it to happen, to simply bear witness to the resolution, even if you have no idea what is going on in the process.

I held the card in my hands and smiled as I read it out loud to my new friends. Nina's mouth hung open, and Sawyer smiled. It was a pretty clear sign that everything I was searching for, asking for, hoping for—was on its way to me.

The next morning, after a much-needed night of rest, I woke up to a missed called from Tess. For some reason, it always made me inherently panic to receive a call from the States instead of a text, so I immediately called her back.

"What's up?" I waited.

"I talked to Tyler..." she began. Shit. I had totally forgotten that while in shroom land I had asked her to do best friend recon and find out if he was okay, how he'd been doing, and, yes, if he was dating someone.

"Okay." My heart immediately started racing.

"He's doing better. He's been having a tough time not talking to you and asked if you were okay. But he said he's been staying busy, spending time with Blue, and trying to get his life back on track." I smiled as my best friend explained from thousands of miles away.

"Good. I'm so happy to hear that."

"He did say he was trying to date. He didn't really go into detail but the way he explained it was that he's dating but no one that he's like...you know...riding off into the sunset with." My heart dropped out of my ass. I let out a big sigh because I knew there was not a damn thing I could do about it—and furthermore, I was the one who had fucking created all of it.

"Okay. Thanks, Tess. I appreciate it," I said, and she heard my hurt through the phone.

"Gabs. He then said, 'There's always going to be a piece of my heart that is waiting for her.'" I took that in.

"Thank you," I told my friend as a little piece of my heart looked up at me from the inside and smiled.

"Of course. I hope you're having an amazing time. We can't wait to have you home."

After breakfast, Nina, Sawyer, Derek and I decided to go on one last adventure before Nina had to leave the following day. We walked on the bamboo bridge through rice fields at the Santichon Village. We rode a human powered Ferris wheel (which is exactly as unique yet mildly terrifying as it sounds), sat on hanging swings that looked out over miles of views while we sipped on tropical smoothies, took photos, laughed, and talked for hours. We very quickly had become the Four Musketeers, and everyone was sad to be losing Nina the next day. But there was one more thing on the agenda before our day around our new favorite place was complete—a tattoo.

To be honest, I wasn't sure I was going to go through with it. In fact, I had been pretty certain that I was going to thank Jeanne for whatever artwork he had drawn up for me, pay him for his time, and let Nina get her first tattoo.

We walked into the shop where Jeanne greeted us with excitement—and I soon found out why. He presented me with his drawing and my whole body froze. It was an image of the map and compass that Tyler had made me for my thirtieth birthday, with my mom's "*I love you*" tucked inside the compass. The main middle line of the compass had been changed to the unalome symbol, which uses spirals to represent the twists and turns in life, leading to the path of enlightenment in the Buddhist culture. And last but not least, the first words I had written in *Eat, Pray, #FML: To the ones who loved me, broke me, lost me, and healed me. You're all the reason I found myself, and for that—I thank you.*

There was not even a question in my mind—I was getting this on my body. It was a decent size, and I decided it would go on the upper center of my back. This tattoo in LA would have been a minimum of $800.00, even more at a well-known shop. In Pai, it was a whopping $99.

I lay on my stomach, the leather table that was in the back of the small shop beneath me, my crew of three accompanying me. As Jeanne prepped the ink and the image, Nina looked at me.

"You realize you're about to get a piece of Tyler put on you—forever," she said. I thought about that for a moment. Because even though someone may not know that image was a direct relation to this person in my life—or the significance it had—I knew. And that was a big deal.

"Yeah. I do," I finally said with a smile. No matter where he and I ended up, he had taught me so very much about this crazy thing that we call life. How to give and receive love in a healthy way. How to laugh until I cried and my stomach hurt. How to never accept *anything* less than I deserve. So yes—it was the *perfect* reminder to keep with me forever.

I took a deep breath, turned on my music, and zoned out as the needle dug into my back for more than an hour. When all was said and done, I looked at the art I had gotten in my new favorite place on earth—and smiled.

"It's perfect."

The Ridiculous Misadventures of...

THE FUCKING LESSON

After saying a tearful goodbye to Nina, who was off to Vietnam now that her knee was good enough to continue her journey, I was headed back to my favorite writing spot, The House Café. On one of the sides there was a riser with a small table, two floor cushions, and views of the pond and greenery all around. I sat and wrote for hours, basking in the glory of comfortable loose-fitting clothes, delicious tea, and no one to answer to except my pen and paper. A bit later, a message from Sawyer came in.

Sawyer: Are you still at the café? I'm walking back from town.

Me: I am. Probably staying another hour or so.

Sawyer: Do you mind if I come join you? I actually wanted to do some writing.

Me: Of course! I'll see you soon.

Since our journey into the psychedelic world, Sawyer had become a totally different (and amazing) version of himself. What was once a quiet, timid soul became an open, invigorated, and expressive human—and it was fucking *awesome* to witness.

He joined me and the two of us sat, both writing, at the serene café I had come to know so well. God, I was going to miss this place.

"Can I read you what I wrote?" Sawyer broke the soundtrack of nature around us.

"Please!" I smiled. It really felt like I was witnessing this human evolve into the person he was always hoping he could be, right in front of my eyes.

"From Hanoi to Pai, days that never end, to days that speed by. This is my journey, from darkness into light."

As he finished reading me the intimate and beautiful words he had put to paper, my eyes lit up and my heart felt full.

"That was so beautiful, dude. Have you ever written before?"

"Never." He chuckled in his Irish accent. "But I've always wanted to. You inspired me."

"What do you mean?"

"I can see how your writing has given you an outlet and changed you as a person. You're so open with everyone you meet—I want to be like that too," he answered.

"Well, thank you. I'm really proud of you. I seriously feel like you've become a totally different person within the last week."

"I feel like I have too. It's amazing. I finally feel like I have some sense of direction in my life. That no matter where I end up, I'll be okay."

"I can't wait for your friends and family back home to meet this new you," I said, smiling at the once-reserved man who had just read truthful, beautiful poetry to me.

After another hour, I said goodbye to Sawyer until our final dinner we had all planned that night. I was heading to town to meet Liz for lunch. I would be heading to Bali next, where she had begun her trip, and knew this would probably be our final time together on this journey. I walked to town with my music in my ears and my thoughts flying around. I had just written a chapter about Tyler. It was so much harder to write about him than it was to write about Daniel or Javier—and I had no idea why. Whatever the reason, it tugged at the aching in my heart that longed for my best friend, which the past few days in Pai had been doing quite a good job at masking.

We sat down across from each other at yet another secret garden style café. After ordering, my new travel sister looked at me.

"What's wrong?" she so poignantly asked.

"I just really miss him. I've never felt like this before," I said.

"So why don't you reach out to him?"

"I can't. There are still too many questions and fears I have to sort through. And I need to do that on my own." I felt my tears coming to the surface.

"Yeah, I understand. Are you afraid he's dating someone else?" she asked. The question jabbed at my heart, hearing it out loud.

"Yes. I know he is. I just don't know to what extent. More than anything, I just want him to be happy. He deserves that." My tears were now creating lined stains on my face.

"Trust the universe, girl. It's always led you exactly where you need to be, hasn't it?"

"It has. It's me who fucks it all up." I laughed as I wiped my tears away. "I just haven't ever felt this type of physical ache for someone—and I don't know how to fix it."

"Maybe there's nothing to fix. Maybe you're supposed to feel it until you come to a conclusion. But it's really clear how much you care about him. I'm rooting for him, and I don't even know him." We both laughed. How lucky was I to have a friend across the entire world that I was able to just sit and cry with? Yes, Pai had been magical, spiritual, and fun—but it had also been undoubtedly difficult because it had made me stop, breathe, and really look at myself. And that...was scary.

I hugged Liz goodbye and hopped on the back of Red's scooter. A group of us, including Derek and Sawyer, headed up to the massive lookout I had gone to when I first arrived. I was sad to be leaving these people, this place. I could have spent the rest of my trip there and been totally content. Red and I hugged and took a photo overlooking the city that had completely captured my heart.

For our last night, we went to dinner at one of our favorite spots. It was on the corner, right where the main night market street started, across from the two-dollar hour-long foot massage place we frequented as much as possible. It had live music mixed in with an eclectic array of songs that played in between their sets. As we sat, ate, and people watched, we indulged in some of the fantastic handcrafted cocktails. A group of girls who'd had their eyes on Sawyer since he'd arrived in Pai walked by on the street and side-eyed me.

"You sure are a hot commodity." I laughed, nodding toward the group of girls.

"They've been pretty relentless."

"Just not interested?" I asked.

"I mean, I'm not really looking for anything serious right now, and they aren't really my type."

"What's your type?" I sipped my drink.

"Uh...I mean...kind of like you? In a not-awkward way." He laughed. "Like if I was back home you would be someone I would date."

"You know a few of my girlfriends messaged me when they saw that picture I posted and asked if we were hooking up."

"Really? Why?"

"Cause you're kind of my type too. If I even have a type. Definitely my travel type." I laughed.

"I know how much you're going through and how much you're struggling with Tyler. So, I would have never attempted anything. And I really connect with you as a friend," he said genuinely. I smiled.

"Cheers to that, friend." We clinked glasses and I leaned my head on his shoulder.

Just then, the song that was played constantly in Pai and therefore constantly on Derek's cell phone when on our adventures, started to play.

"Yessss!" Derek smiled as the song began.

I hopped up from the cushions at our low table, set my drink down, and ran into the now less busy street. I danced with the owner of the restaurant, some random people that were heading home, and the energy in the streets of Pai. I felt at home.

Once we finally arrived back at the hostel after a few cocktails, my first since the party cruise, we found the photographer from Germany sitting down by a fire that had been built earlier in the night. We all sat and talked for a while before deciding to stargaze. Let me paint this hilarious picture for you: Three men (and me) lying side by side flat on our backs, on the cold ground, with one thin-ass blanket covering us as we gazed up at the most brilliant sky you've ever seen. I had Trevor Hall playing on my phone (because I had gotten everyone hooked on him by this point), and the four of us just lay there, silent, looking up at what has always made me remember what tiny and seemingly insignificant little blips we are on the grand scale of the universe.

As the minutes passed, everyone was forced to huddle tighter together so as to not freeze in the cold Pai night. I was on the end, with Sawyer on my right. Eventually, the German photographer said goodnight, and we were left with our little group of three. Then Derek retired to warmth, and Sawyer and I were left alone. The music soaked into our souls as we counted shooting stars flying across the sky. And then, out of absolutely nowhere, I grabbed Sawyer's hand. We lay there for what seemed like another thirty minutes, squeezing each other's hands tightly until I tugged on his arm and pulled him over to wrap around me. It wasn't sexual. It felt like, without words, I said, *I need to be held right now because I miss him so much.* And without hearing it, he answered, *You're safe, I'll hug you for him.*

When the cold had infiltrated us beyond what we could handle, we headed back to the main area of the hostel. Sawyer looked at me.

"I don't know what to do," he said.

"What do you mean?" I asked.

"We just had that talk at dinner...but, I mean, you're gorgeous and I care about you."

I looked at him, thinking. Then I put my arms around him. He squeezed me tightly and we stood there for a long minute just breathing.

I know what you're probably all thinking: *Oh, great, Gabrielle, didn't you learn this lesson in Vietnam already? This isn't going to lead anywhere good.* To be completely honest with you, Sawyer did genuinely care about me as a person—and that feeling was mutual. And quite frankly, he is someone, even now looking back on it all, I could have trusted with my heart. Was I longing for that connection? Yes. Was I sad and wanting to feel better? Definitely. But all I could think of in this moment, for once, *was myself.* I had learned my lesson: *I will never break in order to falsely protect myself, ever again.*

"I don't know if I should kiss you or not," he finally said, breaking me out of my thoughts. A pause.

"Let's say goodnight," I said, looking at him.

"Okay." He smiled.

"Okay." I smiled back.

That night, I went to sleep in my own bed, with a new sense of total empowerment. The old Gabrielle would have felt so lonely, she would have used that opportunity to be close to someone—even if it wasn't the answer. But here I was, my last night in Pai, reveling in the fact that even with the loneliness, the abandonment fears, and the dangling bait...I had finally learned the fucking lesson: *I, am, enough.*

The Ridiculous Misadventures

of...

LEAVING COMFORT

I opened my eyes after not nearly enough sleep and came to the sobering realization that this would be my last day in Pai. This place had unintentionally become my home over the past week and a half, and I was so not ready to leave it. In fact, it flat-out scared me. Pai had ripped my heart wide open, forced new perspectives on me, and healed a part of me that was buried so deep I never even knew it existed.

As my body continued to wake up, I remembered what had taken place with Sawyer a few hours before. It was so strange—every girl at the hostel had been pining over him and swooning over his Irish accent. But over the past seven days, I had gotten to know his soul, and that was what had made me reach for his hand the night before. I did, however, feel like we needed to talk about it so there were no misunderstandings.

"Morning." He smiled as I walked into the common area, looking out at the view I had never really gotten used to but appreciated so much.

"Morning." I smiled back. There seemed to just be an understanding between us.

"What time do you leave?"

"My bus leaves at two," I answered with a sadness in my voice.

"We'll take you." He motioned to Derek, who was pouring a cup of tea.

"Okay. I want to hit Art in Chai one more time before I leave."

"Perfect. After our session?" he asked.

"Great. And uh...maybe you and I should go first and chat about last night?" I offered.

"Yes. Definitely. But we're good." He smiled.

"I know." I smiled back.

That day the hostel had a man coming who did light and sound therapy. It's a meditation practice that uses noise canceling headphones to play sounds that match the beat and rhythm of a bright light flashing on your closed eyelids. Sawyer, Derek, and I had signed up to do it together, and I had no idea what to expect.

After making sure none of us were epileptic or had a history of seizures, the man took us into one of the empty upper-level rooms, where we lay side by side on a big mattress. When I was sandwiched in the middle of my two new friends, he explained to us that if it ever became too intense to raise our hand and let him know, and that it was normal to feel our eyes flicker vigorously.

"Sometimes you will see vivid pictures like you're dreaming. Some people just see colors and shapes that have certain feelings attached to them."

We put our headphones on, looked at each other as if to say, *When in Pai,* and closed our eyes. The music suddenly overwhelmed my eardrums, and I felt the intense light pulsing at my eyelids. I could feel my arms touching Sawyer and Derek on each side of me, but after a few moments, all my senses felt as if they were gone and I was in a green tunnel. It was so intense at first, as I felt my eyeballs wiggle in their sockets, that I thought for a moment I was going to have my first seizure. *This has to be what it feels like,* I thought. I took a deep breath and tried to relax into it all. Then the tunnel started to dance. It was like I was free-floating in the universe, in my purest form—no body, just energy, the way I imagine we exist when we die. The beat of the music shifted, and the visuals became vibrant reds, oranges, and yellows. It morphed into what looked like a big fireball, but it felt like something very different—it felt like *anger.* I watched as I continued to breathe deeply, and my body twitched. *Why anger?* I asked my subconscious. Just then, a bright green ball of fire broke off the sunlike circle and separated itself like an amoeba. *Let the anger go,* I heard as the red began to disappear and the electrifying green ball became larger and larger until it was all I saw. I stayed in the green heaven for the rest of the time, although I had no concept of how long it actually was.

When the music finally subsided and the intense light faded out, I wiggled my toes to get the feeling of being back in my body. The three of us sat up, looked at each other, and tried to gather what our different experiences could mean.

"I felt like I was traveling through space at the speed of light. Like I was the light. It was amazing," Derek said.

"I was traveling down a river in this huge canyon," Sawyer said.

"Wow, you saw actual images?" Derek asked, intrigued.

"Yeah, it was like an actual dream. Gabrielle, what did you see?"

"I saw energy. And emotion. In color," I told them.

I went inside to pack up all of my things, then headed out to sit on the edge of the lookout platform in the main area of the hostel. *What anger am I still holding?* I asked myself. I mean, my ex-husband is a dick, but I don't really feel anger toward him anymore. Javier and I have had a long road of exhausting emotions, but we left things on a good note—and I know everything with him changed me and my life. I don't feel anger toward him. Tyler is the exact opposite of anger—so who the hell is left? *Me. What if it's me I'm angry at?* One last Thought Onion in my new favorite place. Superficial thought?

- You're an idiot who left the best man on this planet, and he's probably currently falling in love with some incredible woman who actually deserves him.

Jesus, harsh much, Gabrielle? I mean, yes, I was in fact angry at myself for not being able to figure out what seemed to be missing in an otherwise perfect relationship. It was frustrating, infuriating, and incredibly confusing. Authentic thought?

- Maybe you're the problem. Maybe you're just too damn broken from Daniel and Javier.

The potential truth of that thought scared the shit out of me—and it angered me. I hadn't really *done* anything to deserve what had happened to me in my past two relationships. Daniel would stomp his feet and tell you our marriage crumbled because we weren't having sex. But that's what a narcissist will do—make you feel like the fact that he chose to have a six-month relationship and many other extramarital affairs was, *of course*, your own fault. Javier, however, would tell you that I'd done nothing wrong. Not one mistake or misstep, even in the aftermath of it all. He would tell you that I'm amazing and that I changed his life—that I in no way deserved to be broken the way he and Daniel had so carelessly broken me. So why on earth did I feel that way? What was under it all?

• I'm now the one abandoning—because I have to protect myself.

Holy shit. It hit me like a fucking semi-truck but made so much goddamn sense. I had been abandoned by every man I had ever loved. My father, my high school sweetheart, my husband, Javier. It was the pattern and fear I had dealt with my entire life—and after 2017, it had become too much for me to handle. So, when a deep, meaningful, strong love came into my life? I fucking panicked—to the point where I abandoned someone I loved. That notion was utterly devastating to me—and it all made sense. I was *so angry* at myself for all of it. Angry that I didn't heal faster, angry that I felt like I had to run, angry that I didn't know how the hell to fix it. It was time to let it go. Time to be compassionate with myself. Time to listen to the lyrics of the song that had affected me so deeply my second night in Pai. *Stop rushing your healing, Gabrielle.* Let yourself learn from the darkness and heaviness you've been walking through. Love, if it's real, isn't going anywhere. Let the anger go. Let yourself be.

I said goodbye to Paula, Red, and the others I had come to know at the hostel.

"I wish you didn't have to leave. I'm going to read your book," Red said, hugging me.

"Here." I smiled, handing her the second copy I had brought with me. "Just leave it at the hostel when you leave. I want it to stay where I healed."

"You got it." She winked at me.

I hopped on the back of Sawyer's motorbike, and we headed into town for one last cup of the best chai I have ever tasted.

We sat in the corner of the café that felt like it was straight off the pages of a fantasy novel. Normally, this type of conversation would be wildly awkward, but neither of us seemed to be nervous or uncomfortable with any of it.

"Do you wanna start or should I?" I laughed.

"Honestly, Gabrielle, I don't feel confused about it at all. I feel like it brought us closer together and it was a nice moment to share. I know you're missing Tyler and having a lot of emotions around it all, and I was happy to be there for you in whatever way that was."

I had to admit, for a twenty-five-year-old, he was extremely self-aware and mature. I don't know if he would have given the same answer a week ago, before he'd had such an intense spiritual awakening.

"I mean, it's not like I'm not attracted to you, of course I am. You're beautiful inside and out, but I know your heart is elsewhere, so my mind never went anywhere past the friendship we've created. It caught me a bit off guard, and if I hadn't come to know you so well and what you're dealing with, I probably would have kissed you last night. But I care about you as a friend and a human, so I'm really glad we didn't do anything to compromise that," he told me, as if we'd been friends for much longer than a week.

"I agree with everything you just said. I don't know what happened. I think I was just wrestling with some feelings of loneliness and missing that connection. It felt good lying there with you and holding your hand—like a best friend that was protecting me. I didn't mean for any lines to get crossed. I am missing Tyler—a lot. And I would never want to muddy the waters of the friendship we've created."

"I'm so glad I met you. I've changed so much during my time here," he said.

"I can see it. We've all seen it. You're like a totally different and better version of yourself." I smiled.

Derek arrived and we all sat, reminiscing on the time we had spent in this wonderful place. Nina had left three days earlier and now it was my time to say goodbye. Every time you leave a new place on your travels, it feels like you're going through a breakup. You look forward to the exciting possibilities the next relationship might hold, but you wonder if you're making the right decision in leaving— or if you should stay and just marry the goddamn place.

We rode over to market street, and they dropped me at the bus stop. I hugged Derek goodbye first.

"I seriously hope I see you again, Gabrielle. You're a rock star. Keep in touch."

"Same here, dude. So glad we met."

Then I turned to hug Sawyer—it was a much longer, tighter hug.

"I'm so glad I met you. I'm gonna miss you," he said softly in my ear.

"Me too. I'm so proud of you." I felt like I was saying goodbye to my brother who had grown exponentially in front of my eyes.

I hopped onto the bus and told myself not to cry. As we started the three-hour trek down the winding road, I sent a photo of our hostel view to Sawyer.

Me: This is from our trip day. So you have your family photo.

Sawyer: Thank you so much. It's not the same without you.

Me: Yeah, I'm feeling it. It's weird. I don't know why I feel very connected to you. Like very certain our paths were supposed to cross. But usually when I meet people like that, it's instant. It wasn't with you. But I feel like I'll miss your energy. Not sure how to really explain it in words.

Sawyer: I feel the same. I can't describe it in words either. It's very strange, something I haven't experienced before. I'm very happy that we spent time together. You allowed me to express myself and feel comfortable doing so, which is out of the ordinary for me. So, thank you for that.

Me: Same. I'm so glad we all came together, and I'm happy to have you in my life. Missing you guys already.

Sawyer: Likewise. I'm sure it's only the beginning of a long friendship between everyone. Anytime you want to chat about absolutely anything, do not think twice about picking up the phone or writing me.

Me: Thank you. Same to you.

Sitting at the airport, I suddenly felt like I was about to have a full-blown panic attack. *Maybe I'll just cancel the silent retreat and go back to Pai.* I knew that wasn't really a practical option since the retreat was paid for and my flight home was from Bali. I had to make it there at some point. Still, this unwavering anxiety bubbled in the pit of my stomach. My heart ached for Tyler—not the boyfriend, the best friend. I grabbed the rock he had given me the day I left on my trip. Looking down at it, I realized the anxiety was because I was officially leaving comfort. Not only was I leaving comfort, I was entering into three days of silence where I would be with the one person I was most afraid to be truly alone with—myself.

I posted a photo of the rock in my hands on my Facebook with the caption, "Currently leaving comfort." As the plane took off, my chest tightened, and my breath felt fleeting. I clutched the rock tightly in my hand and shut my eyes. I sent energy from my heart to Tyler. *Hey, dude. I just really need a sign. I need a sign that I'm okay and that we're still connected. I need to know you're still here.*

I wiped tears from my eyes, took a deep breath, and opened up my photos on my phone. I scrolled back—way back—to photos of Tyler and me. Our heavenly trips to Hawaii, camping, Lake Arrowhead. I looked at his eyes, smiling back at me. I looked at the way he seemed to be holding onto me for dear life in the happiest way possible. Back to our first New Year's Eve together in 2017. Back to the first photos we had ever taken together when we met filming on set in Michigan. I only had three of them on my phone that I had saved from the director's Facebook when we had started dating. We had both changed so much and yet not at all at the same time. I stared at those three old photos during our descent as the music that had become my calming balance played in my ears.

As I stood waiting for my bag to appear on the carousel in Bali, I connected to Wi-Fi to let Nina and Liz know I had made it. Three Facebook notifications popped up on my screen. *That's weird, it's like 2 a.m. in LA*, I thought as I clicked on the blue icon.

Tyler Thomas liked three photos you're tagged in.

My jaw dropped. I stood, frozen, looking at the exact three photos I had been staring at on the plane. Photos that could only be found in the utter depths of Facebook. Photos that were taken back in 2010. Photos of Tyler and me.

You asked for a sign, Gabrielle. Here it fucking is.

The Ridiculous Misadventures of...

SILENCE

I awoke the following morning after my one-night stay at an Airbnb close to the airport. In two hours, I would be picked up to head to the silent retreat, where I'd be putting away my cell phone, headphones, and my voice for three days. Three days might not seem like that big of a deal to some, but to disconnect in such a way, without the music that had been keeping me grounded for the past week, without conversing with random strangers who may or may not become friends, was scary.

I rolled over and looked at my phone. I had a message from Tess.

Tess: Tyler texted me. Do you want to know what he's been saying or no?

For whatever reason, the way I read this text immediately gave me the surge. *What if he's telling her he met someone and fell in love? What if he's finally realized I suck at life and have been dragging him through emotional hell and wants nothing to do with me anymore? What if he's not okay?* I'm notorious for letting my brain play out all the worst possible scenarios with little to no proof that anything of the sort is *actually happening.* Talk about a trauma brain.

Me: Was it late last night?
Me: Call me.

After all, the night before I had received that massive sign too coincidental for reasonable explanation. I waited—and waited. No answer. Cue the panic scenarios escalating.

Me: I'm at this villa for the next two hours before I head up to the silent retreat so call me as soon as you can.

Me: Tess, you're killing me. You have to check your phone if you're going to send a text like that!

The anxiety I was already feeling about disconnecting from the world was now majorly amplified awaiting this piece of information. The driver from the retreat arrived, and I headed out to load up my stuff. I sat in the backseat and stared out the window while I had a complete conversation with myself in my head. *He's gone. He's totally gone. He went on another date with Nicole Conrad, fell madly in love, went away to spend a week in a cabin together, and is now telling Tess he needs me to never contact him again. I'm going to puke.*

Me: I have an hour and a half drive right now before I have to put my phone away. Please call me when you get this.

As we drove closer and closer, I realized that there was a very good chance that I would be entering this already unnerving situation with no clarity about the outlandish scenario I had created, which I now completely swore by and believed. Just as we were making our way up the final fifteen-minute hill to the grounds, my phone buzzed.

Tess: Omg I'm so sorry! I'm on a date!

Fucking time change.

Tess: He said this:

A photo came through. It was the photo I had posted on my Facebook of my little petrified hand clutching the heart-shaped rock. Tyler's message was underneath the screenshot: *Where is she going? That's the rock I gave her right before she left. Wherever she finds herself...please tell her that I'm right there. ALWAYS.*

Tears came to my eyes. *He felt it. He felt when I sent him that energy on the plane yesterday. He isn't gone. He hasn't left. He hasn't abandoned me.* I laughed as I realized how ridiculous my trauma brain scenarios were and how much unnecessary anxiety I had caused myself for the last four hours.

Me: Oh, thank God. I thought it was something bad.

Tess: Nooo I'm sorry! I was making out in the car with a guy, I'm sorry! Lol.

Me: Hahaha! Yes, can't wait to hear about all that. For the rest of the trip, if he messages you, don't tell me. I just need to focus. But the craziest thing happened last night.

I sent my best friend a voice note about what I had done on the plane, the photos I looked at, and the Facebook notifications once I landed.

Tess: Oh yeah. He's super in sync with you. It's wild how he can feel things. It's crazy.
Tess: Have an amazing time at the retreat! Love you!

I read this last message as we pulled into the drop-off area. Instead of panic, I suddenly felt totally at ease. I felt like my soul had gotten a hug from its mate back home with that simple message he had written. *I'm right there. ALWAYS.*

I checked in with one of what the retreat calls Office Angels, and she began my orientation. Bali Silent Retreat is "*A wellness sanctuary of spiritual wisdom and nature's abundance.*" Everything you eat there is made fresh from the food they grow and harvest on the grounds. There is no electricity in the rooms, no air-conditioning, and if you couldn't guess by the name, no talking. It's not that you aren't allowed to speak. If you're there with a partner or a friend and you choose to converse in your room, you may do so in a whispered tone. You can also talk if you have a question for one of the staff members. But I was committed—full silence. I turned my phone off, placed it into my designated locker in the common area, and took a deep breath. No Wi-Fi. No cell phone. I truly needed this.

After walking me around the beautiful property and showing me all the different areas—the yoga/meditation tent, eating area, library, labyrinth, water meditation center, and crying bench (yes, a bench where you can go to just...cry)—she took me to my room. I had an upper-level single room that faced the jungle. Why is that an important detail, you ask? Because it was a three-wall room. So my view (and fourth wall) was quite literally the jungle. It was a simple single bed with a mosquito net to sleep under, a small open-air shower, and a toilet. They provided bedding, a towel, and a kimono. Like at a traditional ashram, you were expected to tidy your living area on your own. You were given your own set of simple dishes and cutlery that you cleaned and reused after every meal to ingrain the idea that you are responsible for the things you need. The property has a no-garbage-in, no-garbage-out rule. Nothing is allowed onto the land that can't be composted or reused. If you bring an item that falls into this category, such as a tube of toothpaste, you must take it with you when you leave. Everything there is very simple—and it is all you really need.

Once I got settled into my new jungle room, I heard a wooden gong sound. There were two types of gongs at the retreat—a wooden one to announce a meal was ready, and a brass one to signify the start of a yoga or meditation class—because, obviously, there were no clocks around.

The food at Bali Silent Retreat was some of the best I've tasted in my life—and it all came straight from the earth. Nothing was processed, canned, or killed. A colorful array of delicious natural options filled the long table at breakfast, lunch, and dinner. It made you look forward to your next meal—and not feel guilty for stuffing your face. I took my beautiful plate of food up to the common area where I sat and stared into the jungle. It's amazing how differently you look at the eating process when you don't have a phone or conversation to distract you. You become aware of the way you take your bites, the art of how you chew, the speed, or lack thereof, with which you eat. You appreciate your surroundings. You appreciate what you're fueling your body with.

I sat and wrote for two hours before looking through the library and deciding on a book to read. I'm not a huge reader, but what else was I to fill my time with over the next three days? I'm also not a huge napper. I either sleep too long and wake up groggy and pissed off that I'm awake, or I don't sleep long enough and wake up irritable and pissed off that I'm awake. Those three days, I took more naps than I had in my entire adult life on giant, colorful cushions, and read two full books. It's amazing what your body will want to do when you allow it to.

That night I went to sleep with a real-life sound machine of croaking frogs, nocturnal birds, and the gentle buzz of the jungle.

I opened my eyes the next morning to the dew still sitting on the lush green wall of the jungle. I had no idea what time it was, but my body seemed to awake with an internal alarm clock. A few minutes later, I heard the brass gong sound as a fifteen-minute warning for the morning meditation and yoga practice.

I arrived at the grand meditation and yoga area. It was a giant wooden circular platform covered by a white tent. Meditation began every morning at 6 a.m. I lay there, the crisp morning air offering a break from the daily humidity that arrived at 8 a.m. sharp. Deep breaths. As our teacher for that morning walked us through a guided meditation with breath work, I sank deep into my subconscious. An hour passed that felt more like ten minutes, and I opened my eyes, knowing I needed to write out what I had just received from my subconscious mind. I jotted a few notes down in my journal before immersing myself in the morning yoga class.

After both sessions, the wooden gong let us know breakfast was served. I decorated my plate with many heavenly creations. They were all equally delicious, though I had no idea what was in most of them.

With a full belly and a clear mind, I sat down to write what I had gotten to in my meditation. It was around a beautiful Hawaiian practice that my mom had once told me about called Ho'oponopono. Step one is to say you're sorry to yourself for the places that exist in you that needed the lesson. Step two is to ask for forgiveness from the part in yourself that needed to experience it all. The third step is to thank yourself for the part that needed healing, which brought the lessons forward. Finally, you tell yourself "I love you" for having love around the entire experience—and for then letting it go. It resonated with me so deeply, in so many different areas of my life—especially, the journey I was currently on. And this time, it was specific to Tyler.

I'm sorry: For the part of me that has gone back and forth and can't decide, which is hurting someone I love and making me feel guilty.

Please forgive me: I forgive myself for needing to go back and forth to figure this all out.

Thank you: Thank you for all the lessons this has brought. Thank you for the guilt, to remind me I am human.

I love you: I love you. It's okay. Let it go.

After journaling about it, I opened up one of the books I had brought on my trip. I'd owned *You Are a Bad Ass* for over a year and had only ever read the very first chapter. I opened it and out fell a note that was apparently holding the place of the last page I had read. I froze. In my hand was a little piece of paper with Tyler's handwriting on it. The note read: *To the prettiest of them all, I hope you smile in your heart today. Love, Tyler.* This whole trip, signs had been appearing right in front of me, but since arriving in Bali, they had been undoubtable, in-your-face, unable-to-file-it-under-coincidence *signs*.

I began to read a section about old stories and false rewards. I realized that I had been living with old stories that were causing me to believe false rewards appearing in my life. It seemed to directly relate to why I couldn't confidently make a decision about Tyler.

The old story:
- I have abandonment issues.
- I don't know what to do and can't make a decision.

The false rewards I'd been getting from them:
- I have an excuse when things hurt me or I'm let down—which keeps me safe because I won't fully let go.
- Not making a decision keeps me in limbo so I never fully feel alone—which gives me a false sense of freedom.

I was sick of it—sick of the abandonment issues, sick of the problems they continually caused in my life, and tired of always being in some type of limbo. It had dishonestly kept me feeling safe when, in reality, it had been keeping me from so much freedom. So there, in silence, I decided to replace it with a new, powerful, story.

- I am always safe, secure, and taken care of.
- I know. I am clear.

I had been constantly searching for clarity on this trip. It was time to stop *searching* for clarity. It was time to just *be* clear. I allowed my body to nap on the giant cushion I'd been journaling on in the humid Balinese air. I slept deep, the way you do when your body is reveling in finally recharging.

When I woke up, I decided to walk the labyrinth. Used for prayer and meditation, a labyrinth is an ancient symbol that relates to wholeness and represents a journey to our own center and back into the world again. It looks like a maze with an opening at the beginning and twists and turns that take you to the very center.

There was a basket of rocks sitting at the entrance with different words written on each. *Knowing, balance, peace, healing...* I looked for one that said clarity. Of course, there wasn't one, because—hello, Gabrielle—you just decided you needed to stop *searching* for clarity and just *know*. I ended up choosing *divine* and *truth*. I stood at the beginning of the labyrinth path, which was made up of tiny little stones. I held the rocks in my hands and set my intention. *I know. I am clear*, I said to myself before I took my first step. As I walked slowly through the labyrinth, I repeated my new mantra over and over again. I took deep breaths as I tried to quiet my mind from all the external thoughts trying to invade my brain.

You don't really know, that's why you're here.
What if you make the wrong decision?
You aren't ever going to find the answers here.

Those thoughts then became questions.

Why am I so scared to commit?
If he is the one, I shouldn't be scared.
Then why has it felt like a piece of my heart is missing?

I continued to walk, slowly and deliberately, breathing deeply. *I know. I am clear.*

As I followed the perfectly positioned rocks leading me to the center, I repeatedly said the words over and over again in my head.

What is missing?
What is it that is missing?

When I reached the center, I looked down at my bare feet. There, right beside my left pinky toe, was a small rock out of its place in the path's manicured formation. One single lone rock out of the thousands that made up this maze. It stared up at me like a nudge sent from whoever the hell up there was still listening to me. Then I heard it.

Nothing is missing. It's just out of place.

It wasn't like I heard a voice from the heavens, or a whisper in the air—it was as if the deepest well inside my soul, which had been locked shut for so many years, finally cracked open just enough to let out the faint voice of a scared and damaged little girl.

Nothing is missing. It's just out of place. I knew exactly what it meant. There was nothing *missing* with Tyler. It was just simply *out of place*. What was it that was out of place? Well, that would be the next piece of the puzzle.

I read an entire book that afternoon. I never knew I could read so much so quickly and actually enjoy it. A few times I would lay my book down on my chest and allow myself to doze off in the hot Bali heat.

In one of the chapters, it spoke about identifying patterns and beliefs. I had done lots of work around this topic both with my mother's healing work and with my own Thought Onions. I decided to write down and really figure out the patterns that had consistently shown up in the area of my life that continually proved to be, for lack of better words, a shit show—the men. First up? The good guys. Starting with my college sweetheart, Wyatt. He was my first serious relationship after Jake's death. So serious that both our families were convinced we were going to get married. He even popped back into my life after Europe, but, lucky for him, he didn't make the final cut of this book.

Wyatt
The behaviors that pushed my buttons.
* Was not compassionate when we fought. This always stuck out to me.
* A dreamer. Which is ironically hilarious because he went on to become a multi-millionaire.

How did that behavior make me act toward him?
* I was let down and disappointed.
* I doubted him.

And finally, what was the belief that showed up with him? What Origin Experience started during my relationship with Wyatt?

* I'm not taken care of when things get tough.
* The good guys won't be enough for me.

That was the big one. *The good guys won't be enough for me.* It played out yet again in my relationship with Tyler.

Tyler
The behaviors that pushed my buttons.
- Who he becomes when he drinks.
- Challenges my past relationships.
- A dreamer.

How did that behavior make me act toward him?
- It made me want to leave.
- Invoked anger and defensiveness that made me feel judged.
- I doubted him.

Looking at the beliefs that showed up from Tyler's patterns was very interesting—because they all had to do with *fear*.

- People like that die. I'd been shown more than once that people with addiction problems die. My grandfather whom I never met. My uncle whom I had just lost.
- Fear of abandoning myself by allowing someone to discredit what I felt was real.
- The good guys won't be enough for me.

The good guys won't be enough for me. I wrote it out for a second time. I stopped and realized the similarities between the two men for the first time. I vividly remember sitting on my mother's front porch after breaking up with Wyatt. "I might have just made the biggest mistake of my life," I'd said to her. Of course, looking back, there was no way I could have stayed with my college love—I had too much to learn, too many mistakes to make, and so much more the universe intended for me before I could settle into a healthy relationship. Ironically, I remember sitting on my own apartment's front step after breaking up with Tyler (lord knows which time) and crying into the phone, saying, "I think I just made the biggest mistake of my life." Because for some reason, I didn't feel safe with the good guys. I felt like it couldn't possibly be that easy—there must come a time when they will choose to abandon me, and it will be even harder, even more devastating, because I would have finally let go and trusted.

I could hear my seven-year-old self screaming inside. The fear of that type of hurt was much too great to allow it to even be in the realm of possibility—which is what always seemed to lead me right into the arms of the *bad guys*.

Daniel

The behaviors that pushed my buttons.

- Jealousy. Again, the fucking irony. The man who made me feel ashamed for doing my job and guilty for living my authentic life was the one who ended up making all of *his* worst fears his own reality.
- Overtly sexual.

Besides the fact that Daniel wanted to have sex—all, the, time— it was also the way he approached it that made my skin crawl. It was always so objectifying and perverted. Don't get me wrong, sometimes I love to have rough, naughty sex—I mean, hello, you've read about it. But there is a time and a place for it, and it takes a certain type of man to make me want it. These patterns definitely made me feel a certain type of way.

How did that behavior make me act toward him?

- Defensive, then *forgiving and accepting*. A vicious and narcissistic cycle.
- Disgusted, irritated, gross.

These two behaviors in my marriage and how I was triggered by them created beliefs that manifested in later relationships.

- Commitment means I'm trapped because he didn't let me be free.
- If you don't love me as I am, I won't give you what you want.

I mean, would you want to sexually fulfill a person who is constantly berating you and making you feel like you can't be yourself or work toward your dreams? Someone who made you feel like you were always doing something wrong and that you should feel guilty for doing a job he literally signed up for?

But the bad guys don't always look like bad guys. In fact, a large majority of the people who know Javier would say he is definitely one of the good guys. In all honesty, one of those people would probably be me. And although it pains him to know it, in my story, he is, unfortunately, a bad guy. Not at all in the same category as my ex-husband, but in the sense that he asked me to place my heart in his hands, vowing to keep it safe, and then promptly catapulted it off to Europe. So, for this comparison, he falls into this category.

Javier
The behaviors that pushed my buttons.
- Non-committal, going back and forth between his feelings.
- Backs out of what he says and his decisions.

I think we can all agree on these two—and who could possibly feel safe when you never know if you're waking up to the boyfriend who's desperately in love with you or the man who panics and wants to run a million miles the opposite way?

How did that behavior make me act toward him?
- Anger and abandonment. Then, *forgiving and accepting.*
- Can't trust what he says.

What was interesting about these two responses is that they were vastly different from my ex-husband—yet they both had one thing in common: I would continually forgive and accept what was so clearly not okay and was so much less than what I deserved. They did, however, instill and validate two very old, very terrifying beliefs.

- The men I love always leave.
- I can't trust when I feel love.

I had attracted two types of men into my life. The good guys, where I always seemed to feel as if something was missing, where they wouldn't leave—*I would*. And the bad guys, who would let me down or abandon me, which I would allow and forgive—and then *they* would leave. It was like my biggest relationships had created ingredients that, when all mixed together, made a dangerous cocktail that ensured a hangover from hell. *Commitment means I'm trapped. The men I love always leave. I can't trust when I feel love. The good guys aren't enough for me.* No wonder I felt like I was drowning in an endless pool of fear. The universe had put Tyler, this amazing man, in front of me and said, *Okay, Gabrielle, here's everything you've always wanted, but you have to walk across this bridge if you really want it.* My subconscious beliefs and fears promptly set that bridge on *fucking fire*—and I *so* did not want to get burned.

The second night at the silent retreat brought a heavy rain just as night was falling. I sat and wrote in my room, reflecting on the day, the rain my sound machine for the night.

The following morning, I awoke to the now familiar brass gong. I threw on a pair of my Thai pants, which made me wonder why jeans were ever even invented, and headed down to enjoy the few cool hours the morning offered.

That morning we had a new instructor, who walked us through a guided meditation. As I lay flat on my back, breathing deeply, with my palms facing up to the sky, I allowed myself to sink really deep. I listened to her soothing voice, the first voice I had heard in almost twenty-four hours.

"Now pick an intention. Make it a big one. Something you want most in your life," she instructed.

Without even thinking, my brain silently shouted: *I am a worldwide best-selling author who is helping people heal, love themselves, and take their power back.*

My lip muscles pushed my mouth into a subtle smile.

"Now repeat it three times," she said. I did so.

I was deep. So deep that her voice felt far away, like when a television is left on in another room.

As I repeated my intention, my right leg suddenly twitched, jolting me back closer to consciousness from the deep state I was in. After that, I fell even deeper into the meditation and, the next thing I knew, a bell sounded to bring us back into reality.

"Come back into the space now. Slowly open your eyes. Stretch. If you want to write down anything that came up for you, now is the time to do that," she said as I started to slowly move my muscles.

I wrote in my notebook: *When I repeated my intention, my right leg twitched hard. What could that mean?*

I walked over to show the instructor the question I had written down. She read it, looked at me, and smiled.

"Maybe you just picked something that your body already knows is yours—and it was confirming it."

It felt like a little message. A nudge to keep going. That, as lost as I may have been feeling in the overall scheme of things, I was on the right path.

After another incredible meal, I decided to sit down and write a letter. Well, three letters, actually. To each of the men who had so greatly affected my life in the past two years. The men who I was, in some form or another, letting go of on this trip. Three letters that were not meant for them—but for me. Letters that I never intended any of them to read. Except, well, if they happen to be reading this book.

For the sake of the catharsis of the writing process, I decided to go in chronological order—starting with the man I'd made the mistake of marrying.

Dear Daniel,
Honestly, it feels so weird to even write your name. There are times where I feel like the five years, our marriage, our entire life together didn't even exist. Probably because I feel like you—at least the you I once knew—doesn't exist anymore. People always say when a relationship ends, it sometimes feels like someone has died. It doesn't feel that way with you—more like I knew the caterpillar but now don't even recognize the transformed butterfly. To be clear,

I don't want to compare you to something pretty—that's not really at all how I think your transformation appears—but you get the point. Everyone expected me to have all this anger toward you—a ton of work to heal around you—the need to forgive you. But to be honest, I'm so fucking grateful toward you. We would have been miserable—I cannot even imagine what my life would look like if I would have been guilted into staying married to you. There was one therapy session where my therapist took me through all the major times in my life where I felt abandoned, so obviously, you came up. I finally got to say everything I wanted to say. Frankly, it wasn't all that much. I wasn't heartbroken when we split because, if I'm being honest with myself, I wasn't in love with you. But I was enraged. Betrayed. Abandoned. You should have done so much better, dude. *So* much better. And how you handled everything after, the shit you've talked and the lies you've spread—doesn't it affect your body? Your brain? Your spirit? It must feel so uncomfortable. I wonder when you read the book if you just went, *well shit, that's all fucking accurate.* You're welcome, by the way, for leaving certain things out. To tell you the truth, I forgive you. And honestly, I did quite a while ago. The freedom and strength I have from being able to say that is one of the greatest experiences of human emotion. Regardless of the shitty way you made it happen—*you set me fucking free,* and I will *always* be grateful for that. You truly are now just a character in my story...and I hope you, too, eventually find your peace.

—Your Ex-Wife.

I've always found it rather amusing that my narcissistic ex portrays that he cheated on me and broke my heart. I wish. Oh, how I wish. Unfortunately, or fortunately, depending on your perspective, the man who broke my heart broke it like my ex-husband never could have done. That place...belonged to Javier.

Dear Javier,

When I left on this trip, I thought I would be going on a journey while simultaneously grieving two different relationships—because that's exactly how I felt before I left. Even though it had been more than two years, while I was in and out of a committed relationship and you had flings, for whatever reason, it had never really *seemed done*—and for that, I want to apologize. So many times you would say things that made me think you were on your way to having some sort of realization or change of heart—but it was ultimately my responsibility for attaching meaning to your words and assumptions to your actions. All of which you have proved to me time and time again is pointless. I could not comprehend that we were connected in so many ways and you thought you could find something more. I've finally realized there is no other meaning, no hidden agendas or deep subconscious blocks. It's just as you flat-out finally said it to me: you just wanted sex. It was my mistake for putting ideas and beliefs on you that you were never capable of fulfilling—at least with me—and for that, I am sorry. You were in many ways my biggest challenge thus far in life. I am so grateful for everything our relationship and heartbreak has taught me—it really did change me, and my life. While the part of me who has always loved and protected you wants to believe you meant it when you said you had to take a step back from me to "do the work"—and I do, more than anything, hope that's true—there is also a part of me that thinks your ego was bruised and you needed to be the one to leave. But it doesn't really matter either way. Turns out I haven't been grieving our relationship on this trip. I've been fully immersed in my relationship with Ty— which, for whatever reason, you doubted from the start. You may have been the hardest man for me to get over, but he is most definitely the strongest connection I have ever had—with anyone in my life. I've thought about you less on this trip than I have in two and a half years, and, truth-

fully, it feels so fucking good. I hope this doesn't sound angry—not that you'll ever be reading it—but it's not. I just
finally feel *free*. I thought I would be on this journey grieving you. Instead, I'm finally accepting you—and everything
you didn't give me that I so badly wanted from you, our
story, and us. Perhaps in another lifetime, we won't have
the wounds we have—you'll be able to love me the way you
almost did, and we'll have a life-changing romance. But for
this lifetime, you were only meant to love the unhealed version of me. You will be the person who opened my eyes and
my heart, broke me into a million pieces, and completely
changed the direction of my life. You will be my Javier. And
for that, with gratitude, I thank you.

—Plum

Then, finally, it was time for the letter to the man who my heart
had been physically aching for. The only man who had truly never
abandoned me—who had shown me what it feels like to be loved
without judgment, jealousy, or boundaries. The man that I still
wasn't sure if I needed to let go of or fly home to.

Dear Tyler,
God, dude. If you only knew. This entire fucking journey
has been about *you*. And yet, I find it so easy to write chapters about Daniel and Javier—and so *incredibly* difficult to
write about you. Even this letter was the last one to be written. There has not been one day—more like one hour—that
I have not thought about you. There were so many times I
felt so sad, like if I didn't call you, I would just crumble. So
many times I felt so happy, like if I didn't call you, I would
just burst. I've talked to so many people about you. I have
genuinely felt like a piece of me is missing. Then came Pai
and my decision to do shrooms—and of course, my entire
trip was about *you*. It had never been clearer to me than

in that moment that I love you—so very deeply. Days later, my conscious mind started to make me question everything again—because I have *so* much guilt for hurting you.
I can't come back if I can't commit to it all—the life, the
house, the step-kid—and to be honest that absolutely terrifies me. Even the thought of being with one person for
the next fifty-some years terrifies me. Every time I left, I
felt so grounded in my decision. It felt hard, but right. So
then why does this keep happening? Why the drug-induced
epiphany? Why *so, many, signs*. Seriously, when I saw you
liked those photos and I told Liz and Nina about it, they
were both floored. Our connection is undeniable. I've never
experienced anything like it. Then, of course, comes all the
bullshit thoughts of you dating someone. I know you are
but not who or how serious. And wondering if you would
be able to forgive me—again—for being with Javier. Having
to tell you about my epic fail of random meaningless sex
in Vietnam that has made me nauseous ever since—where
I thought about you the entire time. But the biggest thing
it all really comes down to is simply this: *I just don't fucking trust myself—and it's terrifying.* I have realized that
maybe there isn't something missing—maybe it's just out
of place. But how do I figure it all out to put it back in hopes
it fits? I hope you understand it has *nothing* to do with *you*.
It's all subconscious. So, then I think, do we go to therapy
about it? And really *do the work* to see? But then this leaves
me in the same fearful position of doing this to you *all over
again*, which I *cannot* do, and you *do not* deserve. Right
before I got here, Tess sent me the message you sent her
that said, *I am always with her*, and it gave me *so* much
peace. I want to make sure I'm not acting out of fear, loneliness, or any other old patterns—*because you deserve so
much more than that.* I honestly thought I was going to
come on this trip to grieve two relationships. However, I
have never felt more healed and complete around Javier.

This *entire* journey has been about you. I'm trying, Jacky.
I'm really fucking trying.

—Peanut

My final night happened to be the full December moon, and
the retreat held a ceremony in the meditation tent. Everyone sat
around the edge of the circular platform as the leader explained to
us the spiritual significance of the full moon and the ceremony we
were taking part in called Agnihotra. It's a healing fire ceremony
that is meant to purify the self and the atmosphere around you. It
can reduce stress, increase energy levels, lead to greater clarity, and
increase openness to love. It is meant to be a time to release, renew,
and transform.

Once the ceremony began, we chanted a mantra all together,
and one at a time someone would walk to the fire and whisper whatever they wanted to let go of. There was so much I was ready to let
go of. People, old beliefs, unwanted feelings that had been plaguing
my energy for far too long. As I chanted the mantra with the people
I had been in silence with for three days, I asked my heart what it
needed to let go of most. *Anything that is no longer serving you*, my
heart whispered back to me.

When it was my turn, I walked to the fire, softly spoke my words
into it, and allowed my energy to release anything that was no longer
serving me. My anger. My guilt. Daniel. Javier. Judgment. Blame.
All of it—it was time to let *all of it* go.

That night, I lay down in my quaint single bed that had turned
out to indeed be all I needed. As I listened to the jungle for the final
time, I thought about what it would be like to live here, without any
of the pressures of life in Los Angeles, the bullshit social media cre-
ates, and the total connection with what really matters—the planet
and myself. What a simpler life it would be.

The final morning, I awoke for the early meditation. In our
mind's eye, our teacher guided us into a shack where there were
four different targets on sticks.

"What do you see on the target?" she asked. I saw four things very clearly. Fear, doubt, commitment, and the unknown. Four things that scared the absolute hell out of me.

"Now, there is something beside you meant to be used on these targets," she continued.

In my mind's eye, I looked to my left and saw an axe. I picked it up and began to hack each of the targets until they were just piles of debris. It felt freeing. More importantly, it showed me the things I needed to give less power to—things I should be less afraid of—and they were all things I was struggling with around Tyler.

Although part of me was sad to be leaving this slice of peaceful heaven, I was definitely ready to immerse myself into the rest of Bali—and you know, talk to people. I sat looking out at the view of the rice fields and wrote a final reflection before I left.

12/12/2019

Three full days of no phone, no human communication, no music. To be honest, there wasn't any huge spiritual aha moment—but there were a few golden nuggets along the way. The labyrinth walk that told me there *isn't* really anything missing, it's just simply out of place. Receiving the confirmation in my meditation that everything I've been working on creating in my life is on its way to me. Seeing the relationship patterns and beliefs they caused that I was so ready to let go of. The days here brought me small clues on this ever-winding path. It's also brought a lot of awareness. I miss human connection—the conversation and the stimulation that comes from it. It's *very* hard for me to quiet my mind and turn off my thoughts. I need much less than I think I do—and my body will sleep if I let it. I most definitely appreciate air-conditioning—the humidity in Bali is no joke. But most importantly, I feel my first little bit of clarity. Well, some peace around my constant search for it, at least. I know no matter which way I end up going with Tyler—it, he, this, is one of my biggest lessons in life. It is making me grow *exponentially*. So, whatever is on the other side of this—whichever side that may be—*will be magical.*

Thank you, Bali Silent Retreat.
Thank you, Mother Earth.
Thank you, Gabrielle.

Gratitude.
Gratitude.
Gratitude.

The Ridiculous Misadventures of...
THE ONLY LOVE

I rode down the hill I had entered Bali Silent Retreat from. I was joined by a fellow guest that I'd seen many times around the property but had never heard speak. We chatted about our experience and laughed that neither of our voices seemed to match what we'd imagined in our heads. I was ready to get back into a world with communication, although I had fully enjoyed my technology-free escape. The retreat had brought me many things, mostly an understanding of the importance of getting quiet and going inward.

As I turned on my phone for the first time and a million notifications flooded my eyes, a message from Liz popped up.

Liz: So...believe it or not, I'm back in Bali. Let me know when you're back in the world!

It was wild—we had only planned on adventuring around some of Vietnam together, but we'd ended up in all three countries at the same time.

Me: I'm here! Dinner?!

Liz: Yes!!!!

Exactly what I needed—a long, heavy conversation with someone who knew me. I couldn't remember the last time I was so excited to just...talk. I said goodbye to the fellow retreat guest and checked into my first real Bali spot. I had purposely chosen an Airbnb to stay in after leaving the retreat—mostly because I assumed I was going to need some peace and quiet to process all that had surfaced during the previous days in silence—and I'm so glad I did.

I walked into the stunning freestanding villa, which was entirely enclosed with floor-to-ceiling windows. A beautiful king bed sat at the center with a flowing white canopy hanging from the tall ceiling. Everything was either sleek wood or bright, airy white. A door led to an outdoor oasis with a shower, surrounded by hanging plants, trees, and a soaking tub. It was as heavenly peaceful as you could hope for—and lying on the king bed felt like you were in the clouds.

Liz met me in the front of the property and the shuttle took us into downtown Ubud. I don't quite know what I was expecting from Bali—it had been on my bucket list for as long as I could remember—and I definitely had high expectations.

We walked through the busy town, popping in and out of shops. The humid air was no joke—no matter what time of day it was. We settled on one of the many restaurants the town had to offer and sat and caught up on the week we'd been apart.

As the sun disappeared and night fell, the city came alive with little lights and a variety of music. We popped into a bar for a drink, where two Brazilians came over to our table.

"You're American!" one of them said after we both introduced ourselves.

"We are!" Liz smiled.

"We're going down the street to this other spot. They have a live band and dancing. Do you want to come?"

Liz looked at me with a *I will be making out with this guy tonight can we please go* face. I laughed. They had me at live band and dancing.

"Sure!" I agreed, as we all stood up to head to the next location.

CP Lounge was a massive outdoor lounge where the ceiling is the starry night sky, the live band's music pulsates through your sweaty pores, and the energy can be felt in the night air. The boys grabbed drinks and ordered a hookah, which has never been my favorite thing, and we chatted for a bit while I broke off to dance on my own whenever a great song came on.

Liz was deep into conversation with her Brazilian of choice, and I was finishing up a drink when it happened—*the live band started playing Gipsy Kings*. My heart immediately jumped up, did a somersault, and started screaming *TYLER* inside.

Blame it on the few cocktails, or the fact that I had been missing this human for three weeks that seemed like an eternity, but in that moment, dancing barefoot to Gipsy Kings in Bali, I wanted him to know I was thinking about him.

I pulled out my WhatsApp, pressed my voice note button, and sent him a recording of our favorite song that was playing. I had no idea what time it was in Los Angeles, or who he might possibly be with. *You just broke your one fucking rule, Gabrielle*, my brain said to myself. *Yep. And I don't fucking care*, my heart danced back.

After another fifteen minutes of dancing and a lot more sweating in the humid Bali night, a notification popped up.

Tyler: Hi. Do you know you pocket dialed me? Hope you're having fun.

Me: Hi. It wasn't a pocket dial. They're playing Gipsy Kings. I feel like I'm letting myself down if I talk to you. But I miss you tremendously and cannot wait to see you.

Tyler: I understand. I miss you every minute of every day.

Me: Same.

I sent the photo of the note I had written at The Note Coffee back in Vietnam that read: *Thank you. I love you. You will always be my unicorn.*

Tyler: Aw. Melting. Thank you, Peanut.

And then, in true Gabrielle fashion, or maybe true love fashion, my heart stomped its feet, threw its little arms up, and said: *fuck this.*

I called Tyler.

"Peanut?" I heard the comforting voice I so desperately missed on the other end.

"Hi, Jacky." The smile on my face grew a thousand sizes.

"Hi, Peanut." I could hear his smile on the other end, too.

"It's so good to hear your voice." My eyes watered.

"You have no idea."

"My mom told me you booked a huge Nissan campaign. I'm so freaking proud of you," I gushed.

"Thank you. Couldn't have come at a better time. How has your trip been so far?"

"It's been a lot. Really great, but definitely some heavy healing. I ended up going to Thailand for a week and a half in between Vietnam and Bali."

"Do you feel like you're getting all the answers you were looking for?" he asked.

"Yes. Little by little, yes. But God, dude, I swear this entire trip has been centered around you." A pause, but I knew it made him smile.

"How so?"

"I've honestly felt like a piece of me was missing. And I just haven't been able to stop thinking about you."

"Well, that makes me really, really happy. And I can't wait to hear all about it. Not talking to you has been insanely hard. But I think it's been good for both of us."

"I really missed hearing your voice," I said again.

"Me too, Peanut. Tremendously."

"Just do me a favor, okay?" I asked.

"What's that?"

"Don't fall in love with anyone yet."

I could feel the electricity shooting through the phone.

"I won't," he finally said.

"Okay." I smiled.

"Okay."

The next morning, I awoke with mixed emotions. *Love*—that I was feeling so much of after hearing Tyler's voice. *Weakness*—feeling like I had broken my golden rule when I caved and contacted him. *Excitement*—to know the person I had constantly been thinking of had been thinking of me too. And *Confusion*—as to what the hell I was supposed to do about it all.

Luckily, I had booked a FaceTime session with Arna that I'd assumed I would be needing after the silent retreat. She had become such a beacon of light for me during dark times.

"It's so good to see your face!" Her kind eyes looked through my phone screen at me. "How has your trip been going so far? Tell me everything."

I divulged everything that I'd been going through—the pit of guilty regret I'd been in after sleeping with Chris 2.0, my confusing inner struggles of missing Tyler, my drug-induced revelations, and the fact that I had spoken to him just a few hours earlier. It was a lot to unpack.

"I feel like I let myself down by contacting him," I admitted.

"Why? It was only a rule you set for yourself. What was the main point of this trip? What were you hoping to gain from it?" she asked.

"Healing myself. And clarity," I answered.

"And have you done a lot of healing so far on your journey?"

"Yes. Definitely."

"So isn't it possible that the healing you've been doing brought you to making the decision to contact him?" she stated.

"Yes, I can see that."

"And what did talking to him bring you?" she asked. I thought about it for a moment.

"Comfort. Love. Happiness."

"All things that come with clarity." She smiled. "So don't beat yourself up for riding the wave to the destination."

I nodded, knowing she was right. It wasn't my job to judge myself—I had done plenty of that over the last few years. I simply needed to just *let go and be.*

"Let me ask you something. Where do you see yourself in the next year? What would be the best and most perfect scene you could set for yourself? Explain it to me as if you are there, in it." I closed my eyes and pictured my perfect setting.

"I'm in a beautiful backyard that is covered with greenery and lush nature. It's the perfect place to write. I can hear the birds singing and feel the warm breeze blowing. It feels safe and serene, like my own little sanctuary," I said as I envisioned myself there.

"That's beautiful. Do you live there?" she asked.

"Yes. It's mine."

"Wonderful. It sounds so peaceful."

"It is." I smiled.

After my session, I made a decision—well, I decided to at least put myself out there for a decision to be made. I texted Tess for assistance.

Me: Can you do me a favor? Can you tell Tyler that I want to see him, and I want to know if he can pick me up from the airport. I don't want to know what he says. I just want him to know I want him to be there. If he's busy, or doesn't want to, that's totally fine. If that's the case, you can still pick me up like we planned.

Tess: Of course. You don't want me to tell you who will be waiting for you?

Me: No. It will either be my best girlfriend or my soul person. Gonna let the universe take this one.

Tess: You got it. Proud of you.

I left my villa feeling much more grounded from my session and peaceful about the decision I'd made to pull the trigger and put my feelings out there. I headed out to do all the touristy things you were supposed to do in Ubud. Swinging from the massive swings that overlooked miles of rice fields and beautiful jungle. Coffee tasting after watching the beans be cleaned and roasted right in front of you. Walking in the intense humidity, sweating from places I didn't know sweat, through the vibrant green rice fields. I went to the Holy Springs Water Temple that everyone had raved about. It was beautiful, although I recommend not visiting on a weekend because it most definitely felt like I was in line for a ride at Disneyland with all the kids and school tours that were there. As I stood in line, freezing in the water, waiting for what I was expecting to be a totally spiritual experience—I made a choice. *Well, Gabrielle, you're here. So you might as well ignore that kid that 100% just peed in this sacred spring and choose to create an experience for yourself instead of expecting one.* At each spout, a ritual is performed, and you are then given a blessing. As I stood at each spout, I thought of something I was truly grateful for and said thank you. By the end of it? Shouting kids, swarms of people, frozen toes and all—I felt so *deeply* blessed.

After my morning of sightseeing, the day had one more very specific and unusual thing on the agenda: *meeting Tyler's ex-girl-friend.*

Jasmine had moved from San Francisco to Bali years ago and, as soon as Tyler found out I was going, he'd connected the two of us. I honestly had no idea what to expect. Tyler was friends with a lot of his exes. He's a very compassionate and loving person, so it didn't really surprise me. I'd heard about her during our past discussions, and Tyler had spoken very highly of her, how kind she was, and that he thought we would totally connect on a soul level. I knew the back-story of their relationship—what I didn't realize was *who he was to her.*

Without a freaking clue as to how this was going to go, I made my way to the vegan restaurant she had chosen with an open mind. I sat there, waiting for my ex-boyfriend's ex-girlfriend to show up like some weird fucked-up Tinder date.

"Gabrielle!" I heard a voice behind me.

"Hi!" I stood up smiling to meet her outstretched arms.

Jasmine was beautiful—she had long dark hair, intense yet caring brown eyes, and an energy that immediately made me feel at ease.

"You're even prettier in person!" she said as she sat down. Always a solid way to start off a first date.

"I was literally thinking the same thing about you." I laughed.

We ordered our meals, which was nearly impossible with all of the incredible options on the menu. Bali is known for having fresh vegan creations everywhere you go. As we exchanged the typical pleasantries, our coffee creations arrived.

"Tell me why you're on this trip. What are you searching for?" She smiled.

"That's such a loaded question." I laughed.

"Sorry, I read energy, so I immediately picked up on it." *Of course*, I thought to myself.

"How much did Tyler tell you?" I asked.

"Not much. Just that you're one of the best souls he's ever met, and he loves you very dearly."

"He didn't tell you we broke up?" Her facial expression answered the question.

"No, he didn't. He just told me to take good care of you."

"I guess I'll start from the beginning then." I chuckled.

As I filled this total stranger in on all that had exploded in my life in 2017 and how I'd become a ball in a fucked-up game of ping pong between Javier and Tyler, her eyes widened as she took in my story. I ended with the highlight reel that my Asia trip had been thus far, including the fact that Tyler and I had spoken for the first time the night before.

"You're not going to believe this." She looked at me. "I've been in almost the exact same situation."

Jasmine began to tell me about her recent year, where she indeed had her own Javier and Tyler. Actually, it was freakishly similar—going back and forth between the two men, feeling this addictive sexual pull from one and a safe, healthy, spiritual bond with the other. The men in her life even looked like the ones in mine. One was Latin and an Aries (of course we had to discuss their signs) and one was a Gemini that absolutely everyone loved. She pulled out her phone.

"I feel like he even kind of resembles Tyler in a way!" She showed me a photo of the healthy love she had ended up choosing.

"Oh my God, I totally see it!"

"Wild, isn't it?"

"So...how did you ever fully realize that he was the person you were supposed to be with?" I asked.

"I just felt it in my heart. Whenever I was away from him, it felt like there was some piece of me missing, I don't really know how to describe it," she said.

It hit me like a fucking bus. It was the same exact thing I had been saying this entire journey.

"Do you think you want to get back together with Tyler?" she asked.

"It's really hard for me to answer that—because while a big part of me does, I know I can't do this to him all over again. I've hurt him too many times and he's just...too good of a human for that," I answered, trying not to get emotional.

"Yeah. He really is."

"Why did you guys break up?" I finally asked.

"It was so long ago, and we were so young. I just don't think it was the right time for our paths to cross. But my mom still brings him up to this day." She chuckled. Then, to my surprise, I realized *she* was getting emotional.

"I'm sorry, I didn't mean to..." My voice trailed off.

"No! It's okay, I don't know why I'm getting emotional about it. It's been forever." Tears fell from her eyes as she quickly wiped them away. "He's just such a good person. He was my first love."

I reached across the table and grabbed her hand. We looked at each other and smiled. Because in that moment, without her even knowing it, she'd given me confirmation. In that moment, I saw in her the full manifestation of what was only a tiny seed inside my heart. I saw exactly what it would look like if I chose to walk away and allow that little piece that felt like it was missing to grow into a life without Tyler—and I didn't want to know that life. I knew there was a Thought Onion in here somewhere. Superficial?

• Get on a plane and fly directly home to Tyler, you stupid, stupid woman.

Superficial indeed. Authentic?

• How can I even trust what I'm feeling anymore?

It was definitely a big fear of mine. I had gone back and forth way too many times between feeling head over heels in love with Tyler to thinking that an important element was missing. So what was at the core of it all?

- What if I've ruined the exact thing I've been searching for?

It was not only shocking—it was terrifying. Because what I saw in her, in that very moment, was the substantiated fear that Javier had left imprinted in me. *What if I never find someone who makes me feel this way.* I had found someone who made me feel that way—in a very different, much more safe and healthy way—and I had totally fled for the hills. And now, as I sat across from someone who knew Tyler's heart as much as I did, I realized that it wasn't just enough love—it was the *only* love.

The Ridiculous Misadventures

of...

THE MONKEY MAFIA

After a few blissful days in the Balinese villa, it was time to move to a more social and bank-account-appropriate location—meaning not splurging on the fifty-seven-dollar villa and moving to a nine-dollar-per-night hostel. Since falling in love with solo travel, I've stayed at some incredible hostels all over the world, and Bali is known for some pretty luxurious ones. Let me tell you, Kuna Bali did not disappoint. The main area had a decent-sized pool, an outdoor bar, lounge chairs, day beds, bean bags to relax in under the shining sun, and an upper level with tons of decorative seating for mealtimes. The rooms felt like cute hotel rooms with spacious bunk beds and came with very welcomed air-conditioning.

One of the main tourist attractions in Ubud is the Monkey Forest. If you couldn't guess from the name, it's an open forest that many Balinese monkeys call home. It's a sacred natural sanctuary and, for a very small fee, you can walk through to admire these long-tailed furry friends. My hostel was super close to one of the entrances so, on my first day in my new spot, I decided I'd venture into what everyone told me shouldn't be missed.

I have to admit, I was slightly nervous. I had heard stories of aggressive and overzealous monkeys grabbing phones out of hands, stealing water bottles from backpacks, and chasing unprepared tourists. So, clutching my phone tightly, I bought my ticket and walked in behind another group of three.

"Can I walk with you? I'm mildly terrified I'm going to get chased by a monkey," I admitted. They all laughed.

"Of course! Where are you from?" one of the girls smiled and asked.

"Los Angeles," I answered.

"Us too! What part?"

"North Hollywood."

"You're kidding! What streets?" she exclaimed. I told her where my little apartment was located, and they gasped in surprised.

"We live directly across the street in those new apartment buildings." The other girl laughed.

"You're kidding! Seriously, what are the odds?"

We all introduced ourselves and started to walk into the center of the forest. One of the girls, Cramer, had long dirty blonde hair, dark brown eyes, and a peaceful smile.

"They leave tomorrow, but I'm staying in Ubud for another week. Let's exchange numbers if you're going to be here a while." She smiled.

"Definitely." We swapped numbers as the first monkey scurried past us.

We reached the center and were suddenly surrounded by monkeys—large and small. There were massive ones that had babies on their backs, medium-sized ones that swung from tree branches, and scruffy-looking ones that would come up and sit right beside you. I had seen countless photos of people with them on their shoulders and even some where the monkey had taken the phone for what they refer to as a "monkey selfie." I was so *not* interested in attempting to pull that one off.

The four of us stuck close and walked around taking photos and videos of funny things the monkeys were doing—it was like being in a live-action video game. There were a few workers standing around who would shoo away any primates that looked like they were getting into trouble. I decided to take my backpack off and sit down on one of the small benches, which were about six feet long. At the other end of the bench, a rather large monkey sat minding his own business.

The *moment* I sat down, this monkey stopped what he was doing and snapped his gaze over at me. They tell you upon entry to the forest to not make direct eye contact with them because they take it as you challenging them. Furthermore, if they start coming toward you, you should just sit still and let them climb on you like you're some freaking human jungle gym. So, after noticing this furry guy setting his sights on me, I quickly did as I had been instructed to— *sat fucking still.*

He swiftly crawled across the six feet between us. I got kind of excited that he was about to crawl onto my shoulder and become my new best monkey pal, like Abu in Aladdin. Maybe we would even get an awesome picture together. He reached my side, placed his cute little human-like miniature hands on my forearm—*AND FUCKING BIT ME.*

It was as if the moment the monkey laid eyes on me, he'd thought, "Yeah, that's the one. *Fuck that chick.*" I didn't scream. I just said, "Oh my God, he just bit me." It was more shocking than painful. Cramer looked over at me in horror. The monkey had already scurried off. I looked down in disbelief as the perfect little teeth marks began to bleed. WHY DID YOU HAVE TO COME TO THE MONKEY FOREST, GABRIELLE?

One of the workers walked me to the first-aid office, where he informed me that I shouldn't worry too much. No one had ever reported rabies from these specific monkeys and bites happen at least once a day. ONCE A DAY? *WHY DOES ANYONE COME TO THE MONKEY FOREST?*

He cleaned and bandaged my arm, and I informed my mother that I was alive and well post primate attack.

Me: At least if I get rabies it'll be a cool press story. "Cujo star's daughter turned rabid by monkey."

I laughed at my hilarious joke. My mother was not amused.

It wasn't until the following day, sharing my crazy day on social media and getting flooded with messages saying I needed to go to urgent care *stat*, that I realized the man at the forest was probably downplaying the seriousness of it for legal reasons. Begrudgingly, I called Liz, and she met me at the local urgent care.

After learning from the doctor that my bite was a category three (yes, out of, you guessed it, *three* categories), I got my first of four rabies shots and an immunoglobulin shot that had to be administered *directly* into my gaping open wound—*twice*.

But sitting in this tiny third-world hospital room, I realized something. When I was in Europe, one of the biggest lessons I learned was that, no matter what happens or where I am, I am totally okay and taken care of. During the last two years of my life, parts of me had lost my true knowing of that. And if there was any moment to full-on freak the fuck out and panic, it would be now—across the entire world, after being an afternoon snack to a rather hefty ape, being shot up with massive needles by someone speaking a language I didn't understand, and hearing that the bill was $2500.00. Instead, I stayed calm as Liz held my hand. I knew the bill would be covered by my travel insurance, and I was totally taken care of by the amazing staff. Here I was, staring all the fear in the face, and I just sat there and smiled because I knew how capable I was. And besides, I'm technically part of the secret monkey mafia now—and have the scar to prove it.

The Ridiculous Misadventures of...

I'VE GOT YOU

While I had planned on leaving Ubud to see Canggu and potentially the Gili Islands, my new battle wound and continued rabies shot schedule meant I was staying in Ubud, close to the urgent care, and, you know, to make sure I didn't turn into a superhero or anything.

I'd become friends with a few different travelers at my hostel—a rough-around-the-edges soul from Ireland, a positive upbeat fellow Californian from San Diego, and an outspoken Dutch girl from the Netherlands.

One of the most talked-about experiences in Bali is the sunrise hike up to Mount Batur. We all woke up at 2 a.m. to be taken to the base of the massive volcano, which boasts an elevation of 5,633 feet. They had told us it was a moderate hike. Now, I don't scale the sides of Half Dome or trek the tough terrain of the Himalayas, but I'm in shape and I hike. This, my friends, was *not* a freaking moderate hike. In fact, after three straight hours, almost all of it uphill, I was not only dripping in sweat, I was pretty sure I needed to see a doctor. But then I turned around to look at the view.

If there is anyone who doesn't believe heaven exists, I dare you to watch the sunrise from the top of Mount Batur and not change your mind. We huddled together in the crisp air and watched the world welcome the sun that morning. Standing high above the clouds, the mountains, and the body of water below, we watched the clouds change from vibrant orange to pale pinks. It was one of the most stunning displays of nature I have ever seen. The universe was just showing off at this point. I was sitting there in this serene peaceful moment when an unsettling yet familiar feeling manifested in my stomach—*panic*. How was it possible to go from such a calm and spiritual feeling to sheer and utter panic? *Thought Onion that shit. Superficial?*

• It's almost the end of my journey.

Yes. The cold realization that my soul-searching month in Southeast Asia was on the last few days. It was a feeling I knew all too well from traveling in Europe—*what if I go home and I'm not healed*. But that wasn't the fear here...authentic thought?

• I feel like I have clarity—but don't trust myself.

Oof. That layer was not only real, it was terrifying. It had been glaringly obvious and abundantly clear that I missed having this human in my life. But did that mean he was supposed to be in it as more than a friend? Did it mean that the fourth time was a charm?

• Tyler is the peaceful sunrise—*and I am the fucking volcano.*

There it was. The biggest fear of all. The fear that Tyler had broken, healed, and started to move forward just for me to erupt back into his life. I thought about the times he'd cried in my arms. The times he'd gone above and beyond what any man should. The times he'd taken me back, despite all the painful things he'd had to endure. And here he was, finally settling back into his life without me. Who the hell was I to mess that up? What if it ended up exactly the way it had the first three times? I couldn't do that again. I couldn't do that *to him* again.

That night, I stayed at the hostel to give my body a break after the strenuous early-morning adventure. I ordered some food and sat at the bar, sipping on a refreshing drink. As I waited for my food, a girl took a seat next to me, and we started chatting about where we were from, where our travels had taken us, and why we were on this trip.

"Let me guess, you're on a soul-searching journey?" She laughed.

"Something like that." I chuckled.

"Is this the first big solo trip you've taken?"

"No, I actually did a month in Europe in 2017, which was my first big solo adventure. Not exactly by choice."

"Oh, girl, I feel like there's a story there."

"You have no idea." I laughed.

We talked about my story, the trip, the book, and how I had ended up across the world yet again in search of something.

"I'm in shock. That's so similar to what I went through," she said. "Only my guy was already in Barcelona and called me to tell me not to come when I was at the airport."

"You're fucking kidding me," I said in disbelief.

"Nope. And I got on the plane and went anyways." God, I freaking love badass women.

We chatted at the bar for over an hour that night, connecting on the familiar theme of *heartbreak*. I had come to know all too well from my readers that heartbreak and grief are universal. No matter if it's from a cheating ex-husband, a quick but deadly love affair, a death, or the loss of something we thought was unwaveringly ours, the core is still the same. *But how beautiful*, I thought to myself. How beautiful that there is something we can all connect on. Something we can all identify with and feel compassion toward. How beautiful that sometimes our fairy tales need to have a heartbreaking end so we can experience beautiful new beginnings. What a human experience that truly is.

The following day I went to a café to get some writing done. As I sat there, the fear from the day before began to grow. I was so scared to misstep—so scared to trust what my heart seemed to be feeling. I took out my phone and sent Tyler a text.

Me: I'm scared.

I had no idea what time it was in LA. *God, Gabrielle, way to send an ominous text that could mean a million different things.* I'm scared of the psychotic monkey who now has a taste for my blood. I'm scared because I might pass out from hiking up to the top of the world. I'm scared that I might break your fragile heart again. I'm scared because *life is fucking scary.* Within seconds, my phone lit up with a response.

Tyler: It's okay to be scared. I got you.

And just like that, all the fear and panic suddenly melted away—because I knew those words. Those words I had said to Javier so many times. Those words that I only ever spoke if I truly had someone's heart in my hands. I knew the weight they carried. *I got you.* Now, more than two years later, I was yet again sitting across the entire world from every comfort I knew. Only this time...*someone finally had me.*

The Ridiculous Misadventures

of...

GABRIELLE

My final night in Ubud, I met Liz and Cramer for one last dinner at a restaurant that looked like it had been crafted deep in the imagination of a spiritual dreamer. There was a massive God-like figure made out of bamboo, colorful seating arrangements that felt like something out of *Alice in Wonderland*, paths that led to different tucked away areas, and brightly colored décor hanging from above.

The three of us sat and laughed as we realized that, while our journeys had been so different, here we were, three girls that lived a mere twenty minutes from each other, bonding across the world. I had connected with so many amazing women on this solo trip, a nice change of pace from my male-heavy Europe adventure. Liz, of course, who had become my travel sister and my center of gravity in each new place I ended up in on my journey. The girls in Vietnam, Kristy, Emily, Kara, and Coco. Even though we only had one night together, they were each an example of strength, love, and fearlessness. Red, the spunky take-no-shit Israeli that I was pretty sure hated me when we first met. Paula, the sweet soul that guided us on our psychedelic journey. And Nina—my friend who will forever have a special place in my heart.

But most importantly, for the first time, I'd met the new me. The me that could recognize her trauma, walk through her fears, and choose to be okay by herself. I was not the same woman that had returned from Europe in 2017. I no longer felt betrayed by the man I'd married or heartbroken by the person I so quickly gave my heart to after. Daniel hadn't ruined my life—he had given me a chance to really go live it. Javier hadn't just broken my heart—*he had broken me open so I could fall in love with myself.* I was no longer scared of what life might throw my way. I had survived the explosions, weathered the storms, and found my way back to the fucking light. *I had survived. I had healed.* And I knew, no matter what catastrophic upheaval the universe might decide to drop into my future world, one thing remained certain: *I would never abandon myself.* So really, when all was said and done, what was there left to fear?

I stepped on the plane, knowing without a doubt the woman I was—*and it was someone I was freaking proud of.* I had boarded my first flight scared, broken, and confused. I had begged, pleaded, and searched for clarity. Then, without any monumental or obvious answer, I found it. There was no right decision. There was no clear and easy path. Life is messy—and brokenly beautiful. The clarity comes when you continue to go inward, do the work, and ask the questions. Tyler had come into my life at what seemed like the worst possible time—when I was so deeply broken, terrified to misstep, and still had such a journey ahead of me. But without our story and all of its heartbreaking back and forth, twists and turns, and highs and lows, I would have never actually found the answer. Tyler was the perfect mirror to show me all of my traumas, all of my fears, and all of my insecurities. He was the essence of the first man I ever lost. His daughter's face reminded me of the little girl whose dad had been taken away twenty-five years ago. He showed me what it felt like to never fear abandonment. And he allowed me to detox from the toxicity I had come to know as love. He had granted me the freedom to leave, to truly heal—and more importantly, to find myself—without ever questioning it. It was time to walk through all the fear. It was time to stop letting my trauma define me. It was time to redefine my oldest Origin Experience. So, as I sat there on the plane, I made the decision. It was no longer, *When I love someone, they die.* From now on, it would be, *When I love someone, they stay.*

Was Tyler going to be there when I landed? Had the past two years happened so that I could become the woman that was able to be loved the way I truly deserved? Or was it all a huge lesson that would end with me losing the person I was now so clear about. He had always made me feel so safe, so protected. But what I had gotten from this journey, this time away from him, this epic quest into the depths of my soul, was that I no longer *needed* his safety or protection. That piece had been officially put back in its rightful place, and I had finally found that within *myself*. Now, I simply wanted to be with the man I had so clearly loved this entire time. Because I finally knew. I finally knew what had been missing all this time. *Me.*

I stepped off the plane, not knowing if I would be seeing the man that felt like home or my best friend who had stuck with me through it all. My heart began to beat fast as I walked through the busy airport, faces flying by in all directions. *Just breathe, Gabrielle. Whoever is here is how your journey is supposed to end.*

I grabbed my bag and headed out onto the crowded street, searching for a familiar face to welcome me home. Even with all the sounds, all I could hear was my heart pounding in my chest.

"Gabrielle!" I froze. My heart stopped. I dropped my bags and turned around.

"You came." My eyes flooded with tears as I ran forward, jumping into Tyler's arms. He picked me up and spun me around, holding me tightly.

"Of course I came," he said into my neck.

I don't think I have ever held onto someone so tightly. He placed me back on the ground, and I looked up at him, still in his arms.

"I have no idea if this is going to work. But I know I want to try." Tears ran down my cheeks. He wiped them away and smiled down at me.

"What was missing?" he asked, knowing I had found the answer.

I looked up at the man all the others had led me to, tears in my eyes, and smiled.

"Me."

EPILOGUE

As I sit in my beautiful backyard, writing, I can hear the birds singing and feel the warm breeze blowing. The scene I described to Arna during our session in Bali has now become a reality. All the heartache, all the drama, and all of the lessons—I would do it all again in a heartbeat if it meant I would end up exactly where I am. Tyler and I didn't have a normal romance—he didn't immediately sweep me off my feet, propose under a waterfall, or attempt to whisk me away to Europe. It happened slowly—and I am so grateful for that. I've never experienced something as deep, or special, as slowly falling more in love with this human and creating a beautiful life together. It is, quite truthfully, why no one else ever fully made sense. I have never felt more healed, more loved, and more at peace than I do right now. So, for all of you that always ask—yes, there is *so* much hope. Every man that came before only deserved to love the unhealed version of me. And this new version? Is really fucking powerful. I am excited for where life is going to take me. I am thankful for the experiences that have made me who I have become—and I am proud as hell of that woman.

None of you will ever truly know what you've done for me. You've changed my life, given me a purpose, and helped me find my voice. You are just as much a part of my journey as any of the characters in this book, and for that, I am so very grateful.

Is life perfect? Of course not—it never is. It's messy, remember? Brokenly beautiful, incredibly intoxicating, fearlessly tragic, and undeniably magical. But what I can tell you, without a shadow of a doubt, is this: *it is so fucking worth it.*

"Peanut! Dad says dinner is ready!"

"Okay, Blue, I'll be right in!"

I have changed so much over the last two years. I don't even recognize the woman who once walked down the aisle. I know now it was never going to work with any of the men before because I hadn't yet found the most important ingredient of a healthy relationship—*myself.* Because, you see, it isn't until we fully love ourselves, daily self-love cocktails and all, that we can attract the type of love we fully and truly deserve. And that love? *It's pretty fucking incredible.*

So, my new best friend—thank you. Thank you for coming on this second journey with me. Thank you for breaking open with me, rooting for me, healing with me, and cheering me on from afar. I have felt you here every step of the way, and I hope I've given you something to take forward into this crazy little thing we call life. But for now, it is time to finish the chapter, close the book, and end this journey.

Until, you know...the next earth-shattering bomb explodes in my life.

Acknowledgements

To every single person who took the time to come on this journey with me—thank you. My FMLers. My new friends. My amazing mother, who I have gotten every ounce of strength, wisdom, and drive from. Erica, my editor, who has kept me grounded and laughing every step of the way. To all the people who gave me their blessing to finish this chapter in my life—and even the ones who didn't. And to the man who held my hand and heart through the discomfort, highs, lows, and pain that it took to write this book: Tay—my unicorn.

Quoted Material

Trevor Hall, "You Can't Rush Your Healing." Track 8 on *Kala.* Welk Records, 2015.

The Cranberries, "Linger." Track 7 on *Everybody Else Is Doing It, So Why Can't We?* Island Records, 1993.

Goldschneider, Gary, and Aron Goldschneider. *The Secret Language of Birthdays: Your Complete Personology Guide for Each Day of the Year.* New York, NY: Avery, 2016.
"Extramarital involvements between these individuals, whether with each other or outside their relationship, are especially tempting to both partners. Marriages will generally prove too much for this combination, since the practical burdens of everyday life do not really suit their preference for the easy pursuit of pleasure."

"These relationships are among the few combinations where the partners can be both friends and lovers before, during, and after their love affair. There is a deep understanding and loyalty in this relationship and a mutual respect, especially on the mental plane. Yet, as well as these two get along, it may not be in the cards for them to marry or even live together, since ease does not necessarily entail either emotional depth or the ability to commit."

Ans. 2019. "These Are the 4 Kinds of Soul Mates and What You Need to Know about Each One." Global Heart. May 29, 2019. https://globalheart.nl/spiritualiteit/these-are-the-4-kinds-of-soul-mates-and-what-you-need-to-know-about-each-one/.

"Healing Soulmate:
One who arrives with an intention to provide you with life lessons that heal your memories by mirroring you. They appear by divine timing—at the time we most need to learn from them. They teach us how to move forward in life. A healing friendship exists only as long as you need it until your purposes are aligned. When your relationship escalates fast, then you'll know you've found a healing soulmate. Sometimes painful, it might not last forever."

"Past Life Soulmate:
You'll feel like you've known them forever. The connection is instant. You may feel like you will be mates for a lifetime—no matter how much time has passed or how far apart you are—and you're probably right. This relationship will likely last forever because you will never feel the need to run or hide from this soulmate. They teach you to trust and believe in yourself. You're both accepted for who you are. The friend who'll help you grow into the person you are meant to be. They can propel you toward your fate without pain or suffering. They'll always have your best interest at heart. This type of friendship can last a lifetime. You just need to stay connected. They're crucial in shaping you into the best version of yourself."

Fairchild, Alana. *Rumi Oracle: An Invitation into the Heart of the Divine*. Glen Waverly, Australia: Blue Angel Publishing, 2015.

"This oracle comes to you with a special message. You are an inspiration. You are helping those around you and even many of whom you are unaware. You are doing this because this is your path, this is your way, this is your gift. You're also being gifted through this oracle with a sign: an issue too difficult for you to understand, no matter how hard you have been working on it, is about to be resolved. You have no need to hold on to it or become 'more worthy' of that resolution. It is going to happen. Your job is to allow it to happen, to simply bear witness to the resolution, even if you have no idea what is going on in the process."

Made in the USA
Las Vegas, NV
30 October 2021